Virtual Machines

Iain D. Craig

Virtual Machines

With 43 Figures

 Springer

Iain D. Craig, MA, PhD, MBCS, CITP
idc@idc.uklinux.net

British Library Cataloguing in Publication Data
Craig, I.
   Virtual machines
   1. Virtual computer systems   2. Parallel processing
   I. Title
   006.8

ISBN 978-1-84996-980-2   e-ISBN 978-1-84628-246-1

Printed on acid-free paper

9 8 7 6 5 4 3 2 1

Springer Science+Business Media
springeronline.com

To Dr P.W. Dale

(Uncle Paul)

Preface

I love virtual machines (VMs) and I have done for a long time. If that makes me "sad" or an "anorak", so be it. I love them because they are so much fun, as well as being so useful. They have an element of original sin (writing *assembly* programs and being in control of an *entire machine*), while still being able to claim that one is being a respectable member of the community (being structured, modular, high-level, object-oriented, and so on). They also allow one to design machines of one's own, unencumbered by the restrictions of a particular processor (at least, until one starts optimising it for some physical processor or other).

I have been building virtual machines, on and off, since 1980 or thereabouts. It has always been something of a hobby for me; it has also turned out to be a technique of great power and applicability. I hope to continue working on them, perhaps on some of the ideas outlined in the last chapter (I certainly want to do some more work with register-based VMs and concurrency).

I originally wanted to write the book from a purely semantic viewpoint. I wanted to start with a formal semantics of some language, then show how a virtual machine satisfied the semantics; finally, I would have liked to have shown how to derive an implementation. Unfortunately, there was insufficient time to do all of this (although some parts—the semantics of ALEX and a part proof of correctness—were done but omitted). There wasn't enough time to do all the necessary work and, in addition, Stärk *et al.* had published their book on Java [47] which does everything I had wanted to do (they do it with Java; I had wanted to define *ad hoc* languages).

I hope to have made it clear that I believe there to be a considerable amount of work left to be done with virtual machines. The entire last chapter is about this. As I have tried to make clear, some of the ideas included in that chapter are intended to make readers think, *even if* they consider the ideas stupid!

A word or two is in order concerning the instruction sets of the various virtual machines that appear from Chapter Four onwards. The instructions for the stack machines in Chapter Four seem relatively uncontroversial. The instructions in the chapter on register machines (Chapter Seven) might seem to be open to a little more questioning.

First, why not restrict the instruction set to those instructions required to implement ALEX? This is because I wanted to show (if such a demonstration were really required) that it is possible to define a larger instruction set so that more than one language can be supported.

Next, most of the jump and arithmetic instructions seem sensible enough but there are some strange cases, the jump branching to the address on the top of the stack is one case in point; all these stack indexing operations constitute another case. I decided to add these "exotic" instructions partly because, strange as they might appear to some, they are useful. Somewhere or other, I encountered a virtual machine that employed a jump instruction similar to the one just mentioned (I also tried one out in one of the Harrison Machine's implementations—it was quite useful), so I included it. Similarly, a lot of time is spent in accessing variables on the stack, so I added instructions that would make such accesses quite easy to compile; I was also aware that things like process control blocks and closures might be on stacks. I decided to add these instructions to build up a good repertoire, a repertoire that is *not* restricted to the instructions required to implement ALEX or one of the extensions described in Chapter Five.

I do admit, though, that the mnemonics for many of the operations could have been chosen with more care. (I was actually thinking that an assembler could macro these names out.) One reason for this is that I defined the register machine in about a day (the first ALEX machine was designed in about forty-five minutes!). Another (clearly) is that I am not terribly good at creating mnemonics. I thought I'd better point these matters out before someone else does.

I have made every effort to ensure that this text is free of errors. Undoubtedly, they still lurk waiting to be revealed in their full horror and to show that my proof-reading is not perfect. Should errors be found, I apologise for them in advance.

Acknowledgements

Beverley Ford first thought of this book when looking through some notes I had made on abstract machines. I would like to thank her and her staff at Springer, especially Catherine Drury, for making the process of writing this book as smooth as possible.

My brother Adam should be thanked for creating the line drawings that appear as some of the figures (I actually managed to do the rest myself). I would also like to thank all those other people who helped in various ways while I was writing this book (they know who they are).

Iain Craig
Market Square
Atherstone
14 June, 2005

Contents

1

Introduction

1.1 Introduction

There are, basically, two ways to implement a programming language: compile it or interpret it. Compilers are usually written for a single target machine; the GNU C compiler is a partial counter-example, containing, as it does, code generators for a number of target architectures (actually, the compiler has to be compiled for a specific target and it is only the full distribution that contains the complete set of code generators). Interpreters are thought to be slow but easy to port.

An interpreter can operate on the source structure of a program (as many LISP interpreters do) or can execute an internal form (for example, polish notation), while virtual machines combine both compilation and interpretation. Virtual machines consist of a compiler and a target architecture implemented in software. It contains a core that deals with the execution of code that has been compiled into the instruction set for the virtual machine's software architecture. The core executes these instructions by implementing the operations defined by the instruction set (which can be seen as a form of emulation or interpretation). Much of the traditional runtime package functionality associated with compiled code is implemented as part of a virtual machine; this clearly serves as an invitation to expand available functionality to provide rich execution environments for programs. It also opens up the possibility that traditional linkage methods (as exemplified by the linkage editor or by dynamic linkage of modules) can be eliminated in favour of more flexible methods.

Virtual machines are used as a method for ensuring portability, as well as for the execution of languages that do not conform well (or at all) to the architecture of the target architecture. As noted in the last paragraph, they afford opportunities to enrich the execution environment as well as greater flexibility.

It is the case that code in compiled form executes considerably faster than interpreted code, with interpreted code running at one or two orders of magnitude slower than the corresponding compiled form. For many, optimising compilers are the *sine qua non*, even though the output code can bear little resemblance to the source, thus causing verification problems (there is, and never can be, a viable alternative to the selection of good or, yet better, optimal algorithms) but optimising compilers are highly platform specific. The virtual machine is also a method for increasing the *general* speed of execution of programs by providing a single site that can be tuned or improved by additional techniques (a combination of native code execution with virtual machine code).

In a real sense, virtual machines constitute an execution method that combines the opportunities for compiler optimisation with the advantages of interpretation.

Although virtual machines in the form of "abstract machines" have been around for a long time (since the mid-1960s), the advent of Java has made them a common (and even fashionable) technique for implementing new languages, particularly those intended for use in heterogeneous environments. As noted above, many languages (Prolog, Curry and Oz, to cite but three) have relied upon virtual machines for a long time.

It is clear that the sense in which the term "virtual machine" is construed when considering execution environments for programs in particular programming languages relates to the other senses of the term. To construct a virtual machine for some programming language or other amounts, basically, to the definition of mechanisms that correspond to the actions of some computational machine (processor) or other.[1]

In the sense of the term adopted in this book, existing hardware imposes no constraints upon the designer other than the semantics of the programming language to be executed on the virtual machine. This view now seems to underpin ideas on the production of more general "virtual machines" that are able to execute the code of more than one programming language and to provide support to executing programs in other ways.

Virtual machines constitute an active research area. This book is intended as an invitation to engage in and contribute to it. This is manifested in a number of ways:

- The use of transitions as a way of specifying virtual machine instructions. (This leads to the idea of completely formal specifications, although this is not followed up in this book—for a formal description of the JVM, [47] is recommended.)
- The use of register-based virtual machines. Most virtual machines are based on stacks. In the register-based approach, it seems possible to widen the scope of virtual machines by providing more general instruction sets that can be tailored or augmented to suit particular languages.

---

[1] This latter sense is the one adopted by the designers of IBM's VM operating system; it implemented the underlying hardware as a software layer.

- The idea of translating ("morphing") code from one virtual machine for execution on another. This raises correctness issues that are partially addressed in this book.

1.2 Interpreters

Since the 1950s, it has been possible to execute programs in compiled form or in interpreted form. LISP was originally implemented in interpreted form, as was BASIC. The LISP interpreter was only a first stage of the project (since then, extremely high-quality LISP compilers have been built) but BASIC was intended from the outset to be an interpreted language. Since then, interpreters have been implemented for a great many languages.

Gries, in his [23], devotes a single chapter to interpreters. He gives the example of the interpretation of the Polish form of a program and describes the organisation of an interpreter, as well as runtime storage allocation. The techniques involved in interpretation are a subset of those in compilation to native code.

1.3 Landin's SECD Machine

In [30], Landin introduced the *SECD machine*. This was originally intended as a device for describing the operational semantics of the λ-calculus. Landin showed how the machine could be used to implement a functional programming language called ISWIM ("If you See What I Mean"[2]). Since its introduction, the SECD machine has been adapted in various ways and used to describe the operational semantics of a great many languages, some functional, some not. The machine has shown itself easy to adapt so that features like lazy evaluation, persistence and assignment can easily be accommodated within it.

Since the SECD machine is arguably the first virtual machine (or "abstract machine" as they used to be called),[3], it is useful to sketch its major points. A brief sketch of the machine occupies the remainder of this section.

The SECD machine gets its name from its main components or *registers* (often erroneously called "stacks"):

S: The state stack.
E: The environment stack.
C: The control list.
D: The dump stack.

---

[2] Many have observed that it should be "Do you See What I Mean"— DYSWIM just doesn't have the ring, though.

[3] I.e., the first thing to be called an "abstract machine" in technical usage and almost certainly the first to be so called in the literature.

Each of these components will be described in turn.

The S, state, register is a stack that is used for the evaluation of expressions. It is usually just called *the stack*. To evaluate an expression such as $5+3$, the values are pushed onto the S register (in reverse order) and then the operator $+$ is applied to them. Just prior to the application of the addition operation, the stack would be:

$$5 \cdot 3 \cdot \ldots$$

After application of $+$, the S register becomes:

$$8 \cdot \ldots$$

(The S register is assumed to grow to the left. The raised dot, $\cdot$, just separates the values.[4])

The E register is the *environment* register (usually just called *the environment*). The environment contains variable bindings. That is, it contains mappings from variables to their values. When a function is called, actual parameters are supplied. The environment for a function will record the mapping from formal to actual parameters, thus allowing the value of each parameter to be looked up when it is required.

For example, consider the unary function $f(x)$. When this function is applied to an argument, say $f(4)$, the binding of 4 to x is recorded somewhere in the E register. Inside f, when the value of x is needed, it is looked up in the environment and the value 4 is obtained. The environment is also used to store the values of local variables. The code to access the environment, both to bind and to lookup variable bindings is stored in the C register and is produced by a compiler generating SECD machine code.

The C register contains a sequence of SECD machine instructions. It is not really a stack but a simple list or vector. A pointer runs down the C register, pointing to each instruction in turn; in other machines, this pointer would be called the *instruction pointer* or the *program counter*; in most SECD implementations, the topmost element in the C register is shown.

The instructions used by an implementation of the SECD machine define what is to be done with the S, E and D registers (it is not impossible for them to define changes to the C register but it is rather rare). For example, the addition instruction states that the top two elements are to be popped from S, added and the result pushed onto S.

The final register is the D register, or the *dump*. The dump is used when the state of the machine must be stored for some reason. For example, when a routine is called, the caller's local variables and stack must be saved so that the called routine can perform its computations. In the SECD machine, the registers are saved together in the dump when a routine is called. When a routine exits, the dump's topmost element is popped and the machine's registers are restored.

---

[4] It will be given a more precise interpretation later in this book.

To make this a little clearer, consider an SECD machine. It is described by a 4-tuple S, E, C, D. When a call is made within one routine to another routine, the current instruction in the C register could cause the following state transition:

$$s, e, c, d \text{ becomes } \langle\rangle, e', c', \langle s, e, c, d\rangle \cdot d'$$

That is, an empty stack is put into the S and a new environment established in the E register; the code for the called routine is put into the C register. Meanwhile, the dump contains a 4-tuple consisting of the state of the calling routine. That state is suspended until the called routine exits.

On exit, the called routine executes an SECD machine instruction that effects the following transition:

$$s', e', c', \langle s, e, c, d\rangle \cdot d' \text{ becomes } s, e, c, d'$$

I.e., everything is put back where it belongs! (Transitions, more completely formalised, will be used later in this book.)

In addition, the SECD machine requires some storage management, typically a heap with a garbage collector. In most implementations, the S, E, C and D registers are implemented as lists. This implies that some form of heap storage is required to manage them. The Lispkit implementation described in [24] implements the three registers in this way and includes the (pseudo-code) specification of a mark and sweep garbage collector.

There are many, different publications containing descriptions of the SECD machine. The book by Field and Harrison [18], as well as Henderson's famous book on Lispkit [24] are two, now somewhat old, texts containing excellent descriptions of the SECD machine.

1.4 The Organisation of this Book

The chapter that immediately follows this (Chapter Two) is concerned with the BCPL OCODE and Cintcode/Intcode machines (in older versions, the bootstrap code was called *Intcode*, while in the newer, C-based, ones it is called *Cintcode*). BCPL is a relatively old language, although one that still has devotees, [5] that was always known for its portability. Portability is achieved through the definition of a virtual machine, the OCODE machine, that executes BCPL programs. The OCODE machine can be implemented from scratch or bootstrapped using Cintcode Intcode, a process that involves the construction of a simple virtual machine on each new processor that is used to implement the full OCODE machine. The OCODE machine and its instruction set are described in that chapter.

Chapter Three contains a relatively short description of the Java Virtual Machine (JVM), possibly the most famous and widely used virtual machine

---

[5] Such as the author.

at the time of writing. The JVM's main structures are described, as is its instruction set.

Doing it yourself[6] is the subject of Chapter Four. First, a simple procedural language, called ALEX, is introduced and informally defined. The main semantic aspects of the language are identified. A simple stack-based virtual machine for ALEX is then described in informal terms; this description is then converted into an Algol-like notation. Some extensions to the virtual machine (driven by extensions to the language) are then considered. An alternative organisation for the virtual machine is then proposed: it employs two stacks (one for control and one for data) rather than one, thus requiring alterations to the definition of the instruction set. This machine is then specified using *transition rules*. A compiler for a large subset of ALEX is specified in Appendix A; the compiler translates source code to the single-stack virtual machine.

The DIY theme continues in Chapter Five. This chapter contains the descriptions of two virtual machines: one for a simple object-oriented language, the other for a language for pseudo parallelism. The base language in both cases is assumed to be the simple dialect of ALEX with which Chapter Four started. In each case, extensions are considered and discussed (there appears to be more to say about the pseudo-parallel language).

The idea of introducing the DIY virtual machines is that they can be introduced in a simple form and then subjected to extensions that suit the various needs of different programming languages. Thus, the ALEX virtual machine starts with a call-by-value evaluation scheme which is later extended by the addition of call by reference; ALEX first has only vectors but records are added at a later stage. In addition, the DIY approach allows the extension and optimisation of the instruction set to be discussed without reference to an existing (and, hence, fixed) language and associated virtual machine.

By way of relief, an event-based language is considered in Chapter Six. This language is somewhat different and has a semantics that is not entirely procedural (although it contains procedural elements) and is not a straight pseudo-parallel language (although it can be related to one); the system was designed (and implemented) as part of the author's work on computational reflection. The virtual machine is a mixture of fairly conventional instructions, instructions for handling events and event queues and, finally, instructions to support (part of) the reflective behaviour that was desired. In order to make the virtual machine's definition clearer, a more mathematical approach has been adopted; transitions specify the instructions executed by the virtual machine. A compiler for the language executed by this virtual machine is specified in Appendix B.

---

[6] For readers not familiar with the term, "DIY" stands for "Do It Yourself". It usually refers to home "improvements", often in kitchens and bathrooms. The result is often reminiscent of the detonation of a medium-calibre artillery shell (or so it seems from TV programmes on the subject). The author explicitly and publicly denies all and any knowledge of home improvements.

An alternative to the stack-based virtual machine organisation is considered in Chapter Seven. This alternative is based on the register-transfer model of computer processors. An argument in favour of this model is first given; this is followed by a short description of the Parrot virtual machine for Perl6 and Python (and, it is to be hoped, many other languages). After this, a DIY register machine is described, first informally and then using transitions. After considering possible extensions, a translation from the two-stack virtual machine code to the register-based virtual machine is presented (it is intended as a motivating example for code translation between virtual machines, an issue, referred to as "code morphing" and discussed in Chapter 9). The correctness of this translation is considered in a semi-formal way. Finally, a more natural translation from ALEX to register-based code is considered before more extensions are discussed.

Register-based virtual machines are discussed because they appear to be an effective alternative to the more usual method of using stack (or zero-address) machines. The author experimented with such a virtual machine as part of the work on the Harrison Machine, the system described in Chapter Six (although not discussed there). The discovery that the Parrot group was using a similar approach for Perl6 appeared a strong basis for the inclusion of the topic in this book.

The implementation of virtual machines is considered in Chapter Eight. Implementation is important for virtual machines: they can either be considered theoretical devices for implementing new constructs and languages or practical ways to implement languages on many and many platforms.

In Chapter Eight, a number of implementation techniques are considered, both for stack- and register-based virtual machines. They include the direct translation to a language such as C and to other virtual machines. The use of different underlying organisations, such as threaded code, is also discussed.

The last chapter, Chapter Nine is concerned with what are considered to be open issues for those interested in pushing forward the virtual machine approach. This chapter is, basically, a somewhat loosely organised list—a brainstorming session—of ideas, some definitely worth investigating, some possibly dead ends, that are intended to stimulate interest in further work.

1.5 Omissions

Virtual machines are extremely popular for the implementation of languages of all kinds. It is impossible in a book of this length to discuss them all; it is also impossible, realistically, to discuss a representative sample.

Prolog is a good example of a language that has been closely associated with a virtual (or abstract) machine for a long time. The standard virtual machine is that of Warren [52] (the *Warren Abstract Machine* or *WAM*). A description of the WAM was considered and then rejected, mostly because of the excellent book by Aït-Kaci [3] on the WAM. Readers interested in logic programming languages would be well advised to read and completely digest [3]; readers just interested in virtual machines will also find it a pleasure to read.

The Scheme language (a greatly tidied-up LISP dialect with static scope) [28] has been associated with compilers since its inception. However, there is a virtual machine for it; it is described in [1] (the chapter on register machines). The implementation there can be used as the basis for a working implementation (indeed, many years ago, the author used it as a stage in the development of a compiled system for experimenting with reflection). Although intended for undergraduates, [1] is highly informative about Scheme (and is also a good read).

Pascal was distributed from ETH, Zürich, in the form of an abstract machine (VM) that could be ported with relative ease. The UCSD Pascal system was also based on an abstract machine. The notion of using a virtual machine to enhance portability is covered below in the chapter on BCPL (Chapter 2). BCPL is simpler in some ways than Pascal: it only has one primitive type (the machine word) and a few derived types (tables and vectors). BCPL's machine is a little earlier than that of Pascal, so it was decided to describe it. (BCPL will also be less familiar to many readers[7] and was a major influence on the design of C.)

Smalltalk [21] also has a virtual machine, which is defined in [21] in Smalltalk. The Smalltalk VM inspired the pseudo-parallel virtual machine described in Chapter 5; it was also influential in the design of the Harrison Machine (Chapter 6). A full description of the Smalltalk VM would have taken a considerable amount of space, so it was decided to omit it.

The Poplog system [42], a system for AI programming that supports CommonLISP, Prolog, Pop11 and Standard ML, uses a common virtual machine. Pop11 is used for all systems programming, so the virtual machine is tailored to that language. However, the Lisp, Prolog and ML compilers are written in Pop11 and generate virtual machine code. The Prolog compiler is based on a continuation-passing model, not on the Warren Abstract Machine, so the Poplog instruction set can be utilised directly. The Pop11 language is, in the author's opinion, worth studying in its own right; the virtual machine and the compilation mechanisms are also worth study. The Poplog system distribution contains on-line documentation about itself.

There are many other virtual machines that could not be included in this book. They include VMs for:

- Functional languages (e.g., the G-machine [25] and derivatives [39]; the FPM [7]);
- Functional-logic programming languages;
- Constraint languages (the Oz language is an interesting example).

---

[7] The author hopes it brings a smile to the lips of British readers, as well as fond and not-so fond memories.

Some readers will also ask why no attention has been paid to Just-In Time (JIT) compilers, particularly for Java. One reason is that this is a technique for optimising code rather than a pure-virtual machine method. Secondly, JIT compilers are a method for integrating native code (compiled on the fly) with a virtual machine. As such, it requires an interface to the virtual machine on which other code runs. In the treatment of the Java virtual machine, the native code mechanism is outlined; this is one method by which native code methods can be integrated.

Given the plethora of virtual machines, the reader might ask why it was decided to describe only three mainstream ones (BCPL, Java and Parrot) and to rely on (probably not very good) home-grown ones. The reasons are as follows:

- If the book had been composed only of descriptions of existing virtual machines, it would be open to the accusation that it omits the X virtual machine for language L. This was to be avoided.

- Home-grown ones could be developed from scratch, thus making clear the principles that underpin the development of a virtual machine.

- In the mainstream, only the Java virtual machine combines both objects and concurrency. It was decided to present new, independent virtual machines so that differences in language could be introduced in various ways. The home-grown approach allows language and virtual machine features to be included (or excluded) *ad libitum* (even so, an attempt has been made to be as comprehensive as possible within the confines of a book of this length—hence the various sections and subsections on extensions and alternatives).

- At the time of writing, the Parrot virtual machine appears to be the only generally available one based on the register-transfer model. The author independently came to conclusions similar to those of the designers of Parrot as to the merits of register-based machines (and on treating virtual machines as data structures) and wanted to argue for this alternative model. As a consequence, the mapping between stack- and register-based models was of importance (as are some of the suggestions for further work in the Chapter 9).

- The derivation of transitions specifying many virtual machines would not have been possible in the time available for the writing of this book. Furthermore, an existing virtual machine is an entity, so the introduction of new instructions (e.g., branches or absolute jumps) would have been less convincing; the *ad hoc* virtual machines described below can be augmented as much as one wishes. [8]

---

[8] Interested readers are actively encouraged to implement the virtual machines in this book and augment them as they see fit, as well as introducing new instructions by defining new transitions.

- Finally, the definition of a virtual machine can be a testing, rewarding and enjoyable exercise. An aim of the current book is to encourage people to do it for themselves and to use their imagination in defining them.

VMs for Portability: BCPL

2.1 Introduction

BCPL is a high-level language for systems programming that is intended to be as portable as possible. It is now a relatively old language but it contains most syntactic constructs found in contemporary languages. Indeed, C was designed as a BCPL derivative (C can be considered as a mixture of BCPL and Algol68 plus some *sui generis* features). BCPL is not conventionally typed. It has one basic data type, the machine word. It is possible to extract bytes from words but this is a derived operation. All entities in BCPL are considered either to be machine words or to require a machine word or a number of machine words. BCPL supports addresses and assumes that they can fit into a single word. Similarly, it supports vectors (one-dimensional arrays) which are sequences of words (multi-dimensional arrays must be explicitly programmed in terms of vectors of pointers to vectors). Routines (procedures and functions) can be defined in BCPL and are represented as pointers to their entry points. Equally, labels are addresses of sequences of instructions.

BCPL stands for "Basic CPL", a subset of the CPL language. CPL was an ambitious lexically scoped, imperative procedural programming language designed by Strachey and others in the mid-1960s as a joint effort involving Cambridge and London Universities. CPL contained all of the most advanced language constructs of the day, including polymorphism. There is a story that the compiler was too large to run on even the biggest machines available in the University of London! Even though it strictly prefigures the structured programming movement, BCPL contains structured control constructs (commands) including two-branch conditionals, switch commands, structured loops with structured exits. It also supports statement formulæ similar to those in FORTRAN and the original BASIC. Recursive routines can be defined. BCPL does support a goto command. Separate compilation is supported in part by the provision of a "global vector", a vector of words that contains pointers to externally defined routines. BCPL is lexically scoped. It implements call-by-value semantics for routine parameters. It also permits higher-order programming by permitting routine names to be assigned to variables (and, hence, passed into and out of routines).

BCPL was intended to be portable. Portability is achieved by bootstrapping the runtime system a number of times so that it eventually implements the compiler's output language. This language is called *OCODE*. OCODE is similar to a high-level assembly language but is tailored exactly to the intermediate representation of BCPL constructs. OCODE was also defined in such a way that it could be translated into the machine language of most processors. Associated with OCODE is an OCODE machine that, once implemented, executes OCODE, hence compiled BCPL. The implementation of an abstract machine for OCODE is relatively straigthforward.

In the book on BCPL [45], Richards and Whitby-Strevens define a second low-level intermediate language called *Intcode*. Intcode is an extremely simple language that can be used to bootstrap OCODE. More recently, Richards has defined a new low-level bootstrap code called *Cintcode*. The idea is that a fundamental system is first written for Intcode/Cintcode. This is then used to bootstrap the OCODE evaluator. The definition of the Intcode and Cintcode machines is given in the BCPL documentation. The BCPL system was distributed in OCODE form (more recent versions distribute executables for standard architectures like the PC under Linux). At the time the book was published, an Intcode version of the system was required to bootstrap a new implementation.

The virtual machines described below are intended, therefore, as an aid to portability. The definitions of the machines used to implement OCODE and Intcode/Cintcode instructions include definitions of the storage structures and layout required by the virtual machine, as well as the instruction formats and state transitions.

The organisation of this chapter is as follows. We will focus first on BCPL and its intermediate languages OCODE and Intcode/Cintcode (Cintcode is part of the current BCPL release and access to the documentation is relatively easy). We will begin with a description of the OCODE machine. This description will start with a description of the machine's organisation and then we move on to a description of the instruction set. The relationship between OCODE instructions and BCPL's semantics will also be considered. Then, we will examine Cintcode and its abstract machine. Finally, we explain how BCPL can be ported to a completely new architecture.

2.2 BCPL the Language

In this section, the BCPL language is briefly described.

BCPL is what we would now see as a relatively straightforward procedural language. As such, it is based around the concept of the procedure. BCPL provides three types of procedural abstraction:

- Routines that update the state and return no value;

- Routines that can update the state and return a single value;
- Routines that just compute a value.

The first category refers to procedures proper, while the second corresponds to the usual concept of function in procedural languages. The third category corresponds to the single-line functions in FORTRAN and in many BASIC dialects. Each category permits the programmer to pass parameters, which are called by value.

BCPL also supports a variety of function that is akin to the so-called "formula function" of FORTRAN and BASIC. This can be considered a variety of macro or open procedure because it declares no local variables.

BCPL supports a variety of state-modifying constructs. As an imperative language, it should be obvious that it contains an assignment statement. Assignment in BCPL can be simple or multiple, so the following are both legal:

```
x := 0;
x, y := 1, 2;
```

It is worth noting that terminating semicolons are optional. They are mandatory if more than one command is to appear on the same line as in:

```
x := 0; y := 2
```

Newline, in BCPL, can also be used to terminate a statement. This is a nice feature, one found in only a few other languages (Eiffel and Imp, a language used in the 1970s at Edinburgh University).

Aside from this syntactic feature, the multiple assignment gives a clue that the underlying semantics of BCPL are based on a stack.

In addition, it contains a number of branching constructs:

- IF ... DO.[1] This is a simple test. If the test is true, the code following the DO is executed. If the test is false, the entire statement is a no-operation.
- UNLESS ... DO. This is syntactic sugar for IF NOT ... DO. That is, the code following the DO is executed if the test fails.
- TEST ... THEN ... ELSE. This corresponds to the usual if then else in most programming languages.
- SWITCHON. This is directly analogous to the case statement in Pascal and its descendants and to the switch statement in C and its derivatives. Cases are marked using the CASE keyword. Cases run into each other unless explicitly broken. There is also a an optional default case denoted by a keyword. Each case is implicitly a block.

In general, the syntax word do can be interchanged with then. In the above list, we have followed the conventions of BCPL style.

BCPL contains a number of iterative statements. The iterative statements are accompanied by structured ways to exit loops.

---

[1] Keywords must be in uppercase, so the convention is followed here.

BCPL has a goto, as befits its age.

BCPL statements can be made to return values. This is done using the pair of commands VALOF and RESULTIS. The VALOF command introduces a block from which a value is returned using the RESULTIS command; there can be more than one RESULTIS command in a VALOF block. The combination of VALOF and RESULTIS is used to return values from functions. The following is a BCPL procedure:

```
LET Add.Global (x) BE
$(
   globl := globl + x;
$)
```

The following is a BCPL functional routine:

```
LET Global.Added.Val (x) =
$(
   VALOF $(
     RESULTIS(x+globl);
   $)
$)
```

From this small example, it can be seen that the body of a procedure is marked by the BE keyword, while functional routines are signalled by the equals sign and the use of VALOF and RESULTIS (BCPL is case-sensitive).

BCPL is not conventionally typed. It has only one data type, the machine word, whose size can change from machine to machine. The language also contains operators that access the bytes within a machine word. Storage is allocated by the BCPL compiler in units of one machine word. The language contains an operator that returns the address of a word and an operator that, given an address, returns the contents of the word at that address (dereferencing).

BCPL supports structured types to a limited extent. It permits the definition of vectors (single-dimension arrays of words). It also has a table type. Tables are vectors of words that are indexed by symbolic constants, not by numerical values. In addition, it is possible to take the address of a routine (procedure or function); such addresses are the *entry points* of the routines (as in C). The passing of routine addresses is the method by which BCPL supports higher-order routines (much as C does).

It also permits the definition of symbolic constants. Each constant is one machine word in length.

BCPL introduces entities using the LET syntax derived from ISWIM. For example, the following introduces a new variable that is initialised to zero:

```
LET x := 0 IN
```

The following introduces a constant:

```
LET x = 0 IN
```

Multiple definitions are separated by the AND keyword (logical conjunction is represented by the "&" symbol) as in:

```
LET x := 0
AND y = 0
IN
```

Routines are also introduced by the LET construct.

Variables and constants can be introduced at the head of any block.

In order to support separate compilation and to ease the handling of the runtime library, a *global vector* is supported. This is a globally accessible vector of words, in which the first few dozen entries are initialised by the runtime system (they are initialised to library routine entry points and to globally useful values). The programmer can also assign to the global vector at higher locations (care must be taken not to assign to locations used by the system). These are the primary semantic constructs of BCPL. Given this summary, we can now make some observations about the support required by the virtual machine (the OCODE machine).

2.3 VM Operations

The summary of BCPL above was intended to expose the major constructs. The identification of major constructs is important for the design of a virtual machine which must respect the semantics of the language as well as providing the storage structures required to support the language.

At this stage, it should be clear that a BCPL machine should provide support for the primitive operations needed for the manipulation of data of all primitive types. The virtual machine support for them will be in the form of instructions that the machine will directly implement. In BCPL, this implies that the virtual machine must support operations on the word type: arithmetic operations, comparisons and addressing. Byte-based operations can either be provided by runtime library operations or by instructions in the virtual machine; BCPL employs the latter for the reason that it is faster and reduces the size of the library. In addition, BCPL supports vectors on the stack; they must also be addressed when designing an appropriate virtual machine.

The values manipulated by these operations must be stored somewhere: a storage area, particularly for temporary and non-global values must be provided. Operations are required for manipulating this storage area. Operations are also required to load values from other locations and to store them as results. More than one load operation might be required (in a more richly typed language, this might be a necessity) and more than one store operation might be required. It is necessary to look at the cases to determine what is required.

BCPL employs static scoping. The compiler can be relied upon to verify that variables, etc., are not required. Static scoping requires a stack-like mechanism for the storage of variables. The virtual machine is, therefore, built around a stack. Operations are required to allocate and free regions of stack at routine entry and exit; the return of results can also be implemented by means of stack allocation and addressing. The compiler generates instructions that allocate and free the right amount of stack space; it also generates instructions to handle returned values and the adjustment of the stack when routines return. Evaluation of expressions can be performed on the stack, so we now are in a position to define the instructions for data manipulation.

With expressions out of the way, the following families of construct must be handled by the compiler and OCODE instructions generated to implement them:

• Control constructs, in particular, conditionals, iteration, jumps;
• ·Assignment;
• Routine call and return;
• Parameter passing and value return from routines and valof.

Note that we assume that sequencing is handled implicitly by the compiler.

Control structure is handled, basically, by means of labels and jumps. There are clear translations between most of the control structures and label-jump combinations. The problem cases are **FOR** and **SWITCHON**. The former is problematic because it requires counters to be maintained and updated in the right order; the latter because the best implementation requires a jump table.

Assignment is a relatively straightforward matter (essentially, push a value onto the stack and pop it off to some address or other). Multiple assignment is also easy with a stack machine. The values are pushed onto the stack in some order (say left to right) and popped in the reverse order. Thus, the command:

```
p,q := 1, 2
```

has the intention of assigning 1 to p and 2 to q. This can be done by pushing 1, then 2 onto the stack and assigning them in reverse order. An interesting example of multiple assignment is:

```
p,q := q, p
```

Swap! It can be handled in exactly the manner just described.

Finally, we have routine calls and **VALOF**. There are many ways to implement routine calls. For software virtual machines, relatively high-level instructions can be used (although low-level instructions can also be employed). The OCODE machine provides special instructions for handling routine entry and exit, as will be seen.

BCPL is a call-by-value language, so the runtime stack can be directly employed to hold parameter values that are to be passed into the routine.

The VALOF ... RESULTIS combination can be handled in a variety of ways. One is to perform a source-to-source transformation. Another is to use the stack at runtime by introducing a new scope level. Variables local to the VALOF can be allocated on the runtime stack with the stack then being used for local values until the RESULTIS is encountered. An implementation for RESULTIS would be to collapse the stack to the point where the VALOF was encountered and then push the value to be returned onto the stack.

2.4 The OCODE Machine

In this section, the organisation of the OCODE machine is presented. BCPL is a procedural programming language that supports recursion. It requires a globally accessible vector of words to support separate compilation. It also requires a pool of space to represent global variables. The language also permits the use of (one-dimensional) vectors and tables (essentially vectors of words whose elements are indexed by symbolic identifiers, much like tables in assembly language). As a consequence, the OCODE machine must reserve space for a stack to support lexical scope and for recursion. The OCODE machine also needs space to hold the global vector and also needs a space to hold program instructions.

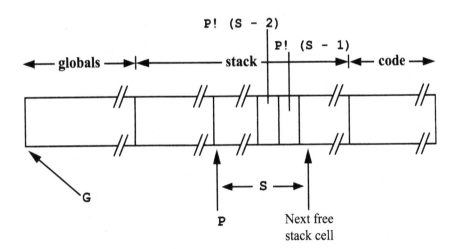

Fig. 2.1. *The OCODE machine organisation.*

The OCODE machine has three memory regions:

- The Global vector;
- The Stack (this is a *framed* stack);
- Storage for program code and static data.

The organisation of the OCODE machine is shown in Figure 2.1.

The *global vector* is used to store all variables declared global in the program. The global vector is a vector of words containing global variables; it also contains the entry points of routines declared in one module that are to be made visible in another. It is pointed to by the G register. The current stack frame is pointed to by the P register. The size of the current stack frame is always known at compilation time, so it need not be represented in code by a register.

There is also a special A register which is used to hold values returned by functions (see below).

Static variables, tables and string constants are stored in the program area. They are referenced by labels which are usually represented by the letter L followed by one or more digits.

The stack holds all dynamic (local) variables.

All variables are of the same size. That is, all variables are allocated the same amount of space in the store. For most modern machines they are 32- or 64-bits in length.

2.5 OCODE Instructions and their Implementation

In OCODE, instructions are represented as integers. Here, we will use only the mnemonic names in the interests of readability. It is important to note that the mnemonic form for instructions and labels must be converted into more fundamental representations when code is emitted by the compiler.

The size of the current stack frame is always known at compile time. When specifying instructions, a variable, S, is used to denote an offset from the start of the current stack frame. This is done only to show how much space is left in the current stack frame by the individual instructions.

When defining abstract machine instructions, an array notation will be employed. Thus, P is considered as a one-dimensional vector. S will still be a constant denoting the size of the current stack frame. Similarly, G will also be considered as an array.

The notation P[S-1] denotes the first free element on the stack.

2.5.1 Expression Instructions

The OCODE instructions that implement expressions do not alter the stack frame size. In the case of unary instructions, the operand is replaced on the top of the stack by the result of the instruction. In the case of binary operations, the stack element immediately beneath the top one is replaced by the result.

The instructions are mostly quite clear. Rather than enter into unnecessary detail, these instructions are summarised in Table 2.1 The table's middle column is a short English equivalent for the opcode.

Only the first instruction deserves any real comment. It is an instruction that considers the current top-of-stack element as a pointer into memory. It replaces the top-of-stack element by the object that it points to. This is the operation of dereferencing a pointer to yield an r-value.

Table 2.1. *OCODE expression instructions.*

Opcode	Description	Definition
RV	r-value	P[S-1] := cts([S-1])
ABS	absolute value	P[S-1] := abs(P[S-1])
NEG	unary minus	P[S-1] := -P[S-1]
NOT	logical negation	P[S-1] := ¬(P[S-1])
GETBYTE	extract byte	P[S-2] := P[S-2] gtb P[S-1]
MULT	multiply	P[S-2] := P[S-2] * P[S-1]
DIV	divide	P[S-2] := P[S-2] / P[S-1]
REM	remainder	P[S-2] := P[S-2] rem P[S-1]
PLUS	add	P[S-2] := P[S-2] + P[S-1]
MINUS	subtract	P[S-2] := P[S-2] - P[S-1]
EQ	equal	P[S-2] := P[S-2] = P[S-1]
NE	not equal	P[S-2] := P[S-2] ≠ P[S-1]
LS	less than	P[S-2] := P[S-2] < P[S-1]
GR	greater than	P[S-2] := P[S-2] > P[S-1]
LE	≤	P[S-2] := P[S-2] <= P[S-1]
GE	≥	P[S-2] := P[S-2] >= P[S-1]
LSHIFT	left shift	P[S-2] := P[S-2] << P[S-1]
RSHIFT	right shift	P[S-2] := P[S-2] >> P[S-1]
LOGAND	logical and	P[S-2] := P[S-2] and P[S-1]
LOGOR	logical or	P[S-2] := P[S-2] or P[S-1]
EQV	bitwise equal	P[S-2] := P[S-2] leq P[S-1]
NEQV	xor	P[S-2] := P[S-2] xor P[S-1]

Table 2.1 employs a notational convention that needs explanation:

- cts is the contents operation (dereferences its argument).
- abs is the absolute value of its argument.
- gtb is the getbyte operator.
- rem is integer remainder after division.
- and is logical and (conjunction).
- or is logical or (disjunction).
- leq is bitwise equivalence.
- xor is bitwise exclusive or (logical not-equivalence).
- $e_1 << e_2$ is left shift e1 by e2 bits.
- $e_1 >> e_2$ is right shift e1 by e2 bits.

Other than this, the "description" of each instruction is just an operation on the OCODE stack. In this and the following cases, the code equivalent is included in the table; when defining virtual machines later in this book, this method will be used to indicate both "descriptions" and implementations of virtual machine instructions.

2.5.2 Load and Store Instructions

The load and store instructions, like those for expressions, should be fairly clear. The code equivalents are included in the right-hand column of Table 2.2. Each instruction is described (middle column of the table).

Table 2.2. *OCODE load and store instructions.*

Opcode	Description	Definition
LPn	load from P	P[S] := P[n]; S := S+1
LGn	load global	P[S] := G[n]; S := S+1
LL Ln	load label	P[S] := Ln; S := S+1
LL Pn	load address	P[S] := P[n]; S := S+1
LL Gn	load global addr	P[S] := G[n]; S := S+1
LLL Ln	load label addr	P[S] := Ln; S := S+1
SPn	store off P	P[n] := P[S]; S := S-1
SGn	store global	G[n] := P[S]; S := S-1
SL Ln	store at label	Ln:= P[S]; S := S-1
LF Ln	load function	P[S] := entry point Ln; S := S+1
LNn	load constant	P[S] := n; S := S+1
TRUE	true	P[S] := *true*; S := S+1
FALSE	false	P[S] := *false*; S := S+1
LSTR n $C_1 \ldots C_n$	load string	P[S] := "$C_1 \ldots C_n$"; S := S+1
STIND	store index	cts(P[S-1]) := P[S-2]; S := S-2
PUTBYTE	put byte	setbyte(P[S-2],P[S-1]) := P[S-3]; S := S-3

There is an instruction not included in Table 2.2 that appears in the OCODE machine specification in [44]. It is the QUERY instruction. It is defined as:

$$P[S] := ?; \quad S := S+1$$

Unfortunately, [44] does not contain a description of it. The remaining instructions have an interpretation that is fairly clear and is included in the table. It is hoped that the relatively brief description is adequate.

2.5.3 Instructions Relating to Routines

This class of instruction deals with routine entry (call) and return. When it compiles a routine, the OCODE compiler generates code of the following form:

```
ENTRY Li n C1 ... Cn
SAVE s
<body of routine>
ENDPROC
```

Here, `Li` is the label of the routine's entry point. For debugging purposes, the length of the routine's identifier is recorded in the code (this is `n` in the code fragment); the characters comprising the name are the elements denoted `C1` to `Cn`. The instructions in this category are shown in Table 2.3.

The `SAVE` instruction specifies the initial setting of the S register. The value of this is the save space size (3) plus the number of formal parameters. The save space is used to hold the previous value of P, the return address and the routine entry address. The first argument to a routine is always at the location denoted by 3 relative to the pointer P (some versions of BCPL have a different save space size, so the standard account is followed above).

The end of each routine is denoted by `ENDPROC`. This is a no-op which allows the code generator to keep track of nested procedure definitions.

The BCPL standard requires that arguments are allocated in consecutive locations on the stack. There is no *a priori* limit to the number of arguments that can be supplied. A typical call of the form:

$$E(E1, \ldots, En)$$

is compiled as follows (see Table 2.3). First, S is incremented to allocate space for the save space in the new stack frame. The arguments E1 to En are compiled and then the code for E. Finally, either `FNAP` k or `RTAP` k instruction is generated, the actual one depending upon whether a function or routine call is being compiled. The value k is the distance between the old and new stack frames (i.e., the number of words or bytes between the start of the newly compiled stack frame and the start of the previous one on the stack).

Table 2.3. *OCODE instructions for routines.*

Opcode	Meaning
ENTRY	enter routine
SAVE	save locals
ENDPROC	end routine
FNAPk	apply function
RNAPk	apply procedure
RTRN	return from procedure
FNRN	return from function

Return from a routine is performed by the `RTRN` instruction. This restores the previous value of P and resumes execution from the return address. If the return is from a function, the `FNRN` instruction is planted just after the result has been evaluated (this is always placed on the top of the stack). The FNRN instruction is identical to RTRN after it has stored the result in the A register ready for the FNAP instruction to store it at the required location in the previous stack frame.

2.5.4 Control Instructions

Control instructions are to be found in most virtual machines. Their function is centred around the transfer of control from one point to another in the code. Included in this set are instructions to create labels in code. The OCODE control instructions are shown in Figure 2.4.

Table 2.4. *OCODE control instructions.*

Opcode	Meaning
LAB Ln	declare label
JUMP Ln	unconditionally jump to label
JT Ln	jump if top of stack is true
JF Ln	jump if top of stack is false
GOTO E	computed goto (see below)
RES Ln	return
RSTACK k	return
SWITCHON n Ld K_1 $L_1 \ldots L_n$	jump table for a SWITCHON.
FINISH	terminate execution

The JUMP Ln instruction transfers control unconditionally to the label L. The instructions JT and JF transfer control to their labels if the top of the stack (implemented as P!(S-1)) is true or false, respectively. Instructions like this are often found in the instruction sets of virtual machines. The conditional jumps are used, *inter alia*, in the implementation of selection and iteration commands.

Although they are particular to OCODE, the other instructions also represent typical operations in a virtual machine. The LAB instruction (really a pseudo-operation) declares its operand as a label (thus associating the address at which it occurs with the label).

The GOTO instruction is used to generate code for SWITCHON commands. It takes the form GOTO E, where E is an expression. In the generated code, the code for E is compiled and immediately followed by the GOTO instruction. At runtime, the expression is evaluated, leaving an address on the top of the stack. The GOTO instruction then transfers control to that address.

The RES and RSTACK instructions are used to compile RESULTIS commands. If the argument to a RESULTIS is immediately returned as the result of a function, the FNRN instruction is selected. In all other contexts, RESULTIS e compiles to the code for e followed by the RES Ln instruction. The execution of this instruction places the result in the A register and then jumps to the label Ln. The label addresses an **RSTACK** k instruction, which takes the result and stores it at location P!k and sets S to $k+1$.

The OCODE **SWITCHON** instruction performs a jump based on the value on the top of the stack. It is used to implement switches (**SWITCHON** commands, otherwise known as case statements). It has the form shown in Table 2.4, where n is the number of cases to which to switch and Ld is the label of the default case. The K_i are the case constants and the L_i are the corresponding code labels.

Finally, the **FINISH** instruction implements the BCPL **FINISH** command. It compiles to **stop(0)** in code and causes execution to terminate.

2.5.5 Directives

It is intended that BCPL programs be compiled to OCODE (or native code) and then executed in their entirety. The BCPL system is not intended to be incremental or interactive. It is necessary, therefore, for the compiler to provide information to the runtime system that relates to the image file that it is to execute. This is the role of the directives.

The BCPL OCODE machine manages a globals area, a stack and a code segment. The runtime system must be told how much space to allocate to each. It must also be told where globals are to be located and where literal pools start and end, so that modules can be linked. The system also needs to know which symbols are exported from a module and where modules start and end.

The BCPL global vector is a case in point. There is no *a priori* limit on the size of the global vector. In addition, two modules can assign different values to a particular cell in the global vector (with all the ordering problems that are so familiar).

The OCODE generator also needs to be handed information in the form of directives. The directives in the version of BCPL that is current at the time of writing (Summer, 2004) are as shown in Table 2.5. The directives are used in different parts of the system, so are briefly explained in the following few paragraphs.

Table 2.5. *OCODE directives.*

Directive
STACK s
STORE
ITEMN n
DATALAB Ln
SECTION
NEEDS
GLOBAL n $K_1 L_1 \ldots K_n L_n$

The STACK directive informs the code generator of the current size of the stack. This is required because the size of the current stack frame can be affected by some control structures, for example those that leave a block in which local variables have been declared.

The STORE directive informs the code generator that the point separating the declarations and code in a block has been reached. Any values left on the stack are to be treated as variable initialisations and should be stored in the appropriate places.

Static variables and tables are allocated in the program code area using the ITEMN directive. The parameter to this directive is the initial value of the cell that is reserved by this directive. For a table, the elements are allocated by consecutive ITEMN directives. The DATALAB directive is used to associate a label with a data area reserved by one or more ITEMN directives.

The SECTION and NEEDS directives are direct translations of the SECTION and NEEDS source directives. The latter are used to indicate the start of a BCPL module and the modules upon which the current one depends.

An OCODE module is terminated with the GLOBAL directive. The arguments denote the number of items in the global initialisation list and each of the K_i are offsets into the global vector and L_n is the label of the corresponding offset (i.e., $K_i L_i$ denotes an offset and the label to be associated with that offset).

Directives are an important class of virtual machine instruction, although little more will be said about them. One reason for this is that, once one becomes aware of their need, there is little else to be said. A second reason is that, although every system is different, there are things that are common to all—in this case, the general nature of directives. It is considered that the directives required by any virtual machine will become clear during its specification.

2.6 The Intcode/Cintcode Machine

The Intcode/Cintcode machine is used to bootstrap an OCODE machine on a new processor; it can also serve as a target for the BCPL compiler's code generator. The code is designed to be as compact as possible. The Cintcode machine was originally designed as a byte-stream interpretive code to run on small 16-bit machines such as the Z80 and 6502 running under CP/M. More recently, it has been extended to run on 32-bit machines, most notably machines running Linux.

The best descriptions of the Intcode and Cintcode machines are [45] and [44], respectively. Compared with OCODE, (Ci/I)ntcode is an extremely compact representation but is somewhat more complex. The complexity arises because of the desire to make the instruction set as compact as possible; this is reflected in the organisation which is based on bit fields. The organisation of the machine is, on the other hand, easily described. The following description is of the original Intcode machine and follows that in [45] (the account in [44] is far more detailed but is essentially the same in intent).

The Intcode machine is composed of the following components. A memory consisting of equal-sized locations that can be addressed by consecutive integers (a vector of words, for example). It has a number of central registers:

A,B: the *accumulator* and *auxiliary accumulator*;
C: the *control register*. This is the instruction pointer; it points to the next instruction to be executed;
D: the *address register*, used to store the effective address of an instruction;
P: a pointer that is used to address the *current stack frame*;
G: a pointer used to access the global vector.

Note that the Intcode machine has a framed stack and a global vector (both necessary to implement OCODE).

Instructions come in two lengths: single and double length. The compiler determines when a double-length instruction should be used.

The operations provided by the Intcode machine are shown in Table 2.6 (the idea is taken from [45], p. 134; the specification has been re-written using mostly C conventions). As in the OCODE instructions, each operation is specified by a code fragment.

Table 2.6. *The Intcode machine functions.*

Operation	Mnemonic	Specification
Load	**L**	B := A: A := D
Store	**S**	*D := A
Add	**A**	A := A + D
Jump	**J**	C := D
Jump if true	**T**	IF A THEN C := D
Jump if false	**F**	IF NOT A THEN C := D
Call routine	**K**	D := P + D
		*D := P; *(D+1) := C
		P := D; C := A
Execute operation	**X**	Various operations, mostly arithmetic of logical operations operating on **A** and **B**.

Each Intcode instruction is composed of six fields. They are as follows:

- Function Part: This is a three-bit field. It specifies one of the eight possible machine operations described in Table 2.6.
- Address Field: This field holds a positive integer. It represents the initial value of the D register.
- D bit: This is a single bit. When set, it specifies that the initial value of the D register is to be taken from the following word.

- P bit: This is single bit. It specifies whether the P register is to be added to the D register at the second stage of an address calculation.
- G bit: This is another single bit field. It specifies whether the G register is to be added to the D register at the end of the third stage of address calculation.
- I bit: This is the *indirection* bit. If it is set, it specifies that the D register is to be relaced by the contents of the location addressed by the D register at the last stage of address calculation.

The effective address is evaluated in the same way for every instruction and is not dependent upon the way in which the machine function is specified.

Intcode is intended to be a compact representation of a program. It is also intended to be easy to implement, thus promoting BCPL's portability (the BCPL assembler and interpreter for Intcode occupies just under eight and a half pages of BCPL code in [45]).

The Intcode machine also uses indirection (as evidenced by the three-stage address calculation involving addresses in registers), thus making code compact.

This has, of necessity, been only a taster for the Intcode and Cintcode machines. The interested reader is recommended to consult [44] and [45] for more information. The full BCPL distribution contains the source code of the OCODE and Cintcode machines; time spent reading them will be rewarding.

3

The Java Virtual Machine

3.1 Introduction

It is arguable that Java and its "compile once, run anywhere" slogan started the current interest in virtual machines; indeed, it would appear to have popularised the term "virtual machine".

This chapter is organised as follows. First, the Java language is briefly introduced. Next, the gross organisation of the Java Virtual Machine—the JVM for short—will be described. In that section, the storage organisation used by the JVM and the organisation of the stack is presented and major concepts such as the Runtime Constant Pool and its contents, including the method areas and class file representation are introduced. The instruction pointer (or program counter—pc in JVM terms) is also briefly discussed. This is followed by a relatively short description of the "class file", a runtime representation of each class; this description is followed by a brief outline of so-called "class resolution," the process of locating and loading classes at runtime.

Section 4 is concerned with the JVM's instruction set. The instruction set can be described in a number of ways. A subset of the instruction set is clearly typed, while another is not. Some instructions are at a relatively high level (e.g., those dealing with locks and exception), while others (e.g., jumps and arithmetic) are not. Finally, there are special-purpose instructions directly tailored to Java's needs: those dealing with locks, monitors, and method and data location, for example.

The final section acts as a summary of the main points. It also discusses the relationship between the main components of the JVM and the source structure of Java programs.

It is not possible, given the space available here, to describe the JVM exhaustively. Instead, all that can be done is to give the reader a general impression that is detailed in some places and superficial in others. Readers interested in the exact details should consult [33]. For information about Java itself, the language definition [22] should be consulted. It is, of course, not possible to understand the details of the JVM in complete detail unless the language is completely understood. It is strongly recommended that interested readers should consult *both* of these texts.

3.2 JVM Organisation: An Overview

This section contains an overview of the JVM's organisation. This description is based upon the published specification [33].

The JVM is a stack-based virtual machine. It contains these basic structures:

- The heap store (main store);
- The stack;
- The method area;
- Runtime Constant Pools;
- The PC register;

The stack and the "class file" objects are stored in the heap, as are the Constant Pools and the method area. In addition, there should be structures to support threads and monitors—they will be considered only (Section 3.9).

The JVM specification is silent on issues pertaining to the heap's management. A JVM can use a mark and scan, stop-and-copy or a generational garbage collector, therefore. A pure reference-counting storage management régime cannot be used, however, unless it is supported by some other mechanism. The reason for this is that circular links can exist between entities stored in the heap (Java has an imperative semantics and, therefore, supports assignment).

There are, in fact, two stacks in the JVM specification: the "native code" stack (or "C stack") and the "Java stack". The first can be disposed of fairly readily. It is the stack used to implement the JVM itself; it is also the stack used for intermediate storage by all the primitive routines in a JVM and by all the code implementing JVM instructions. Additional primitives, as well as *native* methods, are implemented using the "native code" stack. In most implementations, this stack will be the one used by the C runtime system. This stack will not be of further interest because it is beyond the control of the JVM specification.

The other stack is the JVM stack proper. It is a framed stack. A stack frame is allocated when control enters a method. It is deallocated when control returns from the method that caused its allocation. There are two cases of return from a method:

- Normal return. This is performed by the execution of a return instruction.
- Abnormal return. This is performed when an exception of some kind is caught by a handler that is not inside the method invocation associated with the stack frame.

The JVM specification uses the term *completion* to refer to return from a method; it also uses the term *abrupt completion* for what is termed "abnormal return" in the above list. A method can return zero or more values; the value can be of a simple (scalar) type, an array type or a class type (i.e., a reference to an instance of a class).

3.2.1 The stack

The frames of the stack are allocated in the heap. Each stack frame consists of:

- A purely local stack called the *operand stack*;
- A set of local variables;
- A reference to the code associated with the method being executed. This is in the Runtime Constant Pool of the class with which the method is associated;
- A slot for the PC register.

The operand stack is for the storage of temporary and intermediate results in the usual fashion. It is used, *inter alia*, for the evaluation of expressions and parameters.

The set of local variables is used to store:

- The variables local to the method whose activation (invocation) caused the stack frame to be allocated. This is called the *local variable array* in [33].
- Parameters passed from the invoking context.
- The this pseudo variable that always points to the instance upon which the method operates.

Each local variable is 32 bits in length; this corresponds to the internal JVM integer length. It generally also corresponds to the length of a pointer on the host machine. When an entity is longer than 32 bits, two consecutive locals are allocated. The index of the entity in such a case is considered to be the lowest of the indices required to represent it. For floating point numbers (which are implemented according to most of the IEEE 444 standard) or long integer values, which occupy 64 bits on a 32-bit machine, two consecutive local variables are allocated. The standard defines a big-endian representation for all values.

Because of these considerations, there will, in general, be more local variables in a stack frame's local variable array than there are local variables in the corresponding method's source code. In addition, the JVM specification permits implementations of the Java compiler to allocate more local variables when they are needed to optimise method code.

The JVM contains instructions to access and update local variables in the current stack frame's variable array. There are also instructions to manipulate the local stack.

When a method is invoked, a stack frame is created for it. The parameters to be passed to it are evaluated and the results stored in the new stack frame. The code of the method is then executed using the newly created stack frame as its context.

If the method is a *class method* (i.e., a method declared as static in the associated class definition), the parameters passed to it begin at the first element of the local variable array. If the method is an *instance method*, the first element of the local variable array is reserved for the *self* (or *this*) pointer; the parameters are then allocated to the second and subsequent elements. The allocation of parameters is, in both cases, contiguous.

In order to return control to its caller in a normal fashion (i.e., a non-error return or *normal completion* as the JVM specification terms it), the method executes one of the return instructions. These instructions are used to return zero or more values.

When normal completion of a method occurs and the result is passed to the calling method, the called method's stack frame is removed from the stack and is garbage collected. The PC in the exiting stack frame is stored in the JVM's PC register as a return point.

If a method makes an *abnormal* return (or *abnormal completion*) by throwing an exception that is not handled within its body, a search is performed along the call chain. The stack frame for each method between the point at which the exception is thrown and that at which it is handled is removed from the stack and left to be garbage collected (in other words, the stack is collapsed). The exception is then handled in the context of the method defining the handler for exception. It must be noted that the handler is *always* the nearest one along the dynamic (call) chain, not along the static chain.

If an exception is thrown by a method called inside a thread and is handled by a handler that is outside that thread, the stack associated with the thread is terminated. Thread termination causes the store allocated for its stack to be reclaimed; other structures associated with the thread also become garbage.

In most implementations of the JVM, there is *always* at least one thread running at any time. In the case in which there is just one active thread, should an exception be thrown and not handled by that thread, an exception must be raised by the JVM itself; the thread's data structures are also consigned to the garbage collector.

There are other cases in which the JVM has to handle exceptions. They will not be documented here. The interested reader should consult [33] for details.

3.2.2 Method areas

Method code is stored in method areas at runtime. The actual location of each method area is within the class file object representing the class to which the method directly belongs (the one in which it was defined in the source code). Method areas contain byte codes and symbolic references.

The method area also contains the Runtime Constant Pool for each class or interface loaded in the JVM. The Runtime Constant Pool is the runtime representation of the constant_pool table in the class file associated with the class or interace. Each Runtime Constant Pool contains a number of different types of constants. The constants it contains range from numeric literals to method and field references; the former are determined at compile time, while the latter are determined (or "resolved") at runtime.

Class files are used to derived a runtime representation of classes. They contain the code for methods (in the method area), as well as the variables associated with the class and other information (initialisation values, for example). Methods and variables can refer to entities within the same class or to entities within other classes. These references are represented in the class file as *symbolic* references that have to be converted at runtime into addresses in the JVM's store. The stack frame of the currently executing method contains a reference to the (runtime representation of the) class associated with that method. This reference permits the *dynamic linkage* of methods.

A class file object is allocated when a class is loaded. When the class is no longer of use (there are no more references to it either on a stack or in the heap), the storage it occupies become garbage (and is reclaimed by the garbage collector).

When a class (or interface—this is discussed in a little more detail below in Section 3.3) is loaded, the data in the class file is processed in various ways. Some of it is used for verification purposes; the rest is stored in a newly allocated space in the method area. Class files will be discussed in more detail below (Section 3.3).

Runtime Constant Pools act in a way that is reminiscent of symbol tables in other languages.

3.2.3 The PC register

This is the program counter or instruction pointer register. It points to the instruction currently being executed by the JVM, provided that that instruction is a Java bytecode (otherwise, the native code stack—the C stack—and the host machine's registers hold the context and code and the PC register's value is undefined). When the JVM is executing more than one thread, each thread has its own stack and its own PC register. At any point during the execution of the JVM, one thread is being executed.

As noted above, the current method's stack frame contains a slot for the PC register. This is used in the normal way to store the return point at which execution continues after the method returns. In order to cope with native code routines calling JVM coded methods, the PC register (and associated slot in stack frames) must be large enough to hold a native code address.

3.2.4 Other structures

The stack structure is permitted by the JVM specification [33] to contain data other than that described above. Additional data can be used for debugging, for example.

A JVM implementation has also to support threads. The actual implementation is relatively free. There are two basic forms of thread implementation: so-called "green" threads and operating system specific ones. The latter is introduced so that the thread mechanisms of the host operating system can be used to implement Java threads (e.g., Linux threads). The former is an independent thread mechanism that is implemented by the JVM itself.

If the JVM implements the thread mechanism directly, storage structures must be provided to support it. For example, monitors and queues must be implemented, as well as a way to store state information for threads and thread groups. These structures will, probably, reside in the JVM's heap.

If the native thread mechanism is used, the structures to implement it are provided by the native operating system and fall outside of the JVM (using the C stack escape mechanism mentioned above).

In addition, structures required to interface to such things as the host's graphics system (say, X Windows), sockets and remote procedure calls are also required. This interface might require the use of the JVM heap to hold the necessary state information. The C stack escape is also used as part of this interface.

3.3 Class Files

The *class file* structure is fundamental. It contains the compiled code for classes in a standard format. The JVM specification states that the output of a Java compiler need not be in class-file format; however, the runtime system depends upon the information contained in class files. Indeed, the first step taken by the JVM in loading a class file is to verify that the entity being loaded is in class file format. The JVM specification defines what a class file should contain and the representation to be used; it defines the order in which class file components appear at runtime. It also defines the verification processes that should take place before a class can be considered to have been loaded into the JVM.

There is one class file for each class currently loaded in the JVM. Class files can be directly input by a Java compiler, loaded from file or from a local database. They can also be loaded from remote sources such as remote files, remote databases, code servers or just from a socket. The class loading mechanism is relatively straightforward but complicated by the fact that it can be replaced by an application-specific mechanism; it is associated with the class resolution mechanism. The loading mechanism is also the place where most of the security mechanisms of a JVM is located (bytecode verification, among other things). The details of the class loader are omitted from this description for reasons of its complexity. Instead, the class-resolution process will be described because it is this, at runtime, that resolves references stored in class files to its own methods (the methods defined inside that class), to its own variables (the variables declared inside that class) and to other classes.

It should be observed that there is also one class file for each interface currently loaded in the JVM. This is reasonable, for interfaces define entities in their own right. It makes even more sense for Java 2 because it has augmented interfaces so that they are, in effect, abstract classes supporting multiple inheritance rather than simply a device for providing multiple inheritance in a single-inheritance language. For this reason, a class file can define a class or an interface.

The organisation of a class file is rather complex. The JVM specification is highly detailed and includes specifications of data formats. Here, the organisation will only be summarised. As usual, the interested reader is directed to the relevant sections of [33] for the details.

The top-level structure of the class file are indicative of the information it contains. The JVM specification ([33], p. 94) defines the structure as containing:

magic The magic number identifying this as a class file. The value should be 0xCAFEBABE.

minor version This, together with the next field, define the version number of the class file. The version number is used by the JVM to determine whether it can execute the class in a class file.

major version

constant pool count This denotes the number of entries in the constant pool field. The actual number of entries is one less than the value of this field.

constant pool The constant pool. This is a vector of bytes at the top level. The bytes are, however, structured internally as a table.

access flags This is a bit mask whose bits represent flags. The flags denote access permissions to and properties of this class (or interface). The flags defined in [33] are as follows (their values are omitted):

public If this flag is set, the class was declared public and can be accessed from outside the package in which it was defined.

abstract If this flag is set, the class has been declared abstract. This means that the class cannot be instantiated and any attempts to instantiate it must cause an error.

final If this flag is set, the class was declared as begin final. This means that it is not permitted to define subclasses of this class.

super If this flag is set, superclass methods should be treated specially when invoked by the invokespecial instruction.

interface If this flag is set, the entity defined by this class file is an interface, not a class.

this class This is an index into the **constant pool** table. The entry in the constant pool at the offset in this field must be a structure of type CONSTANT_Class_info that represents the class or interface defined by this class file. This must be a valid index.

super class If this class file defines a class, the value of this field must either be zero or a valid index into the **constant pool**. If the value is non-zero, the entry at the offset it specifies must be a CONSTANT_Class_info structure that represents the *direct* superclass of the class defined by this class file. It is not permitted that any of the superclasses of this class be declared as final.

interfaces count This is the number of direct super interfaces of the class or interface defined by the contents of this class file. It must be a valid index.

interfaces This is an array of offsets into the **constant pool** table. Each entry indexed by this array must be a CONSTANT_Class_info structure that represents an interface that is a direct super interface of the class or interface defined by the contents of this class file.

fields count This is another numeric field whose value represents the number of elements in the **fields** table.

fields Each element of this table is a field_info structure representing a complete description of a field in this class or interface. The table only includes those fields that are declared by this class or interface (so excludes inherited ones). A field can be a class or an instance variable.

methods count This numeric field contains the number of methods declared in this class or interface. It is used as the size of the **methods** table that immediately follows.

methods Each element of this table must be a method_info structure giving a complete description of a method that this class or interface defines. The method can be **native** or **abstract** (in which case, no JVM instructions are included). If the method is neither **native** nor **abstract**, the JVM instructions that implement the method are included in the structure. The table includes *all* methods declared (defined) by the class or interface defined by this class file; therefore, it includes **static** (class) methods and any class or interface initialisation methods that are inherited from superclasses or superinstances.

attributes count This is another numeric field. It contains the size of the **attributes** table that ends the class file.

attributes This is a table of attributes for the class. In [33] (p. 98), it is stated that the only attributes causing the JVM to take any action are the **SourceFile** and **Deprecated** attributes; all other values are ignored by the JVM.

In the JVM definition, when field names in the above list are composed of more than one word, connecting underscores ("_") are used to create a valid C (Java) identifier. The underscores have been omitted above in order to render them more legible. It should be noted that, below, what should be spelled as "constant_pool" will always be spelled *without* the underscore.

The class file description refers to the fact that constant pool entries are structured. In addition, it refers to structures of type CONSTANT_Class_info, field_info and method_info. These will be described in the next few paragraphs. The description is necessarily limited, so the interested reader is referred to [33], Chapter 4 (the relevant sections and page numbers are included below). The constant pool entries ([33], Section 4.4, p. 103 *et seq.*) are structures containing a tag and some information. The tag is of fixed size and indicates the type of the constant. The possible tags and their interpretations are:

Class A reference to a class or interface. The information associated with this tag must be a valid constant pool index. The entry at that index must be a Utf8 structure (essentially a string[1]) that represents a fully qualified class or interface name in the internal form (this is a form containing slashes instead of periods separating the path name of the package containing the named class).

Fieldref, Methodref, InterfaceMethodref A reference to a field, method or interface method, as appropriate. The information associated with these three tags have the same format (this justifies their common treatment here):

class_index This field must contain a valid constant pool index. The corresponding entry must be a CONSTANT_Class_info structure that represents the class or interface type containing the field or method declaration.

name_and_type_index This should be another valid constant pool index. Its entry must be a CONSTANT_NameAndType_info structure indicating the name and descriptor of the field or method as appropriate. If this is a Methodref and the entry is of the appropriate type, the entry can begin with the character <, the name must be the special <init> name (thus representing an instance initialisation method—these methods should return no value, note).

String This represents a constant string. The information associated with it is an index into the constant pool. The element at that index must be a string (encoded as a Utf8 object).

Integer This represents a constant integer. The associated information represents the value of that integer constant. The bytes are stored in big-endian format (high-order byte first).

Float This represents a floating point numeric constant in IEEE 754 floating point single format. The bytes are stored in big-endian format (high-order byte first).

Long This represents a long integer constant. The associated information represents the value of the long in the form four highest-order bytes followed by four lowest-order bytes.

---

[1] The JVM structure type Utf8 will just be regarded as a string. Its name will always be written in this font for ease of reading. It is actually defined as a length and a sequence of suitably encoded bytes representing the characters of the string.

Double This represents a double constant in IEEE 754 double format. The high-order four bytes appear first and are followed by the four low-order bytes.

NameAndType This is used to represent a field or method. It does not indicate the class or interface to which it belongs. Its associated information is in the form:

> **name_index** This must be a valid constant_pool index. The entry at that index must be a Utf8 structure (string) representing the name of the field or method; it must be a valid identifier as defined by the Java language specification [22]; it can be the special identifier <init>, denoting an initialiser (see below, Section 3.5).
>
> **descriptor_index** The contents of this field must again be a valid constant pool index. The entry corresponding to this value must be a Utf8 structure representing a valid field or method descriptor.

Utf8 An object of this type is, basically, a text string. It contains a field containing the length of the string and another containing the sequence of characters.

(The actual tag name has the string CONSTANT_ as a prefix.) It should be remembered that the values stored in these entries are *constants*.

Table 3.1. *Flags describing method access and properties.*

Name	Meaning
PUBLIC	can be accessed outside its package
PRIVATE	accessible only within its defining class
PROTECTED	accessible within subclasses
STATIC	static (class method)
FINAL	cannot be overridden
SYNCHRONIZED	must be wrapped in a monitor lock
NATIVE	not implemented in Java
ABSTRACT	no implementation provided (permitted in defining class)
STRICT	FP-strict floating point mode

The structure type method_info ([33], Section 4.6, p. 114 *et seq*) has five fields as follows:

access_flags These are defined in Table 3.1. A class method can only specify one of PUBLIC, PRIVATE or PROTECTED. If such a method has ABSTRACT set, it may not have FINAL, NATIVE, PRIVATE, NATIVE, STRICT or SYNCHRONIZED also set. All interface methods must have PUBLIC and ABSTRACT set. A named initialisation method can have at most one of PRIVATE, PROTECTED and PUBLIC and, possibly, STRICT but no other flags set. Only the value of the STRICT flag is used by the JVM if the method is a class or initialisation method; the other values are ignored. (The actual flags are all spelled with an ACC_ prefix; it has been omitted in order to improve legibility.)

name_index This must be a valid constant pool index. The corresponding entry must be a Utf8 string that represents one of the special method names, <init> for instances or <clinit> for classes, or a valid method identifier as defined by the Java language definition [22]. The special initialisation methods are described in Section 3.5 below.

descriptor_index This is another constant pool index; it must be valid. The corresponding entry is a Utf8 string representing a valid method descriptor.

attributes_count The number of attributes appearing in the following field of this structure type.

attributes The only attributes of interest are the code and exception attributes. All others are silently ignored by the JVM.

A *method descriptor* is a (Utf8) string that is specified as:

$$(ParameterDescriptor^*\ )\ ReturnDescriptor$$

where (and) represent open and close parenthesis; these parentheses appear literally in the method descriptor. The *ParameterDescriptor* part allows for zero or more parameters, each of which is a field descriptor. The *ReturnDescriptor* has the form:

$$ReturnDescriptor:\ FieldType\ |\ \mathbf{V}$$

where $\mathbf{V}$ denotes the void type and where *FieldDescriptor* has the following syntax:

FieldDescriptor: FieldType
ComponentType: FieldType
FieldType: BaseType | ObjectType | ArrayType

The *BaseType* denotes the specification of one of Java's primitive types, while *ObjectType* and *ArrayType* specify object or array types. In a descriptor, a standard encoding for types is employed (it is defined in [33], p. 101). Typically, the encoding is a single character for primitive types and more complex strings for object and array types. The basic encoding is shown in Table 3.2.

The codes shown in Table 3.2 are sufficient to describe any valid Java type. For example, the array type:

double d[ ][ ]

is encoded as:

$$\mathbf{[[[D}$$

while an ordinary integer is denoted by $\mathbf{I}$ (just that: the letter "I" on its own). Finally, the type Object is denoted by the descriptor **Ljava/lang/Object**.

As noted above, there are two attributes of particular importance to methods: the code and exception attributes. They are considered in turn.

Table 3.2. *JVM basic descriptor type codes.*

Encoding	Designated Type	Meaning
B	byte	signed byte
C	char	unicode character
D	double	double-precision floating point
F	float	single-precision floating point
I	int	integer
J	long	long integer
L<classname>;	reference	instance of class **classname**
S	short	signed short
Z	boolean	boolean value
[	reference	one array dimension

The **code** attribute is another variable-length attribute. As will be seen, this attribute contains the JVM instructions implementing the method, as well as other information, as will now be outlined.

attribute_name_index This must be a valid index into the **constant pool** whose corresponding entry is a Utf8 structure representing the string "Code".

attribute_length This numeric field denotes the length of the entire attribute *minus* the first six bytes (i.e., the first two fields of this structure).

max_stack This numeric field denotes the maximum size to which the operand stack can grow during execution of the method represented by this attribute.

max_locals This numeric field denotes the size of the local variables array in the stack frame for each invocation of this method. The value includes the number of elements required for passing parameters into the method represented by this structure.

code_length This field contains the length of the **code** field (which follows). The length is expressed in bytes.

code This is a vector containing the actual JVM instructions that implement the method represented by this structure.

exception_table_length This field contains the number of entries in the exception_table attribute (which follows).

exception_table This is a table whose entries are structures of the form:

start_pc, end_pc These two values indicate the range in the **code** vector in which the exception handler is active. The value of start_pc must be a valid index of the opcode of an instruction in the **code** vector. The value of end_pc must either be a valid index of the opcode of an instruction in the **code** vector or must be equal to code_length. The value of start_pc must be less than that of end_pc. The value of start_pc is inclusive and that of end_pc is exclusive.

handler_pc The value of this field indicates the start of the exception handler. This must be a valid index into the code vector and must be the index of an instruction's opcode.

catch_type If this has a non-zero value, it must be a valid constant pool index whose corresponding entry must be a CONSTANT_Class_info structure that represents an exception class (class Throwable or one of its subclasses) that this handler is intended to handle. The handler will be called only if the thrown exception is an instance of the stated class or of one of its subclasses. If the value is zero, this handler is called for all exceptions; this is used to implement finally clauses.

attributes_count This field contains the number of entries in the last attribute.

attributes The attributes for the method. There are many such attributes. They are ignored here.

When the code in a code attribute is read into store on a byte-addressable machine, if the first byte of the vector is aligned on a 4-byte boundary, the 32-bit offsets in the *tableswitch* and *lookupswitch* instructions will be correctly aligned (on 4-byte boundaries).

The exception attribute is another variable-length structure. It records the exception types that a method can throw. It contains four fields as follows:

attribute_name_index This must be a valid constant pool index which points to a Utf8 structure containing the string "Exception".

attribute_length This numerical field records the length of the exception attribute structure minus the first six bytes (this attribute and the previous one).

number_of_exceptions This numerical field records the number of entries in the following field.

exception_index_table Each element of this vector must be a valid constant pool index which refers to a Utf8 structure representing a class type that the method is declared to throw.

A method can throw an exception if at least one of the following conditions is met at runtime:

- The exception is an instance of class RuntimeException or one of its subclasses.
- The exception is an instance of Error or one of its subclasses.
- The exception is an instance of one of the exception classes (or one of its subclasses) specified in the exception_index_table described in the last list.

Finally, the structure type field_info ([33], Section 4.5, p. 112 *et seq*) has five fields as follows:

access_flags The permitted values are as shown in Table 3.3. (Note that the actual flags have the prefix ACC_ which is omitted in the table.) Only one of the flags PUBLIC, PRIVATE and PROTECTED can be set for any field. Only one of FINAL and VOLATILE can be set for any field. All interface fields must be PUBLIC, STATIC and FINAL; no other flags may be set in this case.

name_index This is a constant pool index; it must be valid. The entry specified by this field must be a Utf8 string representing a field name that is a valid identifier according to the Java language standard [22] and the syntax is as shown above.

descriptor_index This is another constant pool index; it must be valid. It must be another Utf8 string representing a valid field descriptor. The coding scheme for the field descriptor is as shown in Table 3.2.

attributes_count This is the number of attributes in the following descriptor field.

attributes The valid attribute values are Synthetic, Deprecated and Constant-Value. The last is the only one that a JVM is mandated to acknowledge.

Table 3.3. *Flags defining field access and properties.*

Flag	Meaning
PUBLIC	can be accessed from
	outside the package
PRIVATE	can only be accessed inside
	the defining class
PROTECTED	can be accessed inside subclasses
STATIC	static (class variable, etc.)
FINAL	no assignment after initialisation permitted
VOLATILE	cannot be cached (thread annotation)
TRANSIENT	not to be written or read by
	a persistent object manager

The JVM specification [33] also defines formats for such things as inner classes. As stated above, there is insufficient space to cover all details of the class file format in this chapter and the interested reader is directed to the JVM specification where all details can be found.

3.4 Object Representation at Runtime

The JVM specification does not impose any special structure on the representation of objects at runtime. JVM implementations are, therefore, free to adopt a representation that is the most convenient for their use.

Some Sun implementations, for example, implement a reference to a class instance as a pointer to a further pair of pointers. One of these pointers is to a table and a pointer to the class object representing the type of the instance. The other pointer is a reference to a data area in heap that is used to store the instance's local variables. The table contains the object's methods (or pointers to them).

The information stored in the constant pool for each class or interface is defined by the specification. When a class or interface is loaded into the JVM, a Runtime Constant Pool is allocated in the method area of the heap for it. The JVM uses the constant pool table in the class file to construct a binary representation when the class or interface is created. The constant pool table in the class file contains symbolic references, as was seen in the last section. The runtime symbolic references in the runtime constant pool are derived from structures in the binary representation of the class or interface in the following ways:

• A symbolic reference to a class or interface is derived from a CON-STANT_Class_info structure. A reference of this type provides the name of the class or interface in the form that is returned by the Java Class.getName method.

• A symbolic reference to a field of a class or interface is derived from a CONSTANT_Fieldref_info structure in the binary class representation. This structure provides the name of the field as well as a descriptor of its contents; in addition it provides a symbolic reference to the class or interface in which it is located.

• A symbolic reference to a method of a class is derived from a CON-STANT_Methodref_info structure. This provides the name and descriptor for the method. It also provides a symbolic reference to the method's class.

• A symbolic reference to an interface is derived from a CONSTANT_Interface-Methodref_info structure. This provides the name and descriptor pertaining to the interface method; a symbolic reference to the interface to which the method belongs is also derived from the structure.

Non-reference types are also derived from the information held in a class file. In particular, the following are performed:

• Runtime constants are derived from the constant pool structures: CON-STANT_Integer_info, CONSTANT_Float_info, CONSTANT_Long_info, as well as CONSTANT_Double_info.

• Runtime constants whose values are literal strings are derived from CON-STANT_String_info structures that specify their component Unicode characters; the result is an instance of type String. There are some complications, however, to string derivation; they are:

 – The Java language definition [22] specifies that strings composed of the same sequence of characters should be implemented as references to a single instance of String. This single instance actually contains the characters. If the String.intern method is called on any string, the result is a reference to the same instance of String that would be returned if the string appeared as a source-code literal.

 – In order to derive a string literal, the JVM examines the characters that are provided by the CONSTANT_String_info structure. If String.intern has previously been called on an instance of String containing an identical sequence of Unicode characters, the result is a reference to that very instance of String. If, on the hand, a new instance of String is created to contain these characters, that instance is the result of string derivation. The String.intern method is then called upon this newly created string.

The final types that can be obtained from the constant pool are CON-STANT_NameAndType_info and CONSTANT_Utf8_info (the class file representation of names, in this case). These structures are used only in an indirect fashion to derive symbolic references to classes, interfaces, methods and fields, as well as during string literal derivation.

It should be remembered that these symbolic references are eventually resolved into actual addresses in the heap. Thus, references become computationally more tractable than the manipulation of indices and complex string-based structures.

Although the process of derivation is specified in [33], the organisation of the method area and the runtime constant pool are not. The precise organisation of the area and the structures that reside in it are implementation-dependent details not specified by the specification.

3.5 Initialisation

The *creation* of a class or interface is performed by creating an implementation-specific internal representation of that class or interface in the method area in the JVM's heap. The process is initiated by some other class or interface referencing the class using its runtime constant pool (which, necessarily, contains a reference to the new class or interface, as the case may be). The invocation of methods can also cause classes and interfaces to be created.

The details of class and interface creation are somewhat complex. They are documented in Chapter 5 of [33] (p. 155 *et seq*). Suffice it to say that the loading of a class or interface can cause a cascade of class and/or interface loads (those of its supers), if those entities are not already loaded. In addition to the derivation of heap structures, a number of verification procedures can be undertaken, and linkage is performed. Linkage can involve runtime searches up super chains and can fail for a variety of reasons documented in Chapter 5 of [33].

The creation and finalisation (destruction) of class instances is a somewhat simpler process. It is outlined in the remainder of this section.

There are two ways in which an instance of a class might be created: an explicit and an implicit way.

The *explicit* way relies upon one of the following to occur. Either the evaluation of a class instance creation expression creates a new instance of the class referenced by name in that expression or the invocation of the newInstance method of the Class class creates a new instance of the class represented by the Class object for which that method was invoked.

The *implicit* way also consists of two cases:

1. The loading of a class or interface containing a literal of type String can create a new String instance to represent that literal (this has been already encountered above in the last section).
2. The execution of a string concatenation operation not part of a constant expression creates a new String instance to represent the result of the concatenation. Temporary wrapper objects can also be created for primitive type values during string concatenation.

When a new class instance is created, the JVM allocates sufficient heap store to contain all the instance variables that are declared in the corresponding class type, as well as for all the instance variables declared by the superclasses of the instance's class type (this includes *all* of those instance variables that might not be visible). Should there be insufficient space available, the JVM raises an exception (OutOfMemoryError); otherwise, the instance variables thus created are initialised to their default values (generally, zero, null or false, depending upon type).

Once the allocation and initialisation have been performed and just prior to returning a reference to the newly created instance, the constructor that is indicated by the creation operation is invoked to perform specific initialisations. There are five main steps to be performed:

1. The actual parameters of the call to the constructor are bound to the formal parameters.
2. If this constructor begins with an explicit call to another constructor in the same class (using this to denote its location), the arguments are evaluated and these five steps are recursively applied. Should this nested constructor terminate abnormally ("abruptly" in the terminology of [33]), the entire constructor-application process also terminates abnormally. Otherwise, the next step is applied.
3. If this constructor does not begin with a call to another constructor in the same class and the class of this instance is other than Object, this constructor executes either an implicit or explicit call to its superclass' constructor (using super). This is another recursive application of these five steps. Otherwise, the next step is applied.
4. The initialisers for the instance variables of the class of this instance are executed in the *left-to-right order* in which they occur in the source text of the class. Should any of these initialisers raise an exception, no further initialisers are executed and this procedure terminates abnormally. Otherwise, the next step is applied.
5. Finally, the rest of the constructor's body is executed. If this execution terminates abnormally, the entire creation process terminates abnormally (the instance becomes garbage). Otherwise, the procedure terminates normally and a reference to the newly created, initialised instance is returned to the caller.

If, during the execution of a constructor, methods are invoked that are over-ridden in the instance that is being initialised, the *overriding* methods are called, even if this requires their invocation *before* the new instance is completely created.

3.6 Object Deletion

Unlike C++, Java does not provide mechanisms for the explicit cleanup and deletion of objects. However, class Object provides a protected method called finalize—this method can be overridden by other classes (all classes are sub-classes of Object). The definition of the finalize method in any particular class is called the *finalizer* of that class's instances.

Before the storage for an object is reclaimed by the garbage collector, the JVM executes the finalizer on that object so that resources are freed that cannot otherwise be released (e.g., file descriptors and other host system structures that do not reside in the JVM heap). If there were no finalizer, there would be no guarantee that such resources would be released.

The Java language makes no prescriptions as to the time at which a finalizer should be run; it merely states that it will occur before the storage for the object is re-used. The language does not specify the thread in which any finalizer will execute. However, if an uncaught exception is thrown during finalization, the exception is ignored and the object's finalization terminates.

The actual finalizer defined in Object is of little use: it takes no action. The existence of a finalizer in Object does guarantee that the finalizer method for any class is always able to invoke the finalize method in its superclass. This is usually desirable. The invocation of the finalizer in the superclass must, how-ever, be performed explicitly via a super call; the JVM does not automatically invoke the finalizers along the superchain (constructors, however, are always invoked along the superchain).

It should be noted that the finalize method can be explicitly called. In this respect, it is just like any other method. Such a call, however, has no effect whatsoever on the object's eventual automatic finalization.

Finally, the JVM imposes no order on the execution of finalizer methods. They can be invoked in any order or even concurrently.

Classes and interfaces can be *unloaded* if and only if its class loader is unreachable. A class loader can be defined and loaded for any class or collection of classes (it is a class) to alter the way in which or the location from which classes are loaded. (The JVM specification [33] contains a detailed description of class loaders and the associated classes.) There is always a default class loader class present in the JVM, so system classes can never be unloaded; most classes use the default class loader and will never be unloaded.

3.7 JVM Termination

The JVM terminates when one of two events occur:

1. All non-dæmon threads terminate.
2. A particular thread invokes the exit method of the class Runtime or the class System. This is permitted only when the security manager permits it to occur.

(Dæmon threads are threads that are created for internal reasons by the JVM.)

In older versions of the JVM, it was possible to specify that finalizers should be called just prior to system exit. The operation, the runFinalizersOn-Exit in class System, is deprecated from Java 2 platform 1.2.

3.8 Exception Handling

This is an interesting feature of the JVM, one whose implementation can be puzzling.

In the JVM, each catch or finally clause of a method is represented by a range of offsets into the code implementing that method. Each exception handler specifies the range of offsets for which it is active, as well as the type of exception it handles. It also specifies the location of the code that handles that exception. A thrown exception matches an exception handler if the offset of the instruction that caused the exception is in the exception handler's range of offsets and the type of exception is the same or a subclass of that handled by the handler.

When an exception is thrown, the JVM searches for a matching handler in the current method. If a match is found, the code for that handler is executed. If there is no match, the JVM begins a search. First, the current method invocation terminates abruptly (abnormally), causing the current stack frame to be discarded. The exception is then *rethrown* in the caller's context. This continues until either the exception is handled or there are no more contexts in which to search. In the latter case, the thread in which the exception was thrown is terminated.

The order in which exception handlers are searched matters. In the class file, the exception handlers for each method are stored in a table (see Section 3.3). At runtime, the JVM searches through the exception handlers in the same order as that in the class file. Java's try commands are structured, so a Java compiler can always order the the exception handler table's entries in such a way that, for any thrown exception and any value of the pc (instruction pointer or program counter) in the method in which the exception is thrown, the first exception handler matching the thrown exception will always correspond to the innermost matching catch or finally clause.

3.9 Instructions

Instructions are represented by bytecodes. A bytecode consists of an operation field and zero or more operands. The bytecode field is eight bits in length (hence the name); the operands, if present, can be any even multiple of eight bits. A maximum of eight bytes is usually imposed, the maximum represents the number of bits required to hold a floating point number. However, some architectures might require sixty-four bits for an address, as well.

The instruction set can be divided into familiar groups:

- Control instructions;
- Data-manipulation instructions;
- Stack-manipulation instructions.

Control instructions perform transfers of control within a program. They include jump, call and return instructions. Java contains an exception mechanism (the throw and try/finally constructs) and operations to throw and handle exceptions are included within this group (there is a code convention that applies to exceptions to make the location of handlers easier). In the data-manipulation group are included instructions that perform arithmetic and logical operations, bit manipulation and so on. The stack-manipulation instructions access and store variables in the local variable array, as well as operating on the stack (swap and dup operations, for example).

The data and stack manipulating instructions must operate on values whose size ranges from eight to sixty-four bits. The runtime storage requirements for each primitive (source-language) type is as shown in Table 3.4.

It can be seen that types requiring fewer than the standard 32 bits are stored in a full 32-bit word at runtime. This is reasonable when it is considered that the local stack elements and the elements of the local variable array are all 32 bits wide. The only types longer than 32 bits are, as noted above (Section 3.2.1), are long (integer) and floating point (double). The float type is only 32 bits wide.

Table 3.4. *Sizes of Java primitive types.*

Type	Size (in 32-bit units)
byte	1
character	1
short integer	1
integer	1
long integer	2
float	1
return address	1
double	2

The instruction set also contains instructions related to object-oriented programming languages. These instructions perform such operations as:

- Creation of class instances;
- Invocation of methods;
- Access and update of instance and class variables.

The second and third of these groups include instructions whose semantics includes search along the superclass chain to locate the methods and variables addressed by the instructions.

Finally, the instruction set has instructions that support threads and monitors. Under this heading are monitor entry and exit operations, as well as operations for handling thread groups.

The JVM specification [33] does not define how thread scheduling should be performed. It does, however, specify the behaviour of the locking operations required to ensure correct access to shared data inside monitors.

When describing instruction sets, there is always the risk that the result will just be a long list, something that is to be avoided. Therefore, rather than describe all of the JVM's instructions, a few interesting ones will be described in detail, while the remainder are summarised and the interesting points addressed.

Before moving on, it is important to observe that a great many JVM instructions encode type information. Thus, what would be a single data movement and arithmetic instruction on another virtual machine is implemented as a set of type-specific instructions in the JVM. For example, the addition instruction comes in the following forms:

iadd – integer addition;
ladd – long addition;
fadd – (single-precision) floating-point addition;
dadd – (double-precision) floating-point addition.

There is similar replication for other operations. Types are often encoded in an instruction by a single letter:

i for integer;
l for long;
s for short;
b for byte;
c for character;
f for (single-precision) floating-point (float);
d for (double-precision) floating-point (double);
a for reference.

Note that the JVM supports a reference type, written reference, below. This type represents references to objects (including arrays). The JVM also supports an address type for code, written returnAddress.

In the following summaries, where an instruction has many typed forms, its general name will have the letter 'T' as a prefix. For example, the addition instruction would be written 'Tadd'.

3.9.1 Data-manipulation instructions

The arithmetic instructions are: addition (Tadd), subtraction (Tsub), multiplication (Tmul), division (Tdiv), remainder (Trem) and negation (change of sign—Tneg). Each of these instructions expects its arguments to be on the top of the local operand stack. They pop them, perform the operation and push the result back onto the stack.

The following are restricted to integer and long operands:

ishl lsh Left shift;
ishr lshr Arithmetic Right shift;
iushr lushr Logical Right shift.

These instructions expect the stack to be:

$$\ldots\ value1,\ value2$$

where *value1* is the mask to be shifted and *value2* is the amount to shift. For integer shifts, both operands should be integers. For long shifts, the shift should be an integer and the mask should be long

The logical operations are the following:

iand land Logical "and";
ior lor Logical "or";
ixor lxor Logical "xor" (exclusive or).

They all expect their operands to be on the top of the operand stack. The result is pushed back onto the stack.

The logical operations provide an opportunity for explaining how the JVM represents values that require fewer than 32 bits (byte, characters, short integers and logical values). It must be noted that there is a bit string class in the Java library, so arbitrary bit strings can be handled in ways other than "twiddling bits".

Quite simply, the JVM represents all smaller types as 32-bit quantities, so the operands to the logical operations just listed should be integers.

In some cases, this requires a proper conversion, while, in others, it just requires a truncation. Some conversions lose information. Sometimes, the sign of the result (Java integers are always signed—there is no unsigned int at present) might not have the same sign as the input.

Since there are type-specific operations for manipulating data, it is clearly necessary to have type-changing instructions. The instructions are listed. Only some of the conversions are explained. The reason for this is that conversions between floating point (both single- and double-length) are somewhat complex.

The type-conversion instructions are as follows:

Integer to T: The instruction expects a single operand to be on the top of the stack. The operand should be an integer. The result is pushed onto the stack.

i2b: Integer to byte. The operand is truncated, then sign-extended to integer. (The result might not have the same sign as the operand. Information can be lost.)

i2c: Integer to character. The operand is truncated, then zero-extended to integer. (The result might not have the same sign as the operand. Information can be lost.)

i2s: Integer to short. The operand is truncated, then sign-extended to an integer. Information might be lost. The sign of the result is not always the same as the operand.

i2l: Integer to long. The operand is sign-extended to a long. This is an exact operation.

i2f: Integer to (single-length) floating point. There might be a loss of precision becaue single-length floats only occupy 24 bits.

i2d: Integer to (double-length) floating point. No information is lost.

Long to T: The instruction expects a single operand to be on the top of the stack. The operand should be a long. The result is pushed onto the stack.

l2i: Long to integer.

l2f: Long to (single-length) floating point.

l2d: Long to (double-length) floating point.

(Single) Float to T: The instruction expects a single operand to be on the top of the stack. The operand should be a (single-length) float (float). The result is pushed onto the stack.

f2i: Float to integer.

f2l: Float to long.

f2d: Float to double.

Double to T: The instruction expects a single operand to be on the top of the stack. The operand should be a (double-length) float (double). The result is pushed onto the stack.

d2i: Double to integer.

d2l: Double to long.

d2f: Double to (single-length) floating point.

lcmp Compare long. Both operands should be long. It expects the stack to be:

$$\ldots \; value1, \; value2$$

The two values are compared. The result is pushed onto the stack. The result is computed as follows:

$$value1 > value2 \quad \text{Result } 1$$
$$value1 = value2 \quad \text{Result } 0$$
$$value1 < value2 \quad \text{Result } 1$$

Tcmpl (T can be f or d.) Compare operands. Both operands are expected on the stack and should be of the same type.

Tcmpg (T can be f or d.) Compare operands. Both operands are expected on the stack and should be of the same type.

The Tcmpl and Tcmpg instructions differ only in the way in which they handle the NaN value defined by the IEEE 754 floating point standard. The way in which these instructions, often referred to as fcmp<op>, work is as follows. First, the stack should be of the form:

$$\dots value1, \ value2$$

A floating point comparison is performed after they have been popped from the stack. A value-set conversion is performed immediately prior to the comparison. The results of the value-set conversion are denoted v_1' and v_2'. The result (an integer) is computed as follows:

- $v_1' > v_2'$, the result is int 1;
- $v_1' = v_2'$, the result is int 0;
- $v_1' < v_2'$, the result is int −1;
- If at least one of v_1' and v_2' is NaN, the result depends upon which instruction is being executed:
  Tcmpg The result is int 1;
  Tcmpl The result is int −1.

The instructions consider $+0 = -0$.

iinc opcode
index
const

Fig. 3.1. *The JVM iinc instruction format.*

Finally, it is extremely useful to be able to increment (and sometimes decrement) a register or memory location in one instruction. The JVM has *exactly* one instruction for this: iinc. The instruction has the format shown in Figure 3.1. The format is similar to that employed in other cases: first, there is the symbolic opcode, followed by the operands. In this case, the opcode is *iinc*, the first operand is *index* and the second operand is *const*. The *index* is an unsigned byte; this must be a valid index into the local variable array in the current stack frame; that local variable must contain an integer value. The *const* is a signed byte, which is first sign-extended and then added to the local variable at *index*.

3.9.2 Control instructions

The following instructions implement nconditional transfer of control:

goto This is a transfer of control whose operand is a 16-bit offset which is added to the address of the goto instruction's opcode to produce the destination address in the current method's code. Control is transferred to the destination address.

goto_w This instruction has an opcode, followed by *four* bytes. The four bytes are shifted and or'ed to produce an offset into the current method's code. The destination address of the jump is computed by adding the offset to the address of the instruction's opcode. There is an *a priori* limit to the size of a method's code of 65535 bytes (this is for "historical reasons").

jsr This instruction is the subroutine call instruction. It consists of an optcode and two bytes, the latter comprising a signed 16-bit offset formed by shifting and or-ing the two bytes. The address is pushed onto the stack as a value of type returnAddress. Control is transferred to that address from the address of (the opcode of) the jsr instruction. The target of the transfer *must* be the opcode of an instruction.

jsr_w This is a second subroutine call instruction. It has a four-byte offset. The destination is constructed by shifting and or-ing to form a 32-bit signed offset. The offset must respect the maximum method code length. The jsr_w and ret instructions are used to implement finally clauses.

ret This instruction has a single (unsigned) byte as its operand. The operand is used to index the local variable array in the current stack frame. The element of the local variable array thus referenced must contain a value of type returnAddress. This value is copied to the JVM's pc register to perform a transfer of control.

return The return instruction is used when the current method's return type is void. It has no operands. When executed, the instruction returns control to the method that called the one in whose code this instruction occurs. It reinstates the caller's stack frame, discarding the current one. If the method in whose code this instruction occurs is declared synchronized, monitor locks must be released. Exceptions can be thrown, causing failure of this instruction.

Treturn Returns a value of type T from the current method (T can be i, l, f, d or a—recall that types requiring fewer than 32-bits are converted to a 32-bit representation). The value to be returned must be on top of the local operand stack; it should be of the appropriate type. If the current method is declared synchronized, monitor locks are released. The instruction pushes the value to be returned onto the local stack of the method that called the current one. Control is returned to the caller by the JVM; the caller's stack frame is reinstated. Exceptions can be thrown, causing failure of this instruction.

The JVM supports a set of conditional branch instructions. They have the general name if<cond> and a common format. The form that each of these

if<cond>
branchbyte1
branchbyte2

Fig. 3.2. *General if<cond> format.*

instructions takes is shown in Figure 3.2. The first element is the one-byte opcode. There follow the two bytes that constitute the destination offset.

The instruction pops the top element from the local stack and performs a test on it. If the test succeeds, the destination offset is constructed in the usual way and added to the address of the if instruction's opcode to form a new offset into the current method's code.

If the value popped from the stack is written as v, the forms for if can be summarised as:

ifeq —if $v = 0$, control transfers to the destination (v must be an integer);
iflt —if $v < 0$, control transfers to the destination (v must be an integer);
ifle —if $v \leq 0$, control transfers to the destination (v must be an integer);
ifne —if $v \neq 0$, control transfers to the destination (v must be an integer);
ifgt —if $v > 0$, control transfers to the destination (v must be an integer);
ifge —if $v \geq 0$, control transfers to the destination (v must be an integer);
ifnull —if v is equal to null, control transfers to the destination (v must be of type reference);
ifnonnull —if v is not equal to null, control transfers to the destination (v must be of type reference).

If the test fails, the instruction immediately following the if<cond> is executed.

The following generic instructions have a three-byte format: opcode followed by two address bytes. If the test succeeds, the two bytes are used to construct a signed 16-bit offset into the current method's code. In both cases, the stack should have the form:

$$\ldots v_1, v_2$$

These values are popped from the stack. For if_icmpOP, these two values should be integers, while if_acmpOP expects them both to be of type reference.

if_icmpOP Branch if an int comparison succeeds. The values taken by OP are:
   eq If $v_1 = v_2$, the branch is executed.
   ne If $v_1 \neq v_2$, the branch is executed.
   lt If $v_1 < v_2$, the branch is executed.
   le If $v_1 \leq v_2$, the branch is executed.
   gt If $v_1 > v_2$, the branch is executed.
   ge If $v_1 \geq v_2$, the branch is executed.

if_acmpOP Branch if a reference comparison succeeds. The values taken by OP
are:
eq If $v_1 = v_2$, the branch is executed.
ne If $v_1 \neq v_2$, the branch is executed.

tableswitch (opcode)
0-3 byte padding
defaultbyte1
defaultbyte2
defaultbyte3
defaultbyte4
lowbyte1
lowbyte2
lowbyte3
lowbyte4
highbyte1
highbyte2
highbyte3
highbyte4
jump offsets . . .

Fig. 3.3. *The tableswitch instruction format.*

lookupswitch (opcode)
0-3 byte padding
defaultbyte1
defaultbyte2
defaultbyte3
defaultbyte4
npairs1
npairs2
npairs3
npairs4
match-offset pairs . . .

Fig. 3.4. *The lookupswitch instruction format.*

The next pair of instructions are used to implement switch commands
in Java source. Both instructions are of variable length. In both cases, the
instruction is padded by up to three bytes; these bytes should be filled with
zero. The padding is required to ensure that 4-byte alignments are maintained.
The *defaultbytes* are used to construct a signed 32-bit value.

tableswitch The format of this instruction is shown in Figure 3.3. The *low-bytes* and *highbytes* are used to form two 32-bit values, referred to as *low* and *high*, respectively. The bytes indicated by *jump offsets* in Figure 3.3 represent 32-bit values representing $high - low + 1$ offsets, the offsets into the jump table. Note that $low \leq high$.

The instruction expects an integer value to be on top of the stack. This value is popped; it is the index into the table. If the index is less than *low* or greater than *high*, a destination address is computed by adding the *default* to the address of the opcode of this instruction. Otherwise, the destination is computed by subtracting *low* from index and, using this as the offset of a *jump offset*. This second offset is added to the address of the **tableswitch** instruction to produce the address to which to jump, thus causing transfer to one of the non-default cases.

lookupswitch The format of this instruction is shown in Figure 3.4. The *match-offset pairs* must be sorted in increasing numerical order by *match*. A value, called *key*, is expected to be on top of the local stack; it must be of type integer. The value of *key* is compared with the *match* values and, if equal to one of them, a destination address is computed by adding the corresponding *offset* to the address of the opcode of this instruction. If there is no match, the destination is computed by adding the *default* to the address of the opcode of this instruction. Execution continues at the address thus computed.

athrow This instruction expects its operand to be on top of the local stack. The operand must be of type **reference** and, therefore, should refer to an object. This object should be of type **Throwable** (or a subclass thereof). The object reference is then thrown. This is done by searching in the local code for a matching exception handler. If a handler is found, its code is executed; otherwise, a search for a suitable handler is begun.

3.9.3 Stack-manipulating instructions

The JVM requires instructions to represent constant values. The interpretation of these instructions is that they have a literal operand which is pushed onto the operand stack. There are constant instructions for integer (**iconst**), long (**lconst**), float (**fconst**), double (**dconst**) and reference (**aconst**).

In addition, there are the following constant operations:

bipush Push the operand (a byte) onto the stack.

sipush Push the operand (a **short** formed by or-ing the two operands) onto the stack.

ldc This instruction consists of the opcode followed by an operand, *index*. This is an unsigned byte representing an offset into the runtime constant pool of the current class. The entity at that location in the constant pool must be of type **int**, **float** or a symbolic reference to a string literal. If the value is an **int** or a **float**, the value is pushed onto the local stack.

Otherwise, the constant pool entry must be a reference to an instance of String; that reference is pushed onto the local stack.

ldc_w This is the same as ldc but has a 16-bit index (represented by operand bytes following the opcode in store).

ldc2_w This is similar to ldc but loads long or double onto the stack.

aconst_null Push null onto the stack.

iconst_<i> This is a family of instructions: iconst_-1 to iconst_5. They push the (integer) value indicated after the underscore onto the stack.

lconst_<l> Similar to iconst but pushes a long.

fconst_<f> Similar to iconst but pushes a float.

dconst_<d> Similar to iconst but pushes a double.

Tload A family of instructions, each composed of a single byte opcode followed by a single byte that must be a valid index into the local variable array. The value located at that index is pushed onto the stack. The type of the value pushed is indicated by T.

Tload_<n> A family of instructions, each composed only of an opcode. The operand is encoded in the instruction; it is used as an index into the local variable array. The value stored at that index is pushed onto the stack. The type of the value pushed is indicated by T.

Tstore This is a family of two-byte instructions: the first byte is the opcode, the second an index into the local variable array. The stack is popped to yield a value that is stored in the local variable array at the indicated index. The type of the value popped is indicated by T.

Tstore_<n> A family of instructions that encode their operand in the opcode. The operand is an offset into the local variable array. The value on the stack is popped and stored into the local variable array at the indicated index. The type of the value popped is indicated by T.

The wide instruction is a complicated instruction, so the reader should consult the description in [33], pp. 360–1. This instruction modifies the behaviour of other instructions. It takes one of two formats, the actual one depending upon the particular instruction being modified. Its first format is used for: Tload, Tstore and ret. Its second format is used for iinc only. The instruction constructs a 16-bit signed offset into the local variable array. The effect of this instruction is to widen the index of its target opcode when the first format is employed. The second format widens the range of the iinc instruction it targets. The instruction that is thus modified *must not* be the target of a control transfer.

The following instructions support direct manipulation of the stack.

pop Pop the local stack.

pop2 Pop the top two values from the local stack.

dup Push a copy of the top stack element onto the stack. This instruction is used only when the top element is 32 bits wide.

dup2 Push a copy of the top stack element onto the stack. This instruction is used only when the top element is 64 bits wide.

dup_x1 Transform the stack as follows. Given:

$$\ldots v_2, \ v_1$$

change it to:

$$\ldots v_1, \ v_2, \ v_1$$

This instruction operates when the v_i are 32-bit quantities.

dup_x2 Transform the stack as follows. Given:

$$\ldots v_3, \ v_2, \ v_1$$

change it to:

$$\ldots v_1, \ v_3, \ v_2, \ v_1$$

if all the v_i are 32 bits wide. If v_1 is 32 bits wide but v_2 is 64 bits, then the stack should be transformed into:

$$\ldots v_1, \ v_2, \ v_1$$

swap This swaps the top two stack elements.

The **dup2_x1** and **dup2_x2** instructions are variations on **dup_x1** and **dup_x2** (see [33], pp. 222–4, for details).

3.9.4 Support for object orientation

The **new** instruction creates a **reference** to a new object on the stack. The instruction is three bytes in length, the second and third forming an index into the constant pool for the current class. The entry thus indexed should be a symbolic reference to a class, interface or array type. The new instance is created in the heap and the **reference** to it returned to the instruction to be pushed onto the local stack.

newarray Create a new array. The length of the array is expected to be on the top of the local operand stack; it must be an integer (it is popped by the instruction). The one-byte operand following this instruction's opcode denotes the type of the array to be created. A **reference** to the newly created array is pushed onto the local stack.

anewarray Create a new array of **reference** (i.e., whose elements are of type **reference**). See [33], p. 181, for details.

multianewarray This instruction creates a multi-dimensional array. (See [33], pp. 339–340 for details.)

The four field access instructions have a common format, shown in Figure 3.5. The opcode is followed by two bytes that, together, form an index into the constant pool of the current class. The element at that index should be a symbolic reference to a field. This reference yields the name and type of the field, as well as a symbolic reference to the class in which it is located.

opcode
indexbyte1
indexbyt2

Fig. 3.5. *Format of the four JVM field instructions.*

getfield This operation obtains the value stored in an object's field and pushes it onto the stack. It expects a reference to an object to be on top of the local stack. It pops that reference and uses the index bytes to access the field.

getstatic This operation is similar to **getfield** but requires the field it accesses to be a static field of the object. The stack only holds the value to be obtained from the static field (there is no object reference).

putfield This operation expects the stack to have, as its top element, the value to be stored. Immediately beneath, it expects to find a reference to the object in which the value is to be stored. The index is used to resolve the field; checks are made to ensure that the assignment is legal (access and type checks are made).

putstatic This is similar to **putfield** but operates on static fields. The stack is expected only to hold the value to be stored. Checks are again made to ensure that the assignment is permitted and of the correct type.

There is a collection of instructions dedicated to arrays, the most general of which are (again, using the convention described above).

Taload (T can be b, s, i, l, f, d, c or a). These instructions expect a valid array index to be on top of the local stack; immediately beneath this should be a reference to an array. These operands are popped from the stack. The array is indexed using the popped value and the element at that index is pushed onto the stack.

Tastore (T can be b, s, i, l, f, d, c or a). This stores a value in an array. The instruction expects three operands to be on the stack: the value to be stored, an index into the array and a reference to the array. All three values are popped from the stack.

arraylength Returns the length of an array.

There are some general object-oriented instructions:

instanceof This instruction determines whether an object is of a given type. It expects the object to be referenced by the top element of the local stack (which it pops). The two bytes following the opcode form an index into the constant pool for the current class, where it should index a symbolic reference to a class, array or interface type.

checkcast Another complex instruction ([33], pp. 193–4). It verifies that the object referenced by the top stack element is of the given type. The two bytes following the opcode are a constant pool index that should refer to a symbolic reference to a class, array or interface type. The instruction pops the object reference from the stack.

opcode
indexbyte1
indexbyt2

Fig. 3.6. *Format of the JVM invoke instructions (except* invokeinterface*).*

invokeinterface
indexbyte1
indexbyte2
count
0

Fig. 3.7. *Format of the* invokeinterface *instruction.*

The following instructions invoke methods in various places. They are all complex operations, so the reader is strongly urged to read the descriptions in [33]; what follows is just an indicative account.

The first three have a common format that is depicted in Figure 3.6. The last of the group has the format shown in Figure 3.7. The *indexbytes* are used to construct an index into the runtime constant pool of the current class. The entity thus addressed must be a symbolic reference to a method of the appropriate kind.

invokespecial Call an instance method on an instance; special handling for superclass, private and instance initialisation method calls. The operation expects the arguments to the method to be on the local operand stack as well as a reference to the object to which the method belongs.

invokevirtual Invoke a method using dynamic dispatch. That is, invoke an instance method. The actual method being dispatched depends upon the class referred to under the arguments on the stack.

invokestatic Similar to invokevirtual but the method must be declared static.

invokeinterface Similar to invokestatic but the method belongs to an interface.

3.9.5 Synchronisation

There are two synchronisation instructions:

- `monitorenter` Enter a monitor;
- `monitorexit` Leave a monitor.

The functioning of these instructions is complex and the interested reader should consult all the relevant sections of [33].

3.10 Concluding Remarks

In this chapter, the Java Virtual Machine (JVM) has been reviewed. The JVM's overall structure consists of:

- A heap region;
- A stack.

The heap region contains the code to be executed by the JVM, as well as a special Constant Pool data structure. The constant pool holds, at runtime, information about the classes that have been loaded into the JVM. The stack is of the framed variety and is also allocated in the heap.

One important aspect of the heap is its storage of *class file* structures in the constant pools. It is the class file that contains information about each class that has been loaded. The overall organisation of this structure and some of its uses have been described in this chpater.

The JVM executes instructions in the usual way. The instructions in the JVM are aligned on byte boundaries. Instructions, called *bytecodes*, are stored in the *method code* vectors located in class files. The instructions executed by the JVM can be divided into two main classes:

1. Simple instructions. In this class are instructions such as jumps (the JVM supports conditional as well as unconditional jumps) and arithmetic instructions. The arithmetic instructions are *typed*: there are arithmetic instructions for the main numeric types.
2. Complex (or High-Level) instructions. In this class are instructions such as those for the allocation of class instances and arrays, accessing arrays, accessing and updating class and instance variables, throwing and executing exceptions, and instructions for invoking methods of all kinds.

In addition to this Java functionality, the JVM also supports so-called "C" stacks. These stacks allow methods implemented in native code (code that executes directly on the host machine) to be integrated with code implemented as JVM bytecodes.

4

DIY VMs

4.1 Introduction

Having seen example virtual machines, this chapter will concentrate on how to construct a virtual machine for a programming language. To do this, it is necessary to understand the semantics of the language and to understand what is required by any implementation of the language in terms of storage structures.

The chapter first contains an overview of the example language. This language is, by necessity, extremely small. Immediately thereafter, the virtual machine is presented. The virtual machine is designed by providing storage structures and instructions to support every semantically important construct in the language. The approach taken here is fairly conventional in the sense that the language is defined in English and the virtual machine is first described in English and then its instructions are described, using an Algol-like notation, as pieces of a program. An alternative approach to the construction of the virtual machine is then presented (the first virtual machine employs a single stack while the second employs two stacks, one for control and one for data). Rather than give programming-notation-like code to define this second virtual machine, its instructions will be described using *transitions* so that a more formal model of the virtual machine is obtained (this model will be used in other places in this book). The design of the virtual machine raises a number of issues that lead to extensions; the issues are considered in detail.

The reader should note that neither the abstract nor the concrete syntaxes of the languages or extensions described below is given. The reason for this is that they are of no significance to the virtual machines that are *really* the centre of interest. Occasionally, though, some example code will be given, written in an *ad hoc* concrete syntax.

4.2 ALEX

ALEX[1] is an imperative programming language of the simplest kind. It supports only integer and boolean values but only integer variables can be declared. To make up for this, integer vectors (one-dimensional arrays) with compile-time bounds are also supported. Boolean values can be manipulated by expressions but they cannot be stored (there are no boolean variables). In a similar fashion, strings are permitted but cannot be declared. The main use for strings is to serve as filenames.

4.2.1 Language Overview

ALEX supports expressions over integers. In particular, it provides:

- Addition;
- Subtraction;
- Multiplication;
- Division;
- Modulo.

These operations all have type $Int \times Int \rightarrow Int$. In addition, there is also unary minus of type $Int \rightarrow Int$.

It also provides comparisons:

- $<$
- $>$
- $\leq$
- $\geq$
- $=$

These operations all have type $Int \times Int \rightarrow Bool$.

The usual boolean operations are also provided:

- and;
- or;
- not.

The first two of these operations have type $Bool \times Bool \rightarrow Bool$, while the last (negation) has the type $Bool \rightarrow Bool$.

Expressions consist of:

- An integer constant;
- An identifier denoting a variable or a function;

---

[1] ALEX denotes something like "Algorithmic Language EXample"—there is no real name for this thing. There are many texts containing the definitions of toy languages called TINY or SAL. The author does *not* want to call what amounts to a fragment SAL when there is the magnificent example of [34].

- A unary operator (unary minus and logical negation) applied to an expression;
- A binary operator applied to two expressions;
- A function invocation.

This is a fairly standard recursive definition of expression. Note that it includes *integer* variables but not booleans.

ALEX provides commands. The set of commands (or statements) is the following:

- Assignment;
- Selection (conditional);
- Repetition (iteration);
- Procedure call.

These commands are very much as would be expected. Assignment has its usual interpretation, here restricted to integer-valued expressions and integer variables.

Selection (conditional) commands can come in a number of flavours:

- One-branch (if ... then, unless ... do);
- Two-branch (if ... then ... else).

As an extension, case commands will be considered.

The repetitive commands defined in ALEX are:

- loop (an infinite loop);
- while;
- until;
- for.

In connection with loops, ALEX defines two structured exit commands: exit and redo. Execution of the exit command immediately terminates the loop enclosing it. The redo command transfers control to the start of the immediately enclosing repetitive command. (exit and redo are analogous to break and continue in the C family of languages.)

Finally, how (and where) variables and routines (procedures and functions) can be declared in ALEX is considered.

ALEX distinguishes between procedures and functions. Collectively, they can be referred to as *routines*. For the purposes of ALEX, a procedure is a routine that may not directly return a value. A function is a routine that directly returns a value. Functions in ALEX can return values of type int, array(int) or bool (for use in conditionals). Values are returned explicitly in ALEX, as in the C family, using the return(<Exp>) command.

In our initial account of ALEX, the parameter-passing régime for routines will be restricted to call by value. Later, it will be extended to include call by reference. This restriction makes procedures somewhat useless because they are unable to return values via their reference parameters; when the restriction is removed, procedures will have their full power. Return of control to the caller of a procedure is effected by the return command.

In ALEX, routines may *only* be defined at top level. That is, nested routine definitions are not permitted.

The definition of routines can be combined with the declaration of top-level constants and variables. Top-level constants and variables are in scope from the point of their declaration up to and including the end of the program text.

Variables and constants (whether top-level or otherwise) can *only* be of type int or Array(int).

ALEX permits recursive and mutually recursive routine definitions. In order to support this, there is a *forward* declaration form that introduces the identifier of the routine to be defined.

The syntactic form of a declaration is:

```
let var v := 0
and const c = 22
and fun foo (x) = ...
and proc pp (x,y) be ...
and forward fun bar
```

This declares a variable, v, a constant, c, and two routines: a function, foo, and a procedure pp. Note that, at present, it is necessary only to list the parameters to routines. When a distinction between reference and value parameters is introduced, it will be necessary to find some way to differentiate between them syntactically. The last declaration in the list is a forward reference to a function called bar.

The above declaration is legal at top level only. Routines are permitted to declare local variables. ALEX is not block structured in the sense of Algol60 in which blocks can occur wherever a command sequence is permitted, as in:

```
if x < y then
  begin
  integer zz;
    zz := ...;
    x  := ...
  end
```

Instead, ALEX routines have a body comprised of an optional declaration part and a command (this is like Pascal). The following is a legal procedure definition in ALEX:

```
proc pp (x,y) be
  let var zz := 0
  in
    zz := x + y
  end
```

The variables declared *inside* a routine are *local* to it.

ALEX is a statically scoped language.

The top-level declarations and definitions have the form indicated above:

```
let decl1
and ...
in Command
```

where Command is the *top-level program*.

Finally, it is necessary to say a word or two about strings. They are included *only* so that operations on such things as files can be defined. These operations are not specified here but it is possible say a few things about how strings are to be handled. First, they must have some concrete syntactic form. Second, they are always constants so can be stored in a literal pool if space is an issue; otherwise, they can be handled by pushing bytes onto the evaluation stack.

4.2.2 What the Virtual Machine Must Support

The ALEX language is representative of most purely procedural languages. The virtual machine must support this language. It does so by providing instructions and storage structures that implement the following classes of construct:

- Storage for and access and update operations on variables. Variables can be local or global;
- Expression evaluation;
- Selective commands (conditionals);
- Iterative commands (looping constructs);
- Routine call (both procedures and functions);
- Return from routines; this involves the return of values from functions.

These constructs are viewed as being the *central* ones of this language.

It should be noted that the initialisation and termination of programs is not explicitly considered in the treatment that follows. This is an issue that can be handled best by a compiler. (The reader might, though, consider what has to be done and how it could be added to the main routine by a compiler; it is a simple exercise.)

Other language classes will have other central constructs. For example, virtual machines for functional languages have constructs for variable binding, function application and selection. A class-based object-oriented language must support the manipulation of class and instance variables (as well as variables local to each method), method and variable location and method call (a very simple class-based language based on the procedural core provided by ALEX is considered in the next chapter).

4.2.3 Virtual Machine—Storage Structures

The simple language, ALEX, has now been defined. In order to commence the virtual machine design, it is necessary to identify the storage structures required to support it.

The easiest item to consider is the storage of code. Code is typically given as integer values, so the code for a routine will, most naturally, be a vector (1-dimensional array) of integers. If a storage-management package is available, the code can be stored in a heap; otherwise, a maximum size will have to be chosen (usually on a fairly arbitrary basis). One big decision that must be made is whether the code for each routine is stored separately or together in a large contiguous area. The former requires more management than the latter; the latter is simpler to handle but does not permit dynamic replacement of code. The former is a scheme that can be used in interactive environments; the latter in production environments. Here, for simplicity, it will be assumed that the code for all routines in a program are stored in a contiguous vector of integers.

ALEX supports recursive routine definitions. This implies that the virtual machine will employ a runtime stack. This is quite correct. Expression evaluation can also be performed on a stack.

It is necessary to make some decisions about the stack organisation. The following are immediate:

- Is a framed stack used? If so, what is its organisation?
- If not, two stacks are required, one for the storage of control information and the other for the storage of data.

The framed-stack approach combines control and data in one stack. When a routine is entered, a frame is pushed onto the stack; it is popped when the routine is left. The frame contains areas for parameters, local variables and control information. The control information includes the return address and the dynamic chain (a pointer to the immediately previous stack frame in the call chain). If ALEX permitted routine definitions to be nested, it would need a pointer to the stack frame of the routine in which the currently executing one so that locals in the defining environment could be accessed.

The framed-stack approach, also referred to below as the "single-stack" approach, is shown in Figure 4.1. The heap is shown as a dashed box. The other storage structures (the stack and code vector, in particular) might be allocated in the heap, so, in a sense, the heap is an all-pervasive module.

The two-stack approach uses a *data stack* to hold the current values of local variables; the top of the stack is used as a workspace. The approach also uses a *control stack* to hold control information required to invoke routines and return from them. Both data and control stack are structured. The data stack holds parameters and local variables and the top of the stack is used as a scratch area. When a routine is entered, the stack top has to be marked so

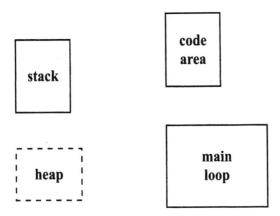

Fig. 4.1. *Virtual machine storage organisation.*

that the new environment can be popped correctly. The control stack holds the return address and other pointers.

In the framed stack approach, the runtime environment is represented by the local variables and the parameters in each frame; frames also hold working storage for expression evaluation. When two stacks are used, the data stack represents the runtime environment as well as working store. In the two-stack approach, the basic idea is that the area above the current environment can be used as a workspace without affecting the contents of the elements of the environment.

Each solution has its advantages and disadvantages. Framed stacks have a more complex organisation than do the stacks in the two-stack approach. However, the framed stack alternative still uses the same space. The two-stack approach requires two stacks to be monitored (and kept in synchronisation) instead just one.

Next, it is necessary to decide how to handle global data. There is no problem with routines because they are compiled to code and the entry point of the command that constitutes the top-level program is always known. The issue relates, more particularly, to the constants and variables declared at top-level in a program. If constants can be restricted so that their initialising expression does not refer to any variables or constants whose values are unknown at compile time, the compiler can remove constants from the program. However, to make constants more generally useful, they must refer to entities whose value remains unknown until runtime. This implies that both constants and variables must be implemented as storage cells (of the appropriate size) at runtime. The distinction will, of course, be that a cell representing a variable will have a write capability, while constant-representing cells will not.

It is possible to arrange for global data to reside on the stack at the bottom-most level. This would be sensible because the outermost declarations in a program are local to the top-level program. Alternatively, the globals could be stored in a separate *global pool*, one variable or constant per cell.

A global pool has some advantages. If the bottom of the stack has to be referenced by following a chain of pointers, the pool implementation is clearly better. If the bottom of the stack can be accessed via a statically declared pointer, there is not much in the choice. Just to make matters a little more interesting, a globals pool will be employed (at least for this exercise).

Next, there must be some way to halt the virtual machine's operation. This can be done with a simple flag that controls the virtual machine's main loop. In addition, it would be quite useful if errors could be reported to the user. There are (at least) two ways to do this:

1. If the language in which the language is to be implemented has an exception mechanism (as do Ada, Java, C++, ML and Ocaml, for example), it can be used.

2. If the implementation language does not have an exception mechanism, it is possible to use a (numeric) variable to hold error codes. When an error occurs, the variable is set to the corresponding code and the virtual machine halted. The value of the error variable is made available to the user in some way.

Finally, strings are an issue. Are they to be allocated as globals of some kind or on the runtime stack? The optimal answer depends upon the frequency with which any given string occurs in the source code. If a string has many references, it is better to store it in a *literal pool* in which all literal data is stored. If a string has few references, it can be allocated on the stack. Strings will *only* be used to name files in ALEX but we will still employ a literal pool. As for globals, this is for expository purposes.

To summarise (in no particular order), the following data structures are required by the ALEX VM:

- The code buffer, which holds the virtual machine instructions into which programs are compiled;
- The stack or stacks used for expression evaluation and for routine call and return;
- The globals area, which holds all global constants and variables.
- The literal pool, which holds all literal constants encountered during the compilation of the program. Frequently encountered integer values (or booleans, for that matter) should not be stored here; its use will be restricted to strings.

4.2.4 Virtual Machine—Registers

The virtual machine is intended to be implemented in some high-level language. Although the term "register" is associated with assembly language programming, in a virtual machine the term refers to a variable (or object of some kind) that holds the state information required by the virtual machine.

The actual set of registers needed by the virtual machine will be larger than those that can be affected by the instruction set. This is because it is necessary to store pointers to stacks, environments, code buffers and so on. Unless the virtual machine is constructed on top of an extremely advanced storage management package, it will usually be necessary to include registers to store the sizes or limit addresses for all the main data structures.

Initially, it can be seen that the following registers are required:

Code A pointer to the start of the code buffer. It can be assumed that the compiler generates correct references into the code buffer, so there will be no check on them.

Stack A pointer to the start of the stack and either a pointer to the end of the storage block allocated for it or a location in which the size of the stack's block is stored. It is necessary to check that the stack has not overflowed. The stack should be wide enough to hold a host-machine pointer (whichever is larger). This is because some instructions will deal with pointers; the majority will operate on integers.

Globals A pointer to the start of the block. It can be assumed that the compiler generates correct references to the elements of the globals table.

Literal Pool A pointer to the start of the block. It can be assumed that the compiler generates correct references to the elements of the literal pool.

The size of the code, globals and literal pool are determined by the compiler. The actual values are passed to the virtual machine as parameters. The size of the stack is typically just a parameter to the virtual machine.

The second pointer or the size value is used, in each case, to determine whether a reference is within limits. If a reference exceeds the limits, an error should be signalled.

The names to be given to each of these registers (assuming a two-stack implementation) are:

CB: Base pointer to code buffer;
SB: Base pointer to the buffer in which the stack is allocated;
SL: The size of the stack's buffer (stack *limit*);
GB: Base pointer to the globals area;
LB: Base pointer to the literal pool.

These registers are used in the implementation of the virtual machine. They are *not* directly programmable by the virtual machine's instructions. They are recorded here as a reminder that these data structures must be allocated somewhere within the software.

To handle each stack, it is necessary to record the current top of stack. For the data stack, it will be called **TD** and, for the control stack, **TE**.

It is also necessary to point to the currently executing instruction. This is the *program counter* or *instruction pointer*. The latter term will be used here, so the register will be called the **IP**.

Termination of the virtual machine is controlled by the **HLT** register. It holds a boolean value (or some encoding thereof). The error register will be called **VME**.

4.2.5 Virtual Machine—Instruction Set

The virtual machine for ALEX requires instructions to implement the following operations:

1. Evaluate expressions;
2. Jump (conditionally or unconditionally) to another location. This is used to support selections and repetitions;
3. Perform assignment;
4. Call routines;
5. Return from routines;
6. Access and update global variables;
7. Access and update local variables;
8. Access literals.

Table 4.1. *Expression-related instructions.*

Opcode	No. operands
add	2
sub	2
mlt	2
div	2
mod	2
minus	1
and	2
or	2
not	1
lt	2
gt	2
eq	2
leq	2
geq	2
neq	2

The instruction set design can start with the instructions required for the evaluation of expressions. These are quite obvious and their behaviour is stereotyped. For a unary operation, the operand is the current top location on the stack. The operator is applied to that value and the top is replaced by the result. For a binary operator, the operands occupy the top two locations on the stack. The two operands are popped from the stack, the operator applied to them and the result is pushed onto the stack.

Expression operators each leave a single integer on top of the stack. Comparison operators each leave a single boolean value on top of the stack. The expression-related instructions are summarised in Table 4.1. In the table, the mnemonics are shown on the left. They were chosen so that they would be relatively easy to comprehend. The operation named minus implements the unary minus (sign changing) operation. It should be noted that the neq (not equal) operation is introduced as a simple optimisation; this is justified by the frequency with which it is encountered in real programs. The number of operands expected by each instruction is shown in the right-hand column of the table. All operands are located on the stack. Each instruction pops its operand(s) off the stack and replaces it (them) by the result.

For expression evaluation to function properly, it is necessary to load constant values onto the stack; this can involve the loading of values stored in the literal pool. It is also necessary to load the contents of global variables and to store them again.

At the moment, call by value is the only evaluation method employed. This implies that expression evaluation need only handle values. When call by reference is added, it will be necessary to handle addresses in some form. Meanwhile, the stack-manipulating instructions can be defined.

Constant integers must be loaded onto the stack. For example, the evaluation of the expression $1 + 2$ requires the values 1 and 2 be pushed onto the stack (in either order, for $+$ is commutative) before the expression can be evaluated. To perform this, there is the pushc (push constant) instruction. It takes the form:

pushc <integer constant>

Occasionally, it will be necessary explicitly to pop a value from the stack. This can be performed by the pop instruction.

If the pushc instruction is executed on a full stack, the virtual machine should raise an error. Symmetrically, should the pop instruction encounter an empty stack, an error should also be raised.

Table 4.2. *ALEX VM stack instructions.*

Opcode	Meaning
pushc n	push constant n onto stack
pop	pop stack
swap	swap top two stack elements
dup	duplicate top stack element

At this point, two additional instructions are introduced. They are the swap and dup instructions (they are assumed to be familiar and are not, therefore, explained). These two instructions will be justified below.

The ALEX virtual machine's stack instructions are summarised in Table 4.2.

The treatment of global variables and constants can be described in terms of stack operations. It must be noted that constants are represented by locations to which only one assignment can be made. Verifying that this condition is satisfied is a matter for the compiler, not for the virtual machine, so it is unnecessary to bother with ensuring that the single-assignment condition holds.

It is necessary to access and set global variables or constants. Global variable access is a matter of locating the variable or constant, retrieving the value stored in it and pushing that value onto the stack. Setting a global variable (but not a constant) consists of popping a value from the stack and storing it in the globals table at the appropriate point. The two instructions are:

getglob n n is the global's index in the globals table.
setglob n n is the global's index in the globals table.

The literal pool only holds manifest constants, so there is no setter instruction required. It is only necessary to refer to the nth element of the literal pool (it will be arranged so that the code that uses literal pool elements will access the data). The single instruction in this group is:

getlit n n is the literal's index in the literal pool.

It is the responsibility of the user of literal pool data to ensure that data lengths are respected. The compiler can generate the appropriate code and/or set the appropriate parameters.

Table 4.3. *ALEX VM global and literal pool instructions.*

Opcode	Meaning
getglob n	Push the nth global onto the stack
setglob n	Pop the stack into the nth global
getlit n	Push the nth literal onto the stack

The ALEX virtual machine instructions for handling globals and literals are summarised in Table 4.3.

The ALEX language supports integer-valued vectors. All vectors have static bounds which are declared at compile time. It is necessary to have some way of allocating vectors, as well as accessing their elements. There are three instructions for handling arrays:

mkvec Create a vector;
vref Access an element of a vector;
vset Update an element of a vector.

The first instruction, mkvec, allocates a new vector. The upper bound of the array is the current top of stack. The instruction pops the bound from the stack, allocates the vector in store and pushes a reference to the newly allocated vector on to the stack. The vector can be allocated directly on the stack or in a heap—the specification is neutral with respect to the place where the allocation is made.

The second instruction, vref, accesses elements of vectors. It expects the current top of stack to hold an index and the element immediately beneath to point to a vector. The instruction pops these values from the stack and checks that the index is within bounds (if not, an error is signalled). Then, it extracts the element from the vector and pushes it onto the stack. In a high-level language, this operation can be represented by:

$$\ldots := a(i)$$

The third instruction, vset, assigns values to vector elements. It corresponds to an assignment in which the left-hand side (l-value) is a vector element reference:

$$a(i) := \ldots$$

The instruction expects the stack to contain, from the top downwards:

1. The value to be assigned to the vector element;
2. The index of the vector element;
3. A reference to the vector.

If the index is out of bounds, an error is signalled.

More stack-manipulating instructions will be introduced when considering routines, below.

Selection and repetitive commands in ALEX introduce jumps. For each of these commands, a schema can be written to define how it is to be translated into the target instruction set. The schemata are independent of any particular instruction set, as will be seen. In the following schemata, the virtual machine instructions for a construct are denoted by the name of the construct enclosed within carets ("angle brackets"). Thus, <condition> denotes a condition part of, for example, a while command.

The schemata are quite simple and standard, so they are presented with little explanation. For a single-branch selection, the schemata are as follows.

For if:

```
<condition>
if-false: goto $end
<thenpart>
$end:
```

For unless:

```
<condition>
if-true: goto $end
<dopart>
$end:
```

For a two-branch selection, the schema is:

```
        <condition>
        if-false: goto $else
        <then-part>
        goto $end
$else: <else-part>
$end
```

For loop (an infinite loop, that is), the schema is:

```
$loop: <body>
        goto $loop
```

For while, the schema is:

```
$start: <condition>
        if-false: goto $end
        <body>
        goto $start
$end:
```

For unless, the schema is:

```
$start: <body>
        <condition>
        if-false: goto $start
$end:
```

The schema for the for command is deferred until later. It introduces some additional complexities.

In the repetitive commands, two labels are shown: one at the start and one at the end of the command. The reason for this is that it makes the definition of the low-level code for exit and redo clear. The scheme for exit is:

```
$start:
        ...
        goto $end
        ...
$end:
```

while that for redo is:

```
$start:
        ...
        goto $start
        ...
$end:
```

A decision has to be made whether to use absolute or relative jumps (i.e., jumps or branches). A branch is usually a jump whose range is restricted to a small region around the current value of the instruction pointer (128 or 256 bytes on many processors). In this virtual machine, only jumps will be used, even though they require an address operand that must be at least as large as the maximum size of the code buffer; it is, though, often easier to make the operand as wide as an implementation-language pointer or integer. For this virtual machine, relative jumps (branches) will not be used; in any case, they make code harder to read and test and require additional work of the compiler. (A genuine branch instruction is considered later, in Section 4.3.1.)

From the above compilation schemata, it can be seen that there are, at least, three kinds of jump needed for their implementation:

- Unconditional jump (a simple **goto**);
- A conditional jump when the result of the test is true;
- A conditional jump when the result of the test is false.

The second instruction will perform the jump if and only if the value on the top of the stack is *true*. For the third, the jump is performed if and only if the value on the top of the stack is *false*.

In the current virtual machine, the instructions will be named as follows:

jmp Unconditional jump;
jeq Conditional jump—perform jump if true;
jne Conditional jump—perform if false.

The names for the second and third instructions are derived from an assumption about the representation of boolean values. In the current virtual machine, the value *true* will be represented by the integer value 1 (one), while *false* will be represented by 0 (zero). The **jeq** instruction performs a jump when there is a 1 on top of the stack (the top of stack is **equal** to 1). The **jne** instruction performs a jump when value on the top of stack is not equal to 1.

These are not the only jump instructions possible (one very powerful instruction jumps to the location that is currently on the top of the stack). They are, with a couple of exceptions, the only ones required to implement ALEX.

As noted above, when the virtual machine encounters a **jeq** or **jne** as the next instruction, it pops the stack. The jump is performed depending upon the value that is popped.

At this point, it is worth adding the instruction to halt execution of the entire virtual machine. It is called **hlt**. When the virtual machine encounters this instruction, it sets the halt register to *true* (or 1).

It is now necessary to consider routine call and return. This naturally requires that the stack's organisation be defined. Stack frames are created on the stack when a routine is entered. There are two cases to consider: one for procedures and one for functions. The differences between these two cases are slight but important. The difference is that the stack frame for a function

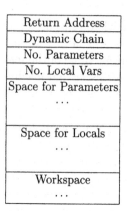

Return Address
Dynamic Chain
No. Parameters
No. Local Vars
Space for Parameters
...
Space for Locals
...
Workspace
...

Fig. 4.2. *Procedure stack frame organisation.*

must reserve space to hold the returned value. Ignoring this difference, stack frames must contain the following:

1. The address of the instruction to be executed when the routine returns;
2. A pointer to the stack frame that appears immediately underneath the new one (the dynamic chain pointer or dynamic chain);
3. The number of parameters;
4. The number of local variables;
5. Space for the values passed as parameters;
6. Space for the local values;
7. Workspace (scratch storage).

The stack frame organisation for procedures is shown in Figure 4.2.

Now, the reader might think that the stack frame organisation for functions would be different from that for procedures. In fact, they are the same. The return sequence for functions is defined in such a way that there is no need to arrange for an independent slot in the stack frame. So, a single stack frame arrangement can be used for both functions and procedures. This is useful because it reduces the number of instructions needed for the virtual machine; it also simplifies the job the compiler must do.

First, local variable access and update is considered. Then parameter access is done. In all cases, the top location of the stack refers to a stack element in the area marked Workspace in Figure 4.2. Where the specifications of the expression-evaluating instructions refer to the top of the stack, it should be understood in the same way.

There are two instructions dealing with local variables. They are:

getlocal n Push the value stored in the local at index $locals + n - 1$) local in the current stack frame onto the stack.

setlocal n Pop the value on the top of the stack and store it the local at index $locals + n - 1$) local in the current stack frame.

Table 4.4. *ALEX VM instructions for parameters and locals.*

Opcode	Meaning
getlocal n	push the nth local onto the stack;
setlocal n	pop the stack and store in the nth local;
getparam n	push the nth parameter onto the stack.

In either case, if n is out of range, an error should be signalled.

Since ALEX does not permit nested routine definitions, there is no need for instructions to get and set non-local variables (variables stored in stack frames below the current one on the stack). However, the introduction of reference parameters will require an addition that is not unlike this. Non-local operations are left until later.

At present, there is only one instruction handling parameters. This is an instruction that reads the value of the specified parameter and loads it onto the stack:

getparam n Access the value stored in the parameter at index $params+n-1$) in the current stack frame and push it onto the stack.

In either case, if n is out of range, an error should be signalled.

It is now possible to define instructions to call routines and to return control from them. This is divided into two tasks:

1. Set up the stack frame of the routine to be called;
2. Transfer control to the called routine.

The stack is set up by the **save** and **frame** instructions, in that order. The **call** instruction is used immdiately after the **frame** instruction to effect a transfer of control. If there are l local variables in the called routine and p parameters to be passed to the called routine, and if the called routine's entry point is e, then the following calls the routine:

```
save l p
<evaluate parameter-1>
...
<evaluate parameter-p>
frame l p
call $e
```

The **save** instruction allocates stack space for the control information and local variables. Specifically, it pushes a spare slot for the return address, then sets the number of parameters, the number of locals and the pointer to the current stack frame, the **fp** register.

The **fp** register has not yet been mentioned. It is a VM register that points to the current stack frame. It is used to facilitate access to stack frame control information and the local variables and parameters stored there.

The operands to the **save** instruction are the number of local variables in the called routine and the number of parameters that are to be passed to it. These operands are the same as for the **frame** instruction. This instruction sets the **fp** register to its new value.

Finally transfer is effected by the **call** instruction:

call *a* Transfers control to the instruction at address *a* in the code buffer. It plants the Return Address into the newly created stack frame.

(It should be noted that, by defining **call** in a slightly different fashion, the **frame** instruction can be omitted. The instruction is retained for the time being in order to make calling sequences a little clearer to those unfamiliar with them.)

Stack frame setup requires the evaluation of parameters. For call by value, this amounts to the evaluation of expressions. It can be assumed that the compiler will check that the correct number of expressions is evaluated.

The **ret** instruction has only to restore the stack pointer, the frame (**fp**) pointer and the instruction pointer. It performs the first two operations so that the previous context is restored; the last is the actual transfer of control back to the caller.

There are three instructions that return values from functions. They are:

reti Return an integer from a function.
retb Return a boolean from a function.
retv Return a vector from a function.

In fact, these three instructions will be implemented in terms of a single one, which will be called **retval**. The reason for this is that they all return a value that is one word wide. There is a little checking that can be performed by each instruction. However, the main function performed by these instructions is identical. The translation of the two type-specific instructions to the actual one can be done by a compiler or by an appropriate assembler.

At the moment a return instruction is executed, the value to be returned is sitting on the top of the stack in the Workspace area. It is necessary to make that value available to the caller, preferably on the top of the caller's stack; that is, the value must be moved to be returned to the top of the caller's Workspace.

When the stack frame is considered, it becomes clear that only the Return Address and Dynamic Chain slots are of any use on return. The other slots in the lower part of the stack frame can be considered scratch information. The return instruction therefore copies the value to be returned to the Number of Parameters slot, sets the **fp** register, returns the context and returns control to the caller.

The instructions for handling routine call and return are summarised in Table 4.5.

Note that the above scheme works only if vectors are stored in the heap. In this case, the top of the stack will be a pointer to the vector. If vectors

Table 4.5. *ALEX VM call-related instructions*

Opcode	Meaning
save *l p*	set up stack frame
frame *l p*	set frame pointer in new stack frame
call *l*	call routine
reti	return integer
retb	return boolean
retv	return value (word)
ret	return from procedure

are allocated sequentially on the stack, a copy operation will have to be performed. For this to work, the return address and dynamic chain must be saved temporarily and the array copied elementwise to the top of the stack of the previous stack frame. The caller can then handle the vector as required. This is a bit messy, so the scheme adopted above was preferred. The allocation of vector elements on the stack can also lead to complex virtual machine code. This is a case in which the abstract nature of virtual machines serves us well.

4.2.6 An Example

Here, an example of a piece of ALEX code, together with the corresponding virtual machine instructions is presented.

```
let fun add2 (x,y) =
  let var z := 0
  in
    z := x + y;
    return(z)
  end
```

Fig. 4.3. *A (very) simple ALEX function.*

Figure 4.3 shows a very simple ALEX function that takes two integer parameters and adds them. The result is assigned to a local variable. The local variable is then returned as the result.

The virtual machine code for this function, called *add2*, is shown in Figure 4.4. In this and all other code examples, it will be assumed that comments start with the percent (%) character and extend to the right, terminating at the end of the line.

The virtual machine code for *add2* begins at the entry point with label $add2 (it is assumed that labels always start with a dollar sign). The first operation is to push zero onto the stack and to assign it to *z*. Local variable *z* is the first local variable; indices into local variables start at zero (for the

```
$add2: pushc 0
       setlocal 0 % z := 0
       getparam 1 % get y
       getparam 0 % get x
       add
       setlocal 0 % z := x + y
       getlocal 0
       reti
```

Fig. 4.4. *Code for the (very) simple ALEX function.*

reason that they are offsets). Next, the two parameters are retrieved in reverse order using `getparam`. Addition is a commutative operation, so the order in which its arguments are pushed on the stack is irrelevant but subtraction and division, for example, are not commutative, so their operands must be pushed in the *reverse* order to which they appear in the program text. Next, the addition is performed (using `add`). The result of the addition is stored in the local variable corresponding to *z*. Next, the value is pushed back onto the stack (using `getlocal`) and returned as the result of the function (using `reti`).

The code sequence in Figure 4.4 shows an inefficiency in the compiler. The `setlocal` pops the result of the addition off the stack; the `getlocal` instruction that *immediately follows* pushes that same value back onto the stack. Any real compiler worth its salt (other than a simple demonstration one) would optimise this sequence to:

```
getparam 1
getparam 0
add
reti
```

Finally, in Figure 4.5, a call to *add2* is shown. The source code is just *add2(1,2)*.

```
% add2(1,2)
    size 1 2
    pushc 2
    pushc 1
    frame 1 2 % frame L P
    call $add2
$L: ...
```

Fig. 4.5. *Code to call the ALEX add2 function.*

Figure 4.5 starts with preparation of the stack frame for the call. Function *add2* has one local variable and two parameters, so the `frame` instruction takes these as values of its L and P operands. A stack frame with space for two parameters and one local variable is created with the **size** instruction. Next, the parameters are pushed onto the stack. In the present case, the actual parameters are constants, so the **pushc** instruction is used. The **frame** instruction is executed next to store the frame pointer in the new stack frame. Finally, the **call** instruction is executed to set the return address in the new stack frame.

Immediately after the **call** instruction, there is the label $L. This label is included only to make clear the point to which control returns after execution of *add2*.

The code for *add2* for the two-stack version of the virtual machine will be given after that alternative model has been described.

4.2.7 Implementation

In this subsection, an outline implementation is presented in an *ad hoc* Algol-like language that should be easily comprehended. It is assumed that unsigned as well as signed variables can be declared (this is not necessary but merely helps us avoid a number of errors and, hence, the need to check for them). It will also be assumed that a **word** type can be defined; this type should coincide exactly with the word type of the underlying hardware.

The implementation's commands will be printed in **this font**. In the text, registers will be printed in **bold face roman**, as above. The names of instructions are printed in this sans font.

First, the registers must be defined:

```
unsigned word fp =   0;
signed   word sp =  -1;
unsigned word ip =   0;
```

Note that the stack is initialised to −1: we are adopting a stack regime that requires an increment of the stack pointer at the start of a push and a decrement at the end of a pop. This initialisation is the reason **sp** was declared as **signed**.

The stack will be denoted by **s**. In a real implementation, this will be derived from the value of **SB**.

The other registers will be ignored: they are initialised when the VM allocates storage and reads the current program.

In the code, the following will be used as follows:

H The size of the header (control information), here = 4.

L The number of local variables in the called routine.

P The number of parameters supplied to the called routine.

For the time being, the method by which operands are obtained is ignored as a complication. (They can be extracted from instructions by incrementing the *ip* appropriately.) Equally, no instruction (except jump instructions) will adjust the *ip* to point to the next instruction in the code buffer; again, this is a minor detail that can be added during implementation.

save L P:

```
if (H + L + P + sp) >= SL then error fi
sp := sp + H
s[sp] := L
s[sp - 1] := P
s[sp - 2] := fp
sp := sp + L
```

frame L P:

```
fp := sp - (L + H + P + 1)
```

call ep:

```
s[fp] := size(call ep) + ip
ip    := ep
```

Here, `size` is a pseudo-function that represents the size of the instruction in appropriate units. The entry point of the called routine, **ep**, will have been converted to a number by the compiler.

getlocal n:

```
sp := sp + 1
s[sp] := s[fp + H + n]
```

setlocal n:

```
s[fp + H + n] := s[sp]
sp := sp - 1
```

getparam n:

What is required is:

```
sp    := sp + 1
s[sp] := s[fp + H + L + n]
```

Since L is not a constant (it varies with the called routine), it is necessary to modify the above slightly:

```
sp    := sp + 1
temp1 := s[fp + 3]
s[sp] := s[fp + H + temp1 + n]
```

Here, the magic number 3 denotes the offset into the stack frame of the Number of Locals slot.

ret:

```
sp := fp
fp := s[sp + 1]
ip := s[fp]
```

retval:

```
s[fp + 2] := s [sp] % overwrite num params
sp := fp
fp := s[sp + 1]
swap
ip := s[sp + 1]
```

Note that this instruction performs a swap operation on the stack; the code denoted **swap** could be a call to a macro or a procedure (it could be directly implemented but a macro is to be preferred).

jmp l:

```
ip := l
```

The label, l, will have been converted to a number by the compiler.

jeq l:

```
if s[sp] = 1 then
  ip := l
else
  ip := ip + size(jeq l)
fi
sp := sp - 1
```

Here and in the next instruction, **size** is a pseudo-function that represents the size of the instruction in appropriate units. The label, l, will have been converted to a number by the compiler.

jne l:

```
if s[sp] /= 1 then
  ip := l
else
  ip := ip + size(jne l)
fi
sp := sp - 1
```

getfglob n:

```
sp := sp + 1
s[sp] := GB[n]
```

setglob n:

```
GB[n] := s[sp]
sp    := sp - 1
```

getlit n:

```
sp    := sp + 1
s[sp] := &LB[n]
```

The getlit instruction returns a *pointer* to the literal string, not the string itself. This avoids copying the string. It also requires that the primitives that take the literal as a parameter must dereference the pointer themselves.

pushc n:

```
sp    := sp + 1
s[sp] := n
```

pop:

```
sp := sp - 1
```

dup:

```
if sp < 0 then error fi
if sp = SL then error fi
sp    := sp + 1
s[sp] := s[sp - 1]
```

swap:

```
if sp < 1 then error fi
temp1 := s[sp]
temp2 := s[sp - 1]
s[sp - 1] := temp1
s[sp] := temp2
```

unop:

```
s[sp] := unop(s[sp])
```

binop:

```
s[sp - 1] := binop(s[sp],s[sp-1])
sp := sp - 1
```

halt:

```
HLT := true
```

At this point, it should be clear that the vref and vset operations have not been specified. If vectors are allocated in a heap, the details of these operations will depend on their representation. Assuming that vectors are defined as something such as a size and a pointer to the actual vector of integers, and assuming an unsigned index and zero-based indexing in the heap object, the operations can be defined in outline form:

vref:

```
index  := s[sp]
sp     := sp - 1
vecptr := s[sp]
if index >= vecptr.size then error fi
s[sp]  := vecptr.elements[index]
```

vset:

```
val    := s[sp]
sp     := sp - 1
index  := s[sp]
sp     := sp - 1
vecptr := s[sp]
if index >= vecptr.size then error fi
vecptr.elements[index] := val
```

The allocation routine, mkvec, is a little harder to specify. To do this, it is essential to assume that there is a routine, allocvec(n), that allocates n units of storage in the heap and uses it to create a vector (there might be additional information added to the structure that is not defined here). With this, it is possible to define:

mkvec:

```
temp1 := s[sp]
s[sp] := allocvec(temp1)
```

The size of the vector is initially on the stack. Note that the stack pointer is not altered. The vector is allocated in the heap and a pointer to it is left on the top of the stack. (Note that errors are not considered.)

4.2.8 Extensions

The extensions considered in this subsection are:

- Reference parameters;
- Case (switch) commands;
- Library routines.

Reference parameters

It turns out that reference parameters are remarkably easy to implement. What is needed is the address of the variable. This leads to two cases:

1. Variables declared on the stack;
2. Global variables.

Variables declared on the stack are local to some routine. The address of such a routine can be represented by the index into the stack vector.

Global variables are a little more interesting. First of all, global variables are always in scope, so they can be accessed and updated using instructions already defined. Second, global variables are stored in a separate vector. If global variables are to be permitted as reference parameters, it is necessary to take their (machine) address, so pointers would be needed to implement reference parameters uniformly.

First, assume that global variables are not permitted as reference parameters. There are two operations, getrefp and setrefp, required. Assuming that all that is required is to pick up a reference to the stack, they can be defined as:

getrefp n:

```
sp    := sp + 1
temp1 := s[fp + 3]
s[sp] := s[s[fp + H + temp1 + n]]
```

Here, the magic number 3 denotes the offset into the stack frame of the Number of Locals slot.

setrefp n:

```
temp1 := s[fp + 3]
s[s[fp + H + temp1 + n]] := s[sp]
sp := sp - 1
```

Here, the magic number 3 denotes the offset into the stack frame of the Number of Locals slot.

Now, assume that reference parameters are implemented as pointers. This gives two simple implementations:

getrefp n:

```
sp    := sp + 1
temp1 := s[fp + 3]
s[sp] := *(s[fp + H + temp1 + n])
```

setrefp n:

```
temp1 := s[fp + 3]
*(s[fp + H + temp1 + n]) := s[sp]
sp := sp - 1
```

Using machine pointers requires that the compiler be able to generate runtime addresses of globals and stacked objects.

Case (Switch) commands

In general, a switch or case command has the general form:

```
switch Exp into
when c1 : C1
    ...
when cn : Cn
    ...
default: Cd
endswitch
```

The Ci are sequences of commands that are not permitted to declare local variables (are not proper blocks). The ci are constant symbols or numerals that need not appear in any particular order (the compiler can perform any ordering and/or scaling).

It is intended that a switch (case) such as the above should be compiled into something like the following:

```
Code for Exp.
Code to perform switch.
$l1: Code for C1.
    ...
$ln: Code for Cn.
    ...
$ld: Code for default.
```

At the end of each of the Ci, there has to be a jump to the end of the construct. Note that the code for each of the Ci is prefixed by a label.

The proposed solution is (a jump table):

```
Code for Exp -- result is on stack top
    switch
    jmp l1
    jmp l2
        ...
    jmp ld
$l1:   -- Code for C1
    jmp $end
```

```
$12:  -- Code for C2
      jmp $end
      . . .
$1d:  -- Code for default
      . . .
$end:
```

The idea is that the `switch` instruction pops the value from the top of the stack and adds it to the instruction pointer so that one of the jump instructions is executed. Execution of one of the jumps causes control to pass to the code for one of the cases. After each case has executed, the `jmp $end` is executed to transfer control to the end of the construct. If the default is applied, its code is executed and control simply falls out of the construct.

Given this description, the definition of `switch` is quite simple:

```
temp1 := pop
ip    := ip + temp1 + 1
```

(the addition of one is required because the `ip` points to the start of the `switch` instruction as this code is executed).

The reader should be clear that it is expected that the compiler will arrange matters so that the expression yields a value appropriate for indexing the cases.

Library routines

In most languages, the number of routines provided to the programmer via the runtime library is quite small; indeed, C provides many routines, not by the standard runtime library provided by the compiler but by a large number of independent library modules.

In principle, if the virtual machine's instructions are adequate, all library routines could be written in that language (e.g., mathematical libraries *could* be written using virtual machine instructions) but they might execute quite slowly. More generally, performance and speed can only be addressed by the provision of virtual machine instructions that perform the relevant operations. This extension to the instruction set implies that more opcodes will be required.

A more powerful mechanism is to provide an interface to native code so that routines coded in some other language can be called directly as if they were written in virtual machine instructions. This is done in the JVM, as was seen in Chapter 3.

4.2.9 Alternatives

The most significant alternative is the use of data and control stacks in place of the single stack employed above. In this subsection, the dual-stack approach

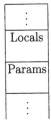

Fig. 4.6. *Organisation of the d stack.*

⋮
Return Address
Old C
Old D
P
L
⋮

Fig. 4.7. *Organisation of the c stack.*

will be described. It should be noted that, for the time being, vectors are ignored.

There are two stacks, the d stack to hold data and the c stack to hold control information. The virtual machine needs to be modified so that it has a base pointer and length (limit) register for each stack. The organisation of the two stacks needs to be determined. Figure 4.6 shows the organisation of the d stack, while Figure 4.7 shows that of the c stack. In both figures, the stack is assumed to grow downwards.

Additional registers are required to address the two stacks. The **dsp** register points to the top of the d stack and the **csp** register points to the top of the c stack. As before, these two pointers are initialised to -1 (so the increment before the push, decrement after the pop protocol is being used). The **D** register will be introduced; it always points to the start of the current local variables area on the d stack. The **C** register is introduced to point into the c stack; it points to the Return Address slot in the top few slots on the c stack.

New instructions are required to:

- Push constants. These are similar to the **pushc** instruction above. They are called: **pushdc** and **pushcc** for the d- and c-stack pushes.
- Pop stack. These are similar to the **pop** instruction above. They are called **popd** and **popc**, respectively.
- An instruction is required to push the contents of a register on the c stack. This will be called **pushrc**.

- Instructions are needed to pop the *c* stack and assign the value to a register. This will be called popcr.

In this case, the save operation is no longer necessary; much of the work that it did can be done by the frame and call operations.

The frame operation is now:

```
csp    := csp + 1
c[csp] := 0 % save for return address
csp    := csp + 1
c[csp] := C
csp    := csp + 1
c[csp] := D
csp    := csp + 1
c[csp] := P
csp    := csp + 1
c[csp] := L
```

The call operation is now:

```
dsp := dsp + c[csp]
C   := csp - 4
c[C]:= 'size(call $p)'+ ip
D   := dsp
```

On the first line, the top element of the stack is accessed. This element just happens to be the number of local variables (L) that was passed to the frame instruction. Next, the new **C** register is set to point to the first word of the new control frame on the *c* stack. Control frames are four words long and the first word of a control frame is always the return address. The third line sets the return address in the control frame. This is done by adding the size of the call instruction to the current value of the instruction pointer. The size of the control instruction is a compile-time constant (and for this reason, it appears quoted above).

The return operation becomes:

```
ip  := c[C]
dsp := D
C   := c[C+1]
D   := c[C+2]
csp := csp - 4
```

The return value operation is now:

```
temp1 := d[dsp]
ip    := c[C]
dsp   := D
C     := c[C+1]
```

```
D      := c[C+2]
dsp    := dsp + 1
csp    := csp - 4
d[dsp] := temp1
```

Note that the value to be returned will always be on the top of the d stack. It is, therefore, copied into the temporary variable `temp1` (it is provided by the virtual machine's implementation). The next four instructions are exactly the same as for `ret`; the final one pushes the return value (in `temp1`) onto the stack top. The top of the stack is now the same as it was before the routine was called.

For the next few instructions, it is necessary to make the following observations. First, the number of local variables (the L parameter to the **frame** instruction) is at location `c[csp]`. The number of parameters to the routine (the P parameter to **frame**) is at location `c[csp - 1]`.

For the next three instructions, the parameter n is a compile-time constant.

getlocal n:

```
dsp    := dsp + 1
d[dsp] := d[D + c[csp] + n - 1]
```

setlocal n:

```
d[D + c[csp] + n - 1] := d[dsp]
dsp := dsp - 1
```

The value to be assigned to the local variable is located on the top of the d stack. The instruction ends by decrementing the d stack top pointer, thus actually popping the value from it.

getparam n:

```
dsp    := dsp + 1
d[dsp] := d[D + c[csp - 1] + n - 1]
```

Unary operators:

```
d[dsp] := 'unop'(d[dsp])
```

Binary operators:

```
dsp    := dsp - 1
d[dsp] := 'binop'(d[dsp],d[dsp+1])
```

or:

```
temp1  := d[dsp]
dsp    := dsp - 1
d[dsp] := 'binop'(d[dsp],temp1)
```

```
let fun add2 (x,y) =
  let var z := 0
  in
    z := x + y;
    return(z)
  end
```

Fig. 4.8. *The (very) simple ALEX function (again).*

```
$add2: pushcc   0
       setlocal 0 % z := 0
       getparam 1
       getparam 0
       add        % x + y
       setlocal 0 % z := x + y
       getlocal 0 % get z for return
       reti
```

Fig. 4.9. *ALEX code for the two-stack VM.*

```
% add2(1,2)
    frame 1 2    % frame L P
    pushcc 2
    pushcc 1
    call $add2
$L:  ...
```

Fig. 4.10. *Calling add2(1,2) on the two-stack VM.*

The translation of the *add2* function (see Figure 4.8) into this virtual machine code is shown in Figure 4.9. The code to perform the call *add2(1,2)* for this version of the virtual machine is shown in Figure 4.10.

To see a call in context, consider the following fragment:

```
a := 1; b := 2; zz := 0;
zz := add2(a,b)
```

This compiles into the following stack code:

```
% assume a = local 0, b = local 1, zz = local 2
pushc 1
setlocal 0
pushc 2
setlocal 1
pushc 0
setlocal 2
% Set up for calling add2
frame 1 2
```

```
getlocal 1
getlocal 0
% call add2
call $add2
% returned value on stack top
setlocal 2
```

The second alternative concerns the introduction of two virtual machine instructions: **getnth** and **setnth**. These are both stack instructions. The first has the form **getnth n** and returns the nth element from the current top of the stack. The second instruction sets the nth element from the current top of the stack to some value—in this case, the value that is currently on the top of the stack.

4.2.10 Specification

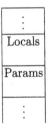

Fig. 4.11. *d-stack organisation.*

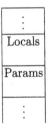

Fig. 4.12. *c-stack organisation.*

The two-stack virtual machine for ALEX is adopted for this model. The organisation of the stacks are repeated in Figures 4.11 and 4.12 for ease of reference (the stacks grow towards the bottom of the page).

The state of the machine will be represented by the tuple:

$$\langle g, d, c, p, \sigma_c, \sigma_d, i_p, \texttt{instr} \rangle$$

where: g is the sequence (vector) of globals, d is the start of the current frame on the d stack, c is the pointer to the start of the current stack frame on the c stack, p is the pointer to the start of the parameter area in the current stack frame, σ_c is the control (or c) stack, σ_d is the data (or d) stack, i_p is the instruction pointer and $\texttt{instr}$ is the current instruction. More generally, $\texttt{instr}$ is taken to be the value of $\kappa(i_p)$, where κ is the code vector.

It is assumed that vector indices start at one.

The length of the sequence s is written as $|s|$ and sequence concatenation is written $s_1 \ddagger s_2$, where s_1 and s_2 are sequences. The concatenation of a single element, v, onto the sequence s, is written as $v \cdot s$ ($v \cdot s = \langle v \rangle \cdot s$, where $\langle x \rangle$ is a sequence containing the single element x). Some sequences will also be expressed using the dot notation. Update of a sequence element is denoted $[v \mapsto i]s$, where s is a sequence, v a value and i an index; this yields a sequence s' that is identical to s except that $s'(i) = v$. Formally, if s is a sequence, v is a suitable value and i and n are numbers, then $[v \mapsto n]s = s'$ is defined by:

$$\forall n \in 1 \ldots |s| \cdot s'(n) = v \Rightarrow (\forall i \in 1 \ldots |s| \cdot i \neq n \Rightarrow s(i) = s'(i))$$

Transitions have a two-part structure separated by $\rightarrow$. The left-hand side denotes the state before the application of the operation, while the right-hand side denotes the state afterwards.

It will be assumed that each instruction has a length of one. This is just a simplification to make notation easier when dealing with the next instruction to execute and with return addresses.

$\texttt{frame} \ \lambda \ \pi$:

$$\langle g, d, c, p, \sigma_c, \sigma_d, i, \texttt{frame} \ \lambda \ \pi \rangle \rightarrow \langle g, d, c, p, s_c \ddagger \sigma_c, s_d \ddagger \sigma_d, i + 1, \kappa(i+1) \rangle$$

where: $s_d = \overbrace{0 \cdot \ldots \cdot 0}^{\lambda \ \text{times}}, \ s_c = \lambda \cdot \pi \cdot d \cdot 0$

$\texttt{call} \ \varphi$:

$$\langle g, d, c, p, f \ddagger \sigma_c, \sigma_c, i, \texttt{call} \ \varphi \rangle$$
$$\rightarrow \langle g, |\sigma_d| - (\lambda + \pi), |\sigma_c| - 5, |\sigma_d| - \pi, f' \ddagger \sigma_c, \sigma_d, \varphi, \kappa(\varphi) \rangle$$

where: $f = \lambda \cdot \pi \cdot d \cdot c \cdot 0$ and $f' = \lambda \cdot \pi \cdot d \cdot c \cdot i + 1$

$\texttt{ret}$:

$$\langle g, d, c, p, f \ddagger f'' \ddagger \sigma_c, \sigma_d, i, \texttt{ret} \rangle \rightarrow \langle g, d', c', p', f'' \ddagger \sigma_c, \sigma_d', \alpha, \kappa(\alpha) \rangle$$

where: $f = \lambda \cdot \pi \cdot d' \cdot c' \cdot \alpha, \ f'' = \lambda_1 \cdot \pi_1 \cdot d'' \cdot c'' \cdot \alpha', \ \sigma_d = s \ddagger \sigma_d'$ and $|\sigma_d'| = d'$ and $p' = d' + \lambda_1$.

`retval`:

$$\langle g, d, c, p, f\ddagger f''\ddagger\sigma_c, v \cdot \sigma_d, i, \texttt{retval}\rangle \rightarrow \langle g, d', c', p', \sigma_c, v \cdot \sigma'_d, \alpha, \kappa(\alpha)\rangle$$

where: $f = \lambda \cdot \pi \cdot d' \cdot c' \cdot \alpha$, $f'' = \lambda_1 \cdot \pi_1 \cdot d'' \cdot c'' \cdot \alpha'$, $\sigma_d = s\ddagger\sigma'_d$ and $|\sigma'_d| = d'$ and $p' = d' + \lambda_1$

`getparam n`:

$$\langle g, c, d, p, \sigma_c, \sigma_c, i, \texttt{getparam } n\rangle \rightarrow \langle g, d, c, p, \sigma_c, v \cdot \sigma_d, i+1, \kappa(i+1)\rangle$$

where: $v = \sigma_d(p+n)$.

`getlocal n`:

$$\langle g, d, c, p, \sigma_c, \sigma_d, i, \texttt{getlocal } n\rangle \rightarrow \langle g, d, c, p, \sigma_c, v \cdot \sigma_d, i+1, \kappa(i+1)\rangle$$

where: $\sigma_d(d+n)$.

`setlocal n`:

$$\langle g, d, c, p, \sigma_c, v \cdot \sigma_d, i, \texttt{setlocal } n\rangle \rightarrow \langle g, d, c, p, \sigma_c, \sigma'_d, i+1, \kappa(i+1)\rangle$$

where: $\sigma'_d = [v \mapsto (d+n)]\sigma_d$.

`jump ℓ`:
$$\langle g, d, c, p, \sigma_c, \sigma_d, i, \texttt{jmp } \ell\rangle \rightarrow \langle g, d, c, p, \sigma_c, \sigma_d, \ell, \kappa(\ell)\rangle$$

`jeq ℓ`:

$$\langle g, d, c, p, \sigma_c, \textit{true} \cdot \sigma_d, i, \texttt{jeq } \ell\rangle \rightarrow \langle g, d, c, p, \sigma_c, \sigma_d, \ell, \kappa(\ell)\rangle$$

`jeq ℓ`:
$$\langle g, d, c, p, \sigma_c, \textit{false} \cdot \sigma_d, i, \texttt{jeq } \ell\rangle \rightarrow \langle g, d, c, p, \sigma_c, \sigma_d, i+1, \kappa(i+1)\rangle$$

`jne ℓ`:
$$\langle g, d, c, p, \sigma_c, \sigma_d, i, \texttt{jne } \ell\rangle \rightarrow \langle g, d, c, p, \sigma_c, \textit{false} \cdot \sigma_d, \ell, \kappa(\ell)\rangle$$

`jne ℓ`:
$$\langle g, d, c, p, \sigma_c, \textit{true} \cdot \sigma_d, i, \texttt{jne } \ell\rangle \rightarrow \langle g, d, c, p, \sigma_c, \sigma_d, i+1, \kappa(i+1)\rangle$$

`getglob n`:

$$\langle g, d, c, p, \sigma_c, \sigma_d, i, \texttt{getglob } n\rangle \rightarrow \langle g, d, c, p, \sigma_c, g(n) \cdot \sigma_d, i+1, \kappa(i+1)\rangle$$

`setglob n`:

$$\langle g, d, c, p, \sigma_c, v \cdot \sigma_d, i, \texttt{setglob } n \rangle \rightarrow \langle [v \mapsto n]g, d, c, p, \sigma_c, \sigma_d, i + 1, \kappa(i + 1) \rangle$$

unop:

$$\langle g, d, c, p, \sigma_c, v \cdot \sigma_d, i, \textit{unop} \rangle \rightarrow \langle g, d, c, p, \sigma_c, \textit{unop}(v) \cdot \sigma_d, i + 1, \kappa(i + 1) \rangle$$

binop:

$$\langle g, d, c, p, \sigma_c, v_2 \cdot v_1 \cdot \sigma_d, i, \textit{binop} \rangle$$
$$\rightarrow \langle g, d, c, p, \sigma_c, \textit{binop}(v_1, v_2) \cdot \sigma_d, i + 1, \kappa(i + 1) \rangle$$

`swap`:

$$\langle g, d, c, p, \sigma_c, v_1 \cdot v_2 \cdot \sigma_d, i, \texttt{swap} \rangle$$
$$\rightarrow \langle g, d, c, p, \sigma_c, v_2 \cdot v_1 \cdot \sigma_d, i + 1, \kappa(i + 1) \rangle$$

dup:

$$\langle g, d, c, p, \sigma_c, v \cdot \sigma_d, i, \texttt{dup} \rangle \rightarrow \langle g, d, c, p, \sigma_c, v \cdot v \cdot \sigma_d, i + 1, \kappa(i + 1) \rangle$$

This completes the specification of the two-stack virtual machine using transition rules. It must be noted that the error cases have not been given; the reason for this is that it would complicate the specification somewhat. In any case, the reader can write them as an exercise (they are not particularly difficult to identify).

Just in case the reader objects to the assumption that all instructions have a length of one, the following is offered. For each instruction, assume there is a function, *size*, which maps each instruction to its length (in some appropriate units, say bytes). This function can be used in transitions that change the value of the instruction pointer.

The point of this approach is that it gives a declarative specification of the virtual machine's instructions that is totally independent of any code or coding convention. Furthermore, it completely specifies the behaviour of the virtual machine without requiring any mental simulation of its operations.

4.3 Issues

In this subsection, some issues raised by the above virtual machine will be considered. In particular, the following will be addressed:

1. Indirect and relative jumps;
2. More data types;
3. Higher-order routines;
4. Primitive routines.

4.3.1 Indirect and Relative Jumps

In an indirect jump instruction, the operand is an address somewhere in the store. At the location specified by the operand, there is another address: that address is the destination of the jump. This is an extremely powerful way to transfer control. Since the address in the operand is a location, the contents of that location can be altered dynamically.

There is a problem with indirect jumps: the simplest algorithms require two passes over the code.

Relative jumps, sometimes called branches, are introduced as a method for compacting code. The BCPL Intcode and Cintcode machines make heavy use of relative jumps, it will be recalled. In a normal jump, the operand is a full address, typically occupying an entire machine word. In a relative jump, the operand can be a byte or 16-bit quantity, depending on the processor architecture. The operand is usually a signed quantity, the sign determining the direction of the jump. The actual address of the destination is usually computed relative to the current instruction pointer value by adding the operand to the instruction pointer to yield an absolute address. When the actual address has been calculated, the jump is performed.

Very often, the address taken as the base (to which the branch instruction's operand, or offset, is added) is the instruction *after* the branch instruction. It must, therefore, be remembered to include the size of the branch instruction in the calculation of the offset. A compiler will have this encoded in its address computation module (if the programmer remembers to include it!)

A second problem with branches is that the insertion of new instructions into the region of program covered by the branch affects the destination.[2] This must be taken into account when patching or otherwise modifying code with branches (another problem that compilers can avoid). A problem for a compiler is that it must keep track of the locations at which branches occur so that the correct offset can be computed; this is a complication for the code generator. A further problem is that the compiler has to make a decision as to whether to generate an absolute or a relative jump (there is ample literature on instruction selection and any modern compiler book will cover this topic)— this complicates the structure of the compiler a little.

Branches can be conditional or unconditional. As usual, an unconditional branch is executed without condition. A conditional branch performs the jump depending on the value of a flag in a register or, in a stack-based virtual machine, on the value on the top of the stack.

For interest, here are the transitions defining three branch instructions for the two-stack virtual machine. The instructions are:

br Unconditionally branch.

---

[2] Personally, I find branches a bit of a pain! So, when doing assembly programming, I include them only when I know the code is in its final form; then I comment them profusely to warn anyone who might modify the code.

beq Branch only if the top of the d stack is the value representing *true*.
bne Branch only if the top of the d stack is the value representing *false*.

In the transitions, o denotes a small signed integer (say, in the range $-128 \ldots + 127$). Again, it will be assumed that all instructions have a length of 1.

So, for br:

$$\langle g, d, c, p, \sigma_c, \sigma_d, i, \text{br } o \rangle \rightarrow \langle g, d, c, p, \sigma_c, \sigma_d, \ell, k(\ell) \rangle$$

where $\ell = i + o + 1$, and $-128 \leq o \leq 127$. Note that 1 is added to the current instruction pointer so the jump destination is computed on the basis of the instruction following the branch.

The two transitions defining beq are:

$$\langle g, d, c, p, \sigma_c, true \cdot \sigma_d, i, \text{beq } o \rangle \rightarrow \langle g, d, c, p, \sigma_c, \sigma_d, \ell, k(\ell) \rangle$$

where $\ell = i + o + 1$ and $-128 \leq o \leq 127$, and for the false case:

$$\langle g, d, c, p, \sigma_c, false \cdot \sigma_d, i, \text{beq } o \rangle \rightarrow \langle g, d, c, p, \sigma_c, \sigma_d, \ell, k(\ell) \rangle$$

where $\ell = i + 1$ and $-128 \leq o \leq 127$.

Finally, the two transitions defining bne are:

$$\langle g, d, c, p, \sigma_c, false \cdot \sigma_d, i, \text{bne } o \rangle \rightarrow \langle g, d, c, p, \sigma_c, \sigma_d, \ell, k(\ell) \rangle$$

where $\ell = i + o + 1$ and $-128 \leq o \leq 127$, and:

$$\langle g, d, c, p, \sigma_c, true \cdot \sigma_d, i, \text{bne } o \rangle \rightarrow \langle g, d, c, p, \sigma_c, \sigma_d, \ell, k(\ell) \rangle$$

where $\ell = i + 1$ and $-128 \leq o \leq 127$.

4.3.2 More Data Types

The addition of data types usually involves changes to the virtual machine: new operations have to be made available to the execution/evaluation process. In addition, it might be advisable to introduce new registers.

Using the same transition notation employed above, vectors will be introduced into the two-stack virtual machine.

Two new registers, the a and s registers are introduced. Their introduction is symptomatic of a general methodological point: if a function can be assisted by the addition of one or two registers, they should be considered. As will be seen, these registers are generally useful; for now, only their use in supporting vectors will be considered.

The operations are as follows. The error conditions are not recorded below; as usual, they are relatively straightforward to define. Vectors will be written as $\mathbf{v}_i$, where i is the length.

The **newvec** operation creates a new vector of length n in the heap. A pointer to the vector is pushed onto the d stack.

$$\langle a, s, g, c, d, \sigma_c, \sigma_d, i, \text{newvec } n \rangle \rightarrow \langle a, s, g, c, d, \sigma_c, \mathbf{v}_n \cdot \sigma_d, i + 1, \kappa(i + 1) \rangle$$

where $\mathbf{v}_n$ is a (pointer to a) vector of length n, allocated in the heap.

The **vset** operation sets an element of the vector currently in the S register. The index of that element is expected to be in the A register.

$$\langle n, \mathbf{v}_i, g, c, d, \sigma_c, v \cdot \sigma_d, i, \text{vset} \rangle \rightarrow \langle n, \mathbf{v}'_i, g, c, d, \sigma_c, \sigma_d, i + 1, \kappa(i + 1) \rangle$$

where $\mathbf{v}' = [v \mapsto n]v$.

The **vref** operation indexes the vector in the S register. The index of the element to be returned is expected to be in the A register. The element is returned by pushing it onto the d stack.

$$\langle n, \mathbf{v}_i, g, c, d, \sigma_c, \sigma_d, i, \text{vref} \rangle \rightarrow \langle n, \mathbf{v}_i, g, c, d, \sigma_c, v \cdot \sigma_d, i + 1, \kappa(i + 1) \rangle$$

where $v = \mathbf{v}_i(n)$.

The **clra** operation clears the A register (sets it to zero).

$$\langle a, s, g, c, d, \sigma_c, \sigma_d, i, \text{clra} \rangle \rightarrow \langle 0, s, g, c, d, \sigma_c, \sigma_d, i + 1, \kappa(i + 1) \rangle$$

The **popa** operation pops the value currently on the top of the d stack and loads it into (assigns it to) the A register.

$$\langle a, s, g, c, d, \sigma_c, v \cdot \sigma_d, i, \text{popa} \rangle \rightarrow \langle v, s, g, c, d, \sigma_c, \sigma_d, i + 1, \kappa(i + 1) \rangle$$

The **pusha** operation pushes the contents of the A register onto the d stack.

$$\langle v, s, g, c, d, \sigma_c, \sigma_d, i, \text{pusha} \rangle \rightarrow \langle a, s, g, c, d, \sigma_c, v \cdot \sigma_d, i + 1, \kappa(i + 1) \rangle$$

The **inca** operation increments the contents of the A register by one.

$$\langle n, s, g, c, d, \sigma_c, \sigma_d, i, \text{inca} \rangle \rightarrow \langle n + 1, s, g, c, d, \sigma_c, \sigma_d, i + 1, \kappa(i + 1) \rangle$$

The **deca** operation decrements the contents of the A register by one.

$$\langle n, s, g, c, d, \sigma_c, \sigma_d, i, \text{deca} \rangle \rightarrow \langle n - 1, s, g, c, d, \sigma_c, \sigma_d, i + 1, \kappa(i + 1) \rangle$$

The **pops** operation pops the d stack. The value popped is loaded into the S register.

$$\langle a, s, g, c, d, \sigma_c, v \cdot \sigma_d, i, \text{pops} \rangle \rightarrow \langle a, v, g, c, d, \sigma_c, \sigma_d, i + 1, \kappa(i + 1) \rangle$$

The **pushs** operation pushes the contents of the S register onto the d stack.

$$\langle a, v, g, c, d, \sigma_c, \sigma_d, i, \text{pushs} \rangle \rightarrow \langle a, v, g, c, d, \sigma_c, v \cdot \sigma_d, i + 1, \kappa(i + 1) \rangle$$

A question arises: should the A register be signed or not? There is no *a priori* answer to this. Sometimes, an unsigned value will be useful, while, at others, a signed one will be better. A signed representation can cause an overflow error when incremented or decremented too far. On the other hand, fewer positive signed values can be represented than with an unsigned value; however, vectors of extreme length (say 2^{24} words) might cause a few problems for the memory manager. Some languages allow negative bounds in arrays; they are, however, normalised to positive values by the compiler, so only positive indices are used at runtime; this indicates that an unsigned representation will be adequate. The wrap-around of unsigned values needs to be checked by the virtual machine, while overflow of a signed value is (as far as the virtual machine is concerned) automatic.

The addition of the *a* and *s* registers are not confined to vectorial operations. In particular, the *a* register can be used when compiling for loops. For example, the following source:

```
for i = 1 to 10 do x := x + 1 od
```

could be translated into the following two-stack code, assuming that x is the nth local variable:

```
        clra        % reg a := 0
$L:     getlocal n
        pushc 1
        add
        setlocal n % x := x + 1
        pushc 10
        pusha
        sub
        pushc 0
        eq          % reg a = 10?
        jne $L
$cont:  ...
```

As an example of the combined use of the A and S registers, the following is offered.

Consider the following fragment:

```
v := newvec(10);
x := 0;
for i = 0 to 10 do
  x := x + v(i)
od
```

If v is the *n*th and x is the *m*th local variable, then:

```
        newvec 10
        setlocal n
```

```
            pushc 0
            setlocal m
            clra
            getlocal n
            pops
    $L:     vref
            getlocal m
            add
            setlocal m
            inca
            pusha
            pushc 10
            sub
            pushc 0
            eq
            jne $L
    $cont: ...
```

These instruction sequences could be somewhat improved by the addition of an instruction that tests the value of the A register. The value to be tested is assumed to be on top of the d stack. This new instruction is called **equa** and is specified by:

$$\langle n, s, g, c, d, \sigma_c, m \cdot \sigma_d, i, \mathbf{equa} \rangle \rightarrow \langle n, s, g, c, d, \sigma_c, true \cdot \sigma_d, i + 1, \kappa(i + 1) \rangle$$

if $m = n$, and

$$\langle n, s, g, c, d, \sigma_c, m \cdot \sigma_d, i, \mathbf{equa} \rangle \rightarrow \langle a, s, g, c, d, \sigma_c, false \cdot \sigma_d, i + 1, \kappa(i + 1) \rangle$$

otherwise.

The last source fragment can now be written:

```
            newvec 10
            setlocal n % v := vec(10)
            pushc 0
            setlocal m % x := 0
            clra       % reg a := 0
            getlocal n
            pops       % reg s := vec
    $L:     vref
            getlocal m
            add
            setlocal m
            inca
            pushc 10
            equa
            jne $L
    $cont: ...
```

The argument for the inclusion of the A and S registers appears convincing. This is because the pure stack code to perform the above summation is considerably longer and *extremely* messy (readers who are unsure of this could profitably write out the stack-only version of the array sum operation). Nested loops require swapping the A and S registers on and off the stack and into/out of temporary variables but this is still considerably simpler than the pure-stack version.

Although the inclusion of the A and S registers improves the loop somewhat, there are still problems with the code, in particular the need to fetch the value of x and store it again. If this could be avoided, the code would run faster. There are two basic ways to do this:

1. Allocate a fixed position on the stack for the running total;
2. Introduce another register.

The first solution leads to code like the following:

```
          newvec 10
          pops      % s := vec(10)
          clra      % a := 0
          pushc 0   % tos = accumulator
$L:       vref
          add       % add to tos
          inca      % a := a + 1
          pushc 10
          equa
          jne $L
$cont:    pushs
          setlocal n
          pusha
          setlocal m
```

This code is not bad. The question arises as to whether it could be improved by the addition of more registers. Perhaps, in this case, the answer is no but if this example were of a nested loop, matters might be different.

Vectors can easily be introduced into the language. Structures (records) can easily be introduced as well. There are different ways to do this, depending upon how structures are represented: if a compact representation is required, there will be one set of methods; if a less compact representation is required, a simple approach based upon vectors can be adopted. This, more wasteful, approach will be considered here.

In this approach, a structure is implemented as a vector. This approach requires at least one word for each structure component, so it is not particularly efficient in storage. The field selectors are either compiler-generated functions or offsets represented by constant values. For example:

```
let s1 = struct(x := 0, y := 0, z := 0)
```

would be represented by a three-element vector and three offsets into it: $0 \mapsto x$, $1 \mapsto y$ and $2 \mapsto z$. The structure:

```
let s2 = struct(x := 0, y := vec(10), z := true)
```

would, again, be represented by a three element vector with the same offsets; the vector is implemented as a pointer that is stored in the second element of the vector and the third component would also be stored in a full word. In this case, however, the initialisation of the structure would be different.

The initialisation code for the first case might be:

```
       newvec 3
       pops
       clra
$L:    pushc 0
       vset
       inca
       pushc 3
       equa
       jne $L
$cont: ...
```

while that for the second might look like:

```
       newvec 3
       pops
       clra
       pushc 0
       vset
       inca
       newvec 10
       vset
       inca
       pushc 0
       vset
$cont: ...
```

An optimising compiler might produce the following, however:

```
       newvec 3
       pops
       clra
       pushc 0
       dup
       vset
       inca
       newvec 10
       vset
       inca
```

```
        vset
$cont:  ...
```

Code to access the second element of either s1 or s2 might be compiled into two-stack code as follows, assuming that the structure is stored in the nth local variable:

```
seta 1
getlocal n
pops        % s points to structure's vector
vref
% top of d contains the value.
```

Here, there is another new instruction: seta. It is defined by:

$$\langle a, s, g, c, d, \sigma_c, \sigma_d, i, \mathtt{seta}\ n \rangle \rightarrow \langle n, s, g, c, d, \sigma_c, \sigma_d, i + 1, \kappa(i + 1) \rangle$$

This new instruction allows the A register to be set without needing to push the initialisation value onto the stack. This is expected to produce another reasonable optimisation.

The implementation of lists is relatively straightforward, requiring the primitive operations *cons* (construct a list cell), *hd* (return the head—the first element—of the list), *tl* (return the list minus its head) and *null* (a predicate returning *true* if its argument is the empty list), as well as a constant value, *nil* (sometimes called *null*, *[]* or 0 in C) to represent the empty list.

Let ℓ be a list and v a value, the empty list is written as (); the list whose head is v and tail ℓ is written as $v :: \ell$. The operations for the two-stack machine are defined by the following transitions:

$$\langle a, s, g, c, d\sigma_c, \sigma_d, i, \mathtt{pushnil} \rangle \quad \rightarrow \langle a, s, g, c, d\sigma_c, () \cdot \sigma_c, i + 1, \kappa(i + 1) \rangle$$

$$\langle a, s, g, c, d, \sigma_c, v \cdot \ell \cdot \sigma_d, i, \mathtt{cons} \rangle$$
$$\rightarrow \langle a, s, g, c, d, \sigma_c, v :: \ell \cdot \sigma_d, i + 1, \kappa(i + 1) \rangle$$

$$\langle a, s, g, c, d, \sigma_c, v :: \ell \cdot \sigma_d, i, \mathtt{hd} \rangle$$
$$\rightarrow \langle a, s, g, c, d, \sigma_c, v \cdot \sigma_d, i + 1, \kappa(i + 1) \rangle$$

$$\langle a, s, g, c, d, \sigma_c, v :: \ell \cdot \sigma_d, i, \mathtt{tl} \rangle$$
$$\rightarrow \langle a, s, g, c, d, \sigma_c, \ell \cdot \sigma_d, i + 1, \kappa(i + 1) \rangle$$

$$\langle a, s, g, c, d, \sigma_d, v :: \ell \cdot \sigma_d, i, \mathtt{null} \rangle$$
$$\rightarrow \langle a, s, g, c, d, \sigma_d, \mathit{false} \cdot \sigma_d, i + 1, \kappa(i + 1) \rangle$$

And finally:

$$\langle a, s, g, c, d, \sigma_d, () \cdot \sigma_d, i, \mathtt{null} \rangle$$
$$\rightarrow \langle a, s, g, c, d, \sigma_d, \mathit{true} \cdot \sigma_d, i + 1, \kappa(i + 1) \rangle$$

With these primitives, as is well known, the other list operations can be defined. Note that the A and S registers can be used to define iterative operations over lists.

An example of list construction is in order. Consider the problem of representing the list (v_1, v_2, v_3, v_4). This can be done as follows (note that the elements are pushed onto the stack in reverse order):

```
pushc nil
pushc v4
cons
pushc v3
cons
pushc v2
cons
pushc v1
cons
```

(Note that it is assumed that nil is defined in some way—a zero pointer is one approach.) The list will be on the top of the stack at the end of this sequence.

As an aside, it will be recalled that the OCODE machine has a special register (called the A register—not to be confused with the A register above) to hold the value returned by a function. This can be adopted in the two-stack virtual machine currently under discussion. This approach can be introduced by the addition of a register, which will be called the R (for "return") register. Another virtual machine operation, called rval, must be introduced: this instruction pushes the contents of the R register onto the d stack. The retval instruction must now be re-defined, as must the return sequence for functions.

The new version of retval can be defined as:

$$\langle r, a, s, g, c, d, f \ddagger f'' \ddagger \sigma_c, v \cdot \sigma_d, i, \texttt{retval} \rangle \rightarrow \langle v, a, s, g, c', d', f'' \ddagger \sigma_c, \sigma_d', \alpha, \kappa(\alpha) \rangle$$

where $f = \lambda \cdot \pi \cdot d' \cdot c' \cdot \alpha$, $f'' = \lambda_1 \cdot \pi_1 \cdot d'' \cdot c'' \cdot \alpha'$, $\sigma_d = s \ddagger \sigma_d$ and $|\sigma_d| = d'$, $p' = \lambda_1 + d'$.

The rval instruction is easily defined:

$$\langle v, a, s, g, c, d, \sigma_c, \sigma_d, i, \texttt{rval} \rangle \rightarrow \langle v, a, s, g, c, d, \sigma_c, v \cdot \sigma_d, i+1, \kappa(i+1) \rangle$$

The calling sequence for a function needs to be modified:

```
      frame l p
      % Code for parameters goes here.
      call $f % perform the call
$cont: rval    % push the returned value onto the d stack.
```

In general, it would appear reasonable to introduce new registers to augment the stack. The introduction of a register avoids the overhead of stack operations, so increases speed at a modest increase in complexity. This is only one issue, though: the addition of special-purpose registers can considerably ease the generation of code by the compiler. This makes the modest introduction of registers a useful technique when extending the range of data types supported by a virtual machine. It must be pointed out, however, that unconstrained introduction of registers might turn out to be self-defeating, making code generation more complex and making the virtual machine overly complex. As in all matters, good judgement is required.

4.3.3 Higher-Order Routines

The usual way to represent higher-order functions is as *closures*. Closures are code–environment pairs. One way to implement them is as two-element vectors: one element of the vector points to the entry point of its code and the other points to an environment. If the stack is implemented as a chain of frames, this can easily be accommodated; if not, an alternative must be sought. This scheme poses no problems as far as creation and manipulation is concerned, as long as an address can be loaded onto the stack. Loading of arbitrary frames onto the stack as well as calling closure code require some care but can be implemented with relative ease.

There are problems associated with closures, however. One such problem is that a closure can be allocated on the stack or in the heap. The compiler has to determine which allocation strategy is best. Further details on the implementation of closures can be found in many modern books on compilers. Appel's books [4] and [5] are suggested.

As far as the current virtual machine and language are concerned, the introduction of closures requires a major change: the addition of a *static chain* to each stack frame. The reason for this is as follows. The current language permits routines to be defined *only* in the global environment; nested routine definitions are not permitted. Thus, there is no real need for a static chain; instead, stack frames are linked by what would otherwise be called the dynamic chain. The static chain is used to point to the environment in which a routine is defined; the dynamic chain is used to point to the environment in which it is called.

Closures represent a form of routine nesting. Non-local (free) variables in a closure refer to the environment in which it is created. This has the implication that closures must have access to that environment. Thus, closures require a static chain. In the current context (the two-stack machine for ALEX), the static chain is implemented by the g register in the virtual machine. Thus, a major addition to the runtime representations would be required. Since this chapter is already long enough, the necessary modifications are left to the reader as an exercise.

4.3.4 Primitive Routines

Some languages, Pascal is an example, have a relatively limited set of runtime primitives (e.g., i/o operations, new and dispose). Virtual machines for these languages can easily implement primitives as instructions in the main case statement. Common Lisp [48], on the other hand, defines something like 400 routines. Clearly, this number of routines cannot be represented in an 8-bit operation (byte) code. Sometimes, primitive functions can be implemented as inline code; some primitives, though, require either extension of the virtual machine's instruction set or some mechanism to call other code.

Frequently used primitives (e.g., some i/o operations) can be implemented as virtual machine instructions. Ones that are used less frequently might be treated in some other way. If primitives are implemented as virtual machine instructions, there is the risk that the case statement in its core will become too big to fit in the cache on some processor architectures and can, therefore, reduce performance.

The Harrison Machine (see Chapter 6) is an example of a system that is rich in primitives. Most of the primitives were not implemented in terms of virtual machine instructions for reasons of speed (many could have been, however). The decision was made to implement them in the language that was used to implement the virtual machine (Java, Scheme or C++, depending upon the implementation). Each primitive was implemented as appropriate. A table of pointers was defined, each element pointing to the code implementing the primitive (or the class containing the method implementing the primitive). On virtual-machine startup, the table was initialised as appropriate. The virtual machine was then extended by *one* instruction, called the *extension* instruction (denoted by the `primcall` opcode). This instruction took a single word operand that denoted the index of the primitive in the primitives table. When the instruction was executed, the virtual machine called the routine in the table at that location and passed a number of arguments to it (stack, environment, etc).

The approach adopted by the Harrison Machine is rather flexible. It does mean a branch out of the main loop's code. It might be preferred to extend the opcode size to 16 bits, thus accommodating primitives as operations. There are, without doubt, many other possible solutions to the implementation of primitives.

4.4 Concluding Remarks

In this chapter, a simple stack-based virtual machine for a very simple language was described and an implementation for it outlined. This machine was then re-defined in terms of a virtual machine with two stacks, one for control information and the other for data. The two-stack machine was then extended to cater for vectors, structures (records) and lists. An alternative mechanism for returning values from functions was considered. The implementations of closures and primitives were also examined.

The chapter has, it is to be hoped, shown how a virtual machine can be defined for a programming language. In order to do this, a very simple language (a toy language, really—it's not much use) was defined and its virtual machine was then specified.

For the virtual machine, the design principles were:

- Identify the semantically meaningful operations that can be used to implement expression evaluation and command execution.
- Identify primitive operations that can be used to implement the operations defined.
- Identify the runtime storage requirements of the language. This requires the identification of such structures as heaps and stacks.
- Identify the operations on these storage structures that implement the storage and retrieval of the data objects required by the programming language. This is closely related to data declarations and definitions.

5

More Stack-Based VMs

5.1 Introduction

The purpose of this chapter is to introduce example virtual machines for a very
small and simple object-oriented language and the core of a pseudo-parallel
language. Each virtual machine is described in some detail; it is to be hoped
that:

- They are sufficiently clear to permit the relationship between the components of each virtual machine to be related to the language concepts it implements. (The languages are described but the detailed mapping is left to the reader to identify.)
- They are sufficiently clear to be used as the basis of a *real* implementation without too much additional work.

Both of the languages are extensions of the ALEX language presented in
Chapter 4. This is done so that the details of the extensions can be the focus of
attention. Furthermore, it allows a would-be implementer to extend an ALEX
virtual machine to one that handles either or both of the extensions presented
in this chapter.

The object-oriented language of Section 5.2 is of an extremely simple kind.
The language is a simple class-based one; it is based upon single inheritance,
thus avoiding any of the problems associated with multiple inheritance (for
a detailed discussion, see [15]). The language, though, does support dynamic
method dispatch; this causes a little problem, for it must always be ensured
that the right method is executed when a request is made of an instance.
Dynamic dispatch is handled in a fairly standard way by means of indirection
tables associated with instances (actually, with classes). This ensures that the
methods associated with the *actual* (not the *declared*) type of an instance are
invoked when a request is made.

The pseudo-parallel language is a simple extension to ALEX; message passing is grafted on, as are some primitives for creating, suspending and killing
processes (the term "process" is used rather than "task" or "thread"). The

virtual machine's definition includes primitives for process management, message passing, queue handling and so on. As with the object-oriented language, the primitives are described in some detail. The storage structures required by the language are also described. It should be noted that, as presented, the language does not support shared memory (this is a proposed extension). Nevertheless, the storage organisation required by the language must be considered when designing a virtual machine for it.

The discussion of the concurrent language ends with a number of suggestions for variations and/or extensions. These suggestions are mostly about more or alternative inter-process communications primitives.

The chapter is arranged so that the object-oriented language is discussed first. This is followed by the presentation of the pseudo-parallel language. A summary section ends the chapter.

5.2 A Simple Object-Oriented Language

This section is about a simple object-oriented programming language, called SOL[1] and its virtual machine. The object-oriented language is quite realistic and in keeping with the most current languages. Readers unfamiliar with object-oriented programming language concepts should consult a suitable text, for example [15].

The language is class-based, so a distinction is made between classes and instances. As is usual, classes define the structure of instances. In this language, a distinction is made between class and instance variables. Methods are associated with classes. Classes are related by single inheritance. Method dispatch is dynamic. Since the virtual machine is the only thing of interest, variance is not relevant (although it would be if a compiler were defined).

The procedural component of this language can be assumed to be defined (alternatively, it can be considered as the relevant subset of ALEX if that makes matters more concrete).

The SOL language is a *pure* object-oriented language, like Java. This means that the only entities that can be defined are objects. The language does *not* permit the programmer to define routines, variables and constants outside of a class. A main class has to be defined for each program.

5.2.1 Language Overview

The programmer defines classes. A class in SOL has a name given by the programmer. It has a single superclass. It has a collection of variables and a collection of methods. The variables define the data elements of the class and can be *mutable* (can be updated as well as read) or *immutable* (can only be

---

[1] This stands for "Simple Object-oriented Language".

read). Class variables can only be of integer type. Boolean values are supported (in exactly the same way as in ALEX) but arrays are not.

Each class defines its set of *instance variables*: these are variables that define the instances of the class. A class can, optionally, define a set of *class variables*: these are variables that are shared by all of its instances.

Methods are defined together with the class to which they belong. The methods defined for a class can be invoked by all of the class' instances. Methods can read and update the slots of its class, as appropriate. Methods can be recursive. Internally, a method constitutes a scope.

Each class has a *single* superclass. It inherits all the variables and methods of its superclass. There is a single root class. This is called Object. Every class is a subclass of Object.

Instances of classes are created by the new function. It returns a reference to the newly created instance. Instance creation consists of two stages:

1. Allocation of the storage for the instance.
2. Initialisation of the new instance's variables.

It is often useful for the methods of a class to refer to the instance on which they were invoked. This can be achieved using a pseudo-variable called self. The reasons for its being a *pseudo*-variable will become clear below.

A pseudo-function called super is used directly to invoke methods in a superclass.

5.2.2 Virtual Machine—Storage Structures

Methods are compiled to virtual machine instructions. A code vector is required to store method code. There are two approaches to code in an object-oriented language. Some languages, Smalltalk being one example, compile method code into separate vectors; these vectors are associated with the class to which they belong at runtime. Other languages, mostly compiled languages like C++, compile all of their method code into a single code vector (C++ does this because it is compiled to native machine code and most operating systems make distinctions between data and code segments for machine code). The approach adopted by Smalltalk is excellently suited to interactive environments in which methods are redefined quite frequently, while the single-vector approach of C++ and others is best suited to production environments. For simplicity, it will be assumed that SOL compiles to a single vector. Each method will have an entry point, just like a routine in ALEX. The entry point denotes the method in the code vector.

Method access is somewhat more complicated, however. This is because methods are accessed with classes. It is necessary, therefore, for each class to have a table containing references to the methods it defines. Dynamic dispatch requires that the methods (and class variables) that can be accessed are those that are defined for the instance's class. This implies that each instance should have some way of indicating its class.

Instances inherit methods and variables. One compilation scheme collects all inherited instance variables and adds them to the instance variables of the class that is being instantiated. The same cannot be done for class variables, since they are shared by all instances of a class. Method references, however, can be collected. It might appear that a slight complication would be that some methods and instance variables might be overridden. This is a matter for the compiler, however, not for the virtual machine.

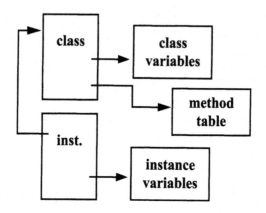

Fig. 5.1. *Class organisation in the heap.*

For the purposes of this chapter, method references will be associated with classes. Instance variables will be collected together. Class variables will be associated with classes. This scheme requires a runtime search for class variables and for methods.

The organisation of a class and one of its instances is shown in Figure 5.1. The figure shows that each instance refers to its class and to a storage area in which its instance variables are allocated. Each class refers to a method table and an area holding class variables. The figure does not show the *superclass* link.

A heap management system is used by SOL. All classes and instances are allocated in the heap.

A runtime stack is required. Its role is identical to that in a procedural language such as ALEX. It contains intermediate results. In the case of SOL, routine references become method references and all variable accesses are relative to a class or instance. A dual-stack scheme could be used for SOL, but a single, framed, stack will be employed here, just as for ALEX. The dual-stack approach will not be discussed in connection with SOL.

A number of procedures and functions are used by the implementation to access and update the heap structures implementing classes, methods and instances. These routines are:

`instvget` *i n* Return the contents of the instance variable *n* of the instance pointed to by *i*.

`instvset` *i n v* Assign value *v* to instance variable *n* of the instance pointed to by *i*.

`instclass` *i* Return a pointer to the class of the instance pointed to by *i*.

`supsuper` *s* Return a pointer to the superclass of the class pointed to by *s*.

`clsvget` *c n* Return the contents of the class variable *n* of the class object pointed to by *c*.

`clsvset` *c n v* Assign value *v* to the class variable *n* in the class object pointed to by *c*.

`mthepget` *c n* Return a pointer to method *n* in class object *c*. This pointer should be the entry point of the method.

A function `alloci` *n* is assumed. This allocates an instance structure in the heap with *n* instance variables. A corresponding `allocc` *n m* can be assumed: this allocates a class structure in the heap with *n* class variables and *m* methods. The `allocc` function will not be used until the extensions are discussed.

Finally, it will be necessary to search along the chain of superclasses of an instance. It is assumed that the compiler can determine how far up the chain to search for a method or variable. The number of steps up the chain is used to locate the desired class object. The following convention is used. If the desired entity is in the class of the instance, the distance is zero (0). If it is in the superclass of the instance's class, the distance is one (1). Each superclass up the chain adds one to the distance.

5.2.3 Virtual Machine—Registers

It might come as a surprise to know that no registers are required in addition to those supplied by the ALEX virtual machine. It is possible to optimise performance by the addition of registers. This will be considered as an extension.

5.2.4 Virtual Machine—Instruction Set

The majority of ALEX instructions can be assumed. In order to support an object-oriented language like SOL, the routine calling instructions of ALEX must be replaced by new ones that access the heap-allocated data structures representing classes, method tables and instances.

Instructions are needed to perform the following operations:

- Create a new instance of a class. (Instance deletion can be performed by the heap management system, as in Java.)
- Get and set instance variables.
- Get and set class variables.
- Refer to self.
- Call a method.

- Return from a method.
- Perform super call.

The instructions will be called:

allocinst: Allocate the storage for a new instance.
initinst: Initialise a new instance.
getiv: Get an instance variable's contents.
setiv: Set a new value into an instance variable.
getcv: Get a class variable's contents.
setcv: Set a new value into a class variable.
save: Set up a stack frame for a method call.
frame: Initialise the frame pointer for a method call.
mcall: Call a method.
retpm: Return from a procedural method.
retval: Return a value from a functional method. Note that this might return
    a reference to an instance.
scall Perform a super call.

The details will depend upon the storage structures employed by the virtual machine.

The reader will note that no mention has been made to self. The reason for this will be made clear below.

Operations not directly related to methods will be defined first. Note that they naturally require the routines described above.

allocinst: Assume that the size is on the top of the stack. A pointer to the newly allocated instance object will replace it when the instruction terminates.

```
s[sp] := alloci s[sp]
```

initinst i: Assume that a pointer to an uninitialised instance structure is on the top of the stack. The operand i is the number of instance variables in the instance. There should be i expressions (results) on the stack immediately below the instance pointer. So:

```
temp1 := s[sp] % get the instance pointer
sp    := sp - 1
for i := 0 to i - 1 do
  instvset(temp1,s[sp],i)
  sp := sp - 1
done
```

Note that the initialising values must be in reverse on the stack (this is natural for stack-based implementations but worth noting).

getivar n: Assume that a pointer to the instance is currently on the top of the stack:

```
s[sp] := instvget(s[sp],n-1)
```

`setivar` n: Assume that the value is on the top of the stack and the pointer to the instance is immediately below:

```
instvset(s[sp - 1],s[sp])
sp := sp - 1
```

`getclass`: Strictly speaking, this is a macro, not an instruction proper. It is used only within instructions in this implementation. So:

```
s[sp] := instclass(s[sp])
```

`getcvar` s n: Assume that the instance pointer is on the top of the stack. The operand s is the offset along the superchain of the class in which the variable (whose offset into the class variables) is n.

```
getclass
if s > 0 then
  for i := 1 to s do
    s[sp] := supsuper(s[sp])
  done
fi
s[sp] := clsvget(s[sp],n)
```

`setcvar` s n: Assume that the value is on the top of the stack and a pointer to the instance is immediately below. The operand s is the offset along the super-chain of the class in which the variable (whose offset into the class variables) is n. So:

```
getclass
if s > 0 then
  for i := 1 to s do
    s[sp] := supsuper(s[sp])
  done
fi
clsvset(s[sp], n, s[sp - 1])
sp := sp - 2
```

The instructions for methods and method calls are the next to be described. In this connection, the pseudo-variable, self, needs to be implemented. The best way to implement self is as an extra parameter to each method, usually the first. To access the value of self, the first parameter in the current stack frame is accessed (this is at offset zero into the parameter area). An instruction can be defined as:

```
self:
```

```
getparam 0
```

The compiler must always insert this extra parameter. It must also arrange method calls so that the instance from which the method call is issued is inserted into the actual parameters of a call.

Calling methods is somewhat more complex than calling ordinary routines. This is because the method must be located in the chain of superclasses starting at an instance's class. A pointer to the method is returned by the search. Other than this (and the inclusion of a pointer to the instance to be bound to self), the calling sequence for methods is similar to that for routines in the single-stack implementation described above. The **call** instruction must be augmented so that the search is included.

An important assumption is made about the search for methods. The method has already been determined to exist by the compiler. A similar assumption is made in connection with class variable access and update.

callmethod *s n*: Assume that a pointer to instance is on the top of the stack.

```
getsuper
if s > 0 then % find the super
  for i := 1 to s do
    s[sp] := supsuper(s[sp])
  done
fi
s[sp] := methepget(s[sp],n) % ep of method on top of stack.
ip    := s[sp]
sp    := sp - 1
```

5.2.5 Extensions

There are many possible extensions. For example, it is possible to:

- Provide more runtime descriptors so that introspection is facilitated;
- Provide dynamic loading and unloading of classes (as in JVM).

A comparison between this example and the JVM (either as outlined in Chapter 3 or [33]) or the Smalltalk virtual machine [21] will soon reveal areas in which extensions are possible. The language for which the current virtual machine was defined is extremely simple and only intended to show the main points—some extensions to the language will have a profound influence on the organisation of the virtual machine.

5.2.6 Alternatives

The main alternative to the class-based approach to object orientation is prototypes. This is an extremely interesting area but there is no space to introduce it here. Interested readers should consult [15] for an introduction to prototypes; for the more knowledgeable, either [10] or [36] are recommended.

5.3 A Parallel Language

This section is concerned with a simple parallel processing language, which will be called LASSIE.[2] This is, in essence, a procedural language extended to support parallel processing. The virtual machine is designed to execute on a uni-processor system, so implements a form of pseudo-parallelism. The basic procedural language will be assumed to be ALEX.

There are differences between the current system and ALEX. ALEX has global variables and literals. In LASSIE, global variables must be understood as having two flavours:

1. Variables that are global to all routines in a process but which are not visible in other processes. These variables must be allocated on the process' stack.
2. Variables that are accessible to all processes in a program (in the system). Variables of this kind must be protected by semaphores or some other mechanism to ensure mutual exclusion. For the time being, this kind of variable will be omitted.

Literals are read-only, so can be handled in exactly the same way as in ALEX. However, if processes can be introduced dynamically, there will be the need to protect the literal pool so that mutual exclusion is ensured.

5.3.1 Language Overview

The language is organised around the concept of a process. A process resembles a little program. It contains a set of global variable and constant definitions and a collection of routines. It has a main program. When a process is first executed, control is passed to its main program which, typically, is an infinite loop (hence our inclusion of the loop construct in ALEX).

The language contains all the constructs of ALEX. As noted above, there are issues relating to global variables and literal pools. In order to make matters as simple and modular as possible, global variables will be stored in the lowest stack frame on a process' runtime stack. This makes them accessible to all of the routines defined within a process. This could increase the cost of global access. However, the virtual machine will be augmented with a **G** register which always points to the globals area at the bottom of the stack. The easiest way to implement the globals areas is to interpret the outermost let of a process as a set of definitions and declarations that are *local* to the process. This has the pleasant implication that what were global variables will now be stored in the local variables part of the bottom stack frame. The **G** register points to the start of the locals section of the bottom stack frame.

This interpretation of an ALEX program has another pleasant consequence: it is now possible to pass *parameters* to a process when it is created.

---

[2] For suitably obscure reasons that are not revealed.

They are stored in the parameters area of the bottom stack frame. Sometimes, the parameters passed to a process are of importance to routines within its body. In particular, the process' identifier is of considerable use. To handle these cases, a set of *additional* global variables will be added to each process by the compiler; code to assign parameter values to these globals will be generated by the compiler and inserted into the process' initialisation code.

The initialisation code added by the compiler is executed when the process is run for the first time. One particular operation is to set the process' identifier as a global variable.

It is necessary for processes to create other processes. This is done using a **create** operation which returns the identifier of the newly created process, so that the creator can send messages to the new process. In some process models, in particular the Unix/Posix model, process creation involves storage sharing and separation. In the model employed here, when a process is created, the virtual machine allocates new storage that is totally disjoint from the creator's. When a child process has been created, the parent continues. The Unix/Posix *fork* model allows the creator to wait until all of its children have been terminated. This is not directly implemented in the current example.

In addition, the language contains syntactic constructs for sending messages. A message, for the virtual machine, is just a header containing routing information and a pointer to a payload. The payload is a vector of bytes (or words) that is supplied by the process' code. As far as the virtual machine is concerned, the contents of a message are of no consequence. For the programming language, they might be described as a record or structure or by a vector.

The message-exchange protocol is initially designed to be asynchronous. One reason for this choice is that it is easier to implement. A second reason is that synchrnonous mechanisms can be implemented on top of asynchronous ones. In an asynchronous scheme, one process sends a message to another and continues processing. At some stage, the receiving process receives the message. The receiving process does not have to wait for a message to arrive if it does not so choose. In a synchronous scheme, both processes must synchronise before they exchange the message(s). One way of implementing synchronous communications on top of asynchronous is for the first process to send a message stating that it wants to communicate. The receiver replies with a message saying that it is ready to receive the message. The message is then exchanged and both processes continue independently. Clearly, to make this work, both processes must recognise that a message has been sent by the other. The receiver must be able to wait until the exchange has been made. When the exchange is made, the receiver might, optionally, then send an acknowledgement message. An implementation of synchronous message exchange will be considered as an extension.

When concurrency in any form is an issue, the question of fairness arises. Fairness is the property that every process is given the processor eventually. The main queue in the virtual machine implements a *round robin* priority system. Processes are added to the end of the queue and removed from the front. Eventually a process will reach the head of the queue and will be executed. It is not permitted to insert a process into the middle of the ready queue, so overtaking is not possible. Equally, there are currently no priorities, so overtaking cannot occur by altering process priorities or by repeatedly introducing a higher priority process. The fairness of the current virtual machine is minimal.

5.3.2 Virtual Machine—Storage Structures

The storage structures for a parallel language are somewhat more interesting than for other languages. Most of the usual storage structures are present but they are often replicated, one for each process. For example, there is a stack for each process so that computations within a process cannot affect those in another.

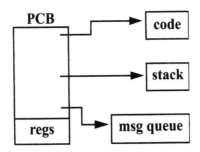

Fig. 5.2. *General organisation of a process table (PCB).*

- A *process descriptor*. This contains information describing a process. It contains:
  – The instruction pointer for the process. Each process has its own instruction pointer.
  – The process' stack. Each process has its own stack.
  – A status field. This records the state of the process.
  – A pointer to the process' code vector. Note that two or more processes can share the same code.
  – A message queue.
  – A termination flag. This is set when the process terminates.
  – A set of processor registers. These are copies of the virtual machine's registers that are made when a context switch removes the process from the (virtual) processor.
- A process table. This holds all the process descriptors of processes that are currently executing or have just been created. The process table is

indexed by a *process identifier*, or *pid*. This allows information in a process descriptor to be accessed rapidly by the virtual machine (and other things). Figure 5.2 shows the general organisation of the process table (also called a *Process Control Block*, hence *PCB* in the figure).

- A process queue called the *ready queue*. This holds the process descriptors of all processes that are ready to execute.
- A stack for each process.
- A code vector for each process.
- A message queue for each process. This holds the messages that the process has yet to process.
- A message header. This is a standard header that consists of:
  - The pid of the sender.
  - The pid of the receiver.
  - A pointer to the message's *contents* (or *payload*).

It will be assumed that the following are defined for process descriptors:

allocpd: Allocate a new process descriptor in the process table. If there are no free slots, an error is signalled.

initpd *ss c*: Initialise a process descriptor. The parameters are:
  ss: The size of the stack for the new process.
  c: The code vector for the new process.

deletepd *p*: Delete the process descriptor *p*.

process_id *p*: Return the pid of the process descriptor *p*.

process_stack *p*: Return the stack in the process descriptor *p*.

process_stack_set *p s*: Set a stack *s* in process descriptor *p*.

process_msgs *m*: Return the message queue in process descriptor *p*.

process_msgs_set *p m*: Set a message queue in process descriptor *p*.

process_status *p*: Return the status of the process descriptor *p*.

process_status_set *p s*: Set the status *s* of the process descriptor *p*.

process_ip *p*: Return the instruction pointer of process *p*.

process_ip_set *p ip*: Set the instruction pointer *ip* in process descriptor *p*.

process_code *p*: Return the code vector in process descriptor *p*.

For queues, the following are required:

create_queue: Create a FIFO queue.

next *q*: Return the next object enqueued on queue *q*.

enqueue *q o*: Enqueue object *o* onto queue *q* using the FIFO discipline.

emptyq *q*: Return *true* if the queue *q* is empty, *false* otherwise.

clearq *q*: Empty the queue of its current contents. This is a rarely used operation.

Stacks also need some operations defined over them:

stack_create *n*: Create a stack of size *n* in the heap.

stack_size: Return the size of the stack.

stack_bottom: Return a pointer to the bottom of the stack.

stack_top: Return the top of the stack.

stack_top_set: Set the new top of the stack.

There are operations associated with messages:

msg_create *src dest conts*: Create a message wrapper with three slots set to *src*, *dest* and *conts*.

msg_src: Return the pid of the sender of the message.

msg_dest: Return the pid of the intended receiver of the message.

msg_conts: Return the contents (payload) of the message.

For the time being, the code vector will be ignored. There are different ways to implement it. The organisation of the code vector is of little interest if processes cannot be added dynamically to the virtual machine.

5.3.3 Virtual Machine—Registers

The virtual machine inherits a number of registers from the sequential language. In addition, it defines a set of registers of its own.

HLT The halt flag to terminate the virtual machine.

SB A pointer to the stack of the process that is currently executing.

SL The length of the current stack (for checking—this is ignored below).

stk A pointer to the start of the current process' stack.

sp The top of the current process' stack.

G The globals start pointer. This is set when a process is made current.

cp A pointer to the current process' descriptor.

ip The instruction pointer.

mq The message queue of the current process.

cpid The pid of the currently executing process.

cpcd A pointer to the current process' code vector (or its entry point if code is compiled into a single vector or segment).

ptab The process table.

rdy The ready queue.

(Again, some of these registers are not programmable by virtual machine instructions. They are, as noted in Chapter 4, essential for the operation of the system.) It is necessary to change the names of registers in ALEX code in order to convert it to run on the current virtual machine. This is a simple but tedious matter.

Stacks, queues and messages will be allocated in a heap.

Figure 3.3 shows the general organisation of the storage structures used by this virtual machine. The figure shows the currently running process as a pointer to a control block (or process descriptor) that refers to a set of registers, a stack and a message queue. (The "regs" box in the figure refers to a location in which the process saves its registers between activations). Figure 3.3 also shows a number of waiting queues. In general, a virtual machine will have a number of waiting queues, one for each shared resource.

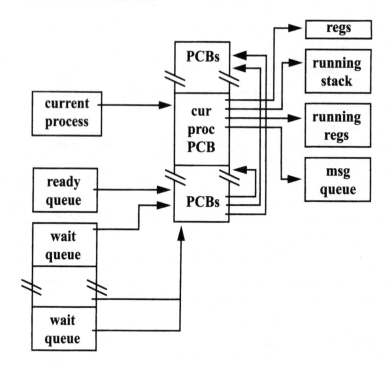

Fig. 5.3. *General organisation of support structures.*

5.3.4 Virtual Machine—Instruction Set

The basic operations determine the instructions.

It is necessary to create and delete processes. The former requires the creation and initialisation of a process descriptor. A stack must be created for the new process and the code vector must be set in the process descriptor; the instruction pointer must be initialised and an empty message queue must be assigned to it. The status is set to *ready*. As far as the source code is concerned, the `process_create` function returns the identifier of the newly created process.

Process deletion can involve the deletion of the process' descriptor. In most operating systems, there is a limit to the number of process descriptors that can be present at any time. This leads to an implementation of the process table as a vector of process descriptors. When a process terminates, its descriptor is marked as free (either by setting a flag or, more usually, by adding it to a free chain—the free chain is used in allocating process descriptors, as well). The deletion operation will be denoted by `delete_pd`, here, and no more details will be given. Similarly, the allocation of a new process descriptor is handled by the `alloc_pd` abstraction.

When a process descriptor has been created, it is placed in the ready queue. At some time, it will come to the top of the queue and will be run.

The process-creation instruction is:
pcreate *ss c*. The operands are the same as for **initpd**. The instruction allocates a new process descriptor in the table and allocates and initialises a stack which is then stored in the new process descriptor. An empty message queue is created and stored in the process descriptor. The code vector is set in the descriptor and the instruction pointer is set to the first instruction. The process status is set to *ready* and the descriptor (process) is enqueued on the ready queue.

The instruction that deletes a process is:
pdelete *pid*. The *pid* operand is the process identifier of the process to be deleted. The operation deletes the stack and message queue of the process and clears the slots in the process descriptor. The process descriptor is then marked as *free* so that it can be re-used.

Sometimes, a process needs to terminate itself voluntarily. This is achieved using the **pdelete** instruction. However, cleanup operations might be necessary. For the current version, there are no cleanup operations. It must be noted that the sudden suicide of a process can lead to deadlocks. In the present case, if there are processes waiting on messages from a process that has just killed itself, they will wait forever for replies.

In the case of a suicide, the compiler must generate code to access the process' identifier. If the identifier is stored as offset *mypid* in the global variables area of the process, the suicide instruction can be implemented as:

```
getglob mypid
pdelete stk[sp]
```

An operation that voluntarily suspends the caller will be useful. This is called the **suspend** operation. It is executed when the process is running. The effect of executing a **suspend** operation is to remove the caller from the processor. A context switch stores its state information in its process descriptor and the descriptor is enqueued on the back of the ready queue.

The suspend instruction is:
psuspend. There are no operands.

The virtual machine executes a cycle. On each cycle, a process is selected from the ready queue. The process that is selected is usually the first in the queue. This is operationalised by selecting a process descriptor (the first) from the ready queue. A context switch is performed to remove the currently running process (storing its state information in its process descriptor) and setting the virtual machine's registers from the newly selected descriptor. The instruction pointer is set in the virtual machine and the newly selected process runs.

In the initial version, only asynchronous message passing will be supported. To support this, a trio of operations is required:
asendmsg *d m*: This sends the message, *m*, to the destination *d*. The destination is a valid pid. The operation creates a message header and sets *m* as its payload. The result is enqueued on the message queue of the process with

pid equal to *d*. The caller is *not* suspended after or during execution of this operation.

anextmsg: This returns a pointer to the next message in the caller's message queue (if there is one); it returns nil if the message queue is empty.

agotmsgs: This is a function that returns *true* if there are messages currently in the caller's message queue and *false* otherwise.

Note that the message-handling operations require us to extend the denotable values of the sequential language with pointers and the value nil. A suitable representation for them must be selected. For a virtual machine, a pointer can be an underlying machine address and nil can be zero (as it is in C).

Since context switches will occur repeatedly, an operation will be defined to handle it. This operation will be used more as a macro than an independent operation. Nevertherless, it is a virtual machine operation, so must be included in a complete specification.

The context-switching operation has the form:
switchctxt *outpid*, where *outpid* is that of the process to be switched out. It saves the state of *outpid* in its descriptor. It obtains the next process from the ready queue and makes it runnable.

When one process decides that the virtual machine should halt, it executes a halt instruction to set the **HLT** flag. This is achieved in the obvious way (which is identical to the way it was done for ALEX).

5.3.5 Implementation

So, the instruction set must be implemented. Luckily, most instructions are the same as in one of the ALEX variants, so a lot of work has already been done. However, it is still necessary to provide implementations (some of which are not trivial) for the following instructions:

1. pcreate.
2. pdelete.
3. psuspend.
4. asendmsg.
5. anextmsg.
6. agotmsgs.

In addition, the **switchctxt** macro will be required.
pcreate *stksz code*: returns *pid* of new process.

```
code  := stk[sp]
sp    := sp - 1
stksz := stk[sp]
sp    := sp - 1
pid := allocpd
```

```
    initpd stksz code
    enqueue rdy  pid
```

pdelete *pid*: Assuming that the process is not on any queues.

```
    deletepd stk[sp]
    sp := sp - 1
```

suicide:

```
    deletepd cpid
```

switchctxt *outpid*:

```
    proc      := ptab[outpid]
    proc.mq   := mq
    proc.sp   := sp
    proc.ip   := ip
    proc.stk  := stk
    proc.SL   := SL
    proc.SB   := SB
    enqueue rdy outpid
    proc := dequeue rdy
    mq    := proc.mq
    sp    := proc.sp
    ip    := proc.ip
    stk   := proc.stk
    SL    := proc.SL
    SB    := proc.SB
```

psuspend:

```
    enqueue rdy cpid
    proc      := ptab[cpid]
    proc.mq   := mq
    proc.sp   := sp
    proc.ip   := ip
    proc.stk  := stk
    proc.SL   := SL
    proc.SB   := SB
    nxtproc   := dequeue rdy
    proc      := ptab[nxtproc]
    mq        := proc.mq
    sp        := proc.sp
    ip        := proc.ip
    stk       := proc.stk
    SL        := proc.SL
    SB        := proc.SB
```

asendmsg *destpid msg*:

```
msg       := stk[sp]
sp        := sp - 1
destpid := stk[sp]
stk[sp] := msg_create cpid destpid msg
destp     := ptab[destpid]
enqueue destp.mq stk[sp]
sp        := sp - 1
```

anextmsg: Returns a message or *nil*:

```
sp := sp + 1
stk[sp] := dequeue proc.mq
```

msgconts *msg*: Assume *msg* is stack top.

```
stk[sp] := msg_conts stk[sp]
```

msgsrc *msg*: Assume *msg* is stack top.

```
stk[sp] := msg_src stk[sp]
```

msgdest *msg*: Assume *msg* is stack top.

```
stk[sp] := msg_dest stk[sp]
```

agotmsgs: Returns true or false, depending upon state of local message queue.

```
sp        := sp + 1
stk[sp] := emptyq mq
```

5.3.6 Extensions

There are a great many possible extensions to LASSIE, some of which are:

- Synchronous message exchange;
- Shared variables and, more generally, critical sections;
- Conditional critical sections;
- Monitors;
- Await constructs;
- Priorities and better scheduling;
- Dynamic process introduction;
- Storage management.

Synchronous messages

As outlined above, it is possible to build upon asynchronous communication to provide a synchronous version. In this subsection, an alternative approach will be adopted: bounded buffers protected by semaphores. Each process is associated with a unique buffer. This buffer is accessed using two semaphores: one for mutual exclusion and one to signal full/empty. The buffer is of a finite size: a size of 1 would be ideal. The actual buffer holds a single pointer to a message of the same structure as that described above.

The operations on the buffer are:

ssend *pid msg*: This is a procedure. The shared buffer associated with the process *pid* is accessed. If no other process is active in the buffer and the buffer is not full, the caller adds the message to the buffer. In either of the other cases, the caller is suspended on the semaphore's queue.

sread: This is a function. It is called by the owner of a shared buffer. It accesses the shared buffer. If no other process is active in the buffer and if the buffer is full, the caller copies the pointer and signals that the buffer is empty. Otherwise, the caller is suspended on the semaphore's queue.

Initially, the buffer is *nil*.

Binary semaphores are quite adequate for this application. The addition of semaphores adds a little complexity because they introduce the possibility that a process can be either on the ready queue or on some semaphore queue.

A semaphore implementation requires three operations:

initsema *s n*: Initialise the semaphore *s* and set the counter to *n*.

wait *s*: Wait on the semaphore (the P operation).

signal *s*: Signal on the semaphore (the V operation).

Shared variables

The conventional way to implement shared variables is to use semaphores. The synchronous message exchange outlined above is an example of a shared variable.

Events

The Unix operating system supports an event-based inter-process communication mechanism (called "signals"). It is relatively easy to implement events in virtual machines like the one described above. More generally, it is possible to include programmable interrupts, as well as introducing those supported by the operating system on which the virtual machine executes. If the virtual machine is implemented in Ada, most of the work of interfacing to operating system interrupts is already done in its library.

Monitors

Monitors, as is well known, are a high-level construct similar to a class. Basically, a monitor is a set of data, an initialisation routine and a collection of *entry* routines. In addition, there is a *monitor* queue of processes that are waiting to enter the monitor and perform an operation.

Await

This construct was introduced by Brinch Hansen [12]. It is a high-level construction of the form:

await condition

where condition is an expression that returns a boolean value.

The caller is suspended until the expression returns *true*. This is the source of the problems associated with the construct. The obvious way to execute the expression is within a busy wait but this, at least on a uni-processor, is not an option. What is required is for the expression to be periodically evaluated and the result used to determine whether to resume the process which originally called the await function.

There is a simple solution to the problems associated with the construct: generate thunks. The construct calls a thunk to evaluate the conditional expression.

5.3.7 Alternatives

In the implementation sketched above, a context switch involved saving the virtual machine registers in the outgoing process and obtaining a new set of registers from the process to which control is switched. This clearly requires space in the process descriptor. One simple alternative is to store the entire context (VM registers) on the top of a process' stack when it is switched out. This is a common approach adopted in operating system kernel construction.

A large question hangs over the approach adopted here. It was decided to design a virtual machine that looks very much like a conventional operating system kernel. If continuations are available to the implementer (see, for example [20] for a series of Scheme interpreters based on continuations), a cleaner approach might be available. This is the way that Concurrent ML was constructed [43].

Using continuations, it is possible to employ the operations of a sequential VM without all the extra structure and operations described above. All the approach requires is that the basic VM provides a way to manipulate continuations. One reply is that continuations are an extremely good way to implement pseudo-concurrency but they are not so good for:

- Implementing VMs for concurrent languages that might execute on a multi-processor;
- Providing such features as tracing and profiling.

5.3.8 Issues

One severe criticism of Java is that its thread operations are at a very low level. The operations defined above are at an even lower level! The defence given by the designers of Java is that it is possible, given their primitives, to implement any other kind of thread operation. This is a defence that will also be offered here. It was a design decision, here, to define a virtual machine as an example. The primitives chosen for this virtual machine are intended to show how they can be implemented and represented in the instruction set. It is quite possible to wrap the primitives defined above in a richer set of constructs, many of which can be implemented by the compiler.

5.4 Concluding Remarks

This chapter contains descriptions of two relatively simple virtual machines:

- One for a simple object-oriented programming language based upon the sequential virtual machine;
- One for a simple parallel language that uses the sequential language as it core.

Again, the purpose of presenting these VMs was to show how, in an informal way, they can be designed. The examples show how more "modern" extensions to a simple algorithmic core can be implemented in a virtual machine.

5.4.1 Some Optimisations

The descriptions of the three virtual machines presented in this chapter and the previous one are not optimal, even though a direct implementation will have reasonable performance. In this subsection, a few optimisations will be considered.

An optimisation that is definitely worth discussing is the replacement of constant references in instructions by pointers. For example, the entry points of routines can be replaced by pointers instead of indices into code vectors. Similarly, jumps of both kinds can be optimised by converting labels into pointers to instructions. If entry points and labels are represented in VM code by words, this usually requires no additional space, assuming that the underlying hardware representations of words and pointers is the same. In code segments that are heavily used, the substitution of pointers for indices is definitely worthwhile because it considerably reduces the number of storage accesses (and cache loading on most processors). This optimisation requires a pre-processing phase before loading into the virtual machine.

In an object-oriented language, access to the super classes of an instance can also be optimised by the replacement of indices by pointers. It was assumed above that the compiler can determine in which superclass a method is to be found. This led to a pointer-chasing exercise. This can be removed if a direct pointer to the method can be obtained; by hypothesis, it can.

Readers interested in a parallel language and virtual machine based on the π-calculus (see, for example, [35]) will find the description of PICT in [40] interesting.

5.4.2 Combining the Languages

One reason for presenting virtual machines for an object-oriented and for a pseudo-parallel language was that they both represent interesting and useful extensions to the basic virtual machine concept. The combination of the two leads to an object-oriented parallel programming language, a so-called "active object" language. Active objects are, at the time of writing, a research area.

Case Study: An Event-Driven Language

6.1 Introduction

In this chapter, a virtual machine of a less conventional nature is presented. This is done to demonstrate to readers that the semantics implemented by a virtual machine need not match that of the von Neumann model or that of a conventional stack model in all details; indeed, any semantics, conventional or otherwise, can be implemented using a virtual machine. Functional languages with lazy evaluation, stream-based languages and functional-logic languages (which require that evaluations be suspended until input unification variables are bound) do not conform to the conventional von Neumann model but can be implemented with relative ease using virtual machines.

The present case is of an event-driven system. In this system, called the Harrison Machine[1] [13, 14], structured objects, called *events*, are used to trigger the execution of pieces of code. The code is organised as small modules. Code execution is guarded by operators resembling those in a temporal logic; the code that is guarded by an operator is called a *rule*. In this system, rules can be nested, providing a structured language for building event-based software.

Rules use the *cause* operation to cause events. This is implemented as the creation and initialisation of event objects which are stored in a *global* event queue. The main loop of the virtual machine removes the next event from the queue (using the FIFO discipline by default) and runs the pattern code of all the rules in the system (this executes nested patterns, as well as top-level ones). Those rules whose pattern is satisfied by the event are stored in a list; those whose pattern is not satisfied are left until the next cycle. Rules whose patterns have been satisfied are then executed in some order (in all the implementations to date, this has been sequentially by iterating down the list, executing each rule in turn). The execution of rules causes new events that

---

[1] Named after John Harrison, the designer and constructor of the first reliable ship's chronometer.

are added to the global FIFO. When all rules have been executed, they are returned to the set of all rules and the cycle continues until there are no more events to be processed or until a rule decides that the machine is to stop.

The last paragraph describes the *basic* or *default* mode of operation for the system. The Harrison Machine was designed in order to explore the following issues:

- Using event-based processing as a looser form of routine call. Rules (actually entire modules) can be added and removed from the system at runtime; new rules can be substituted for old ones as the system executes.
- Computational reflection using events. Computational reflection is the ability of a process to inspect and modify itself as it executes.

The second of these issues imposes some interesting requirements on the Harrison Machine's virtual machine. First, since the system is concerned with event-driven execution, it was necessary for the *entire* virtual machine to be represented as rules to be executed by the system itself. This permits a collection of rules running on the virtual machine to implement the functions of that machine and, thereby, act as another virtual machine upon which to run rules. In particular, it permits the execution of virtual machines in a hierarchy or in pseudo parallel, some (or all) of which can implement different instructions and execution cycles (thus, providing a set of *different* virtual machines all executing within the same image). Communication between such nested virtual machines is effected using the global event queue.

The fact that the event queue is global is both a blessing and a nuisance. It provides a means of communication between *all* of the rules in the system. It also acts as something of a bottleneck. However, its role as a focus for control decisions turns out to be of some utility. The library of functions included with the virtual machine includes operations for handling queues (in fact, all queues, including the global event queue, are implemented as DEQueues) and for replacing the global one with a local one. In the rule language, queues are first-class entities (as are rules), so the language provides primitives for setting and accessing the global event queue as an object. This enables rules to replace the global event queue with queues of their own. These queues are intended to hold events that have been generated by virtual machines implemented as rules. There are also library routines implementing the DEQueue protocol, as well as those that search the queues. This enables rules to implement FIFO, LIFO and other control régimes within a virtual machine (when implementing virtual machines as rules, these operations can be performed on queues stored in variables local to a rule).

To implement this properly, events must be treated as first-class entities, also. This has the implication that the virtual machine must be able to create and operate upon the entities representing events.

The virtual machine also contains primitives for setting and accessing the rule that is to be executed next, thus permitting rules to decide what to run next. There is also a **suspend** primitive that a rule can execute to remove itself from the processor and cause the next rule to be run.

The fact that rules are first-class entities has less impact upon the virtual machine. The rule-language compiler is also a routine in the runtime library, so rules can be compiled from source text or abstract syntax trees (there are also primitives for their construction) and then either stored on an external medium or immediately loaded into the system. There are also primitives for loading rules from external media such as files or a database. Rules can also be stored, singly or in sets, in variables local to rules; they, like queues and events, can be stored in components of events, thus permitting the exchange of state and operation between rules at runtime.

This collection of primitives allows rules to control the execution of other rules, as well as maintaining a collection of event queues. It also allows rules to control the contents of the rule store at any point in the execution of the virtual machine.

The Harrison Machine has been implemented a number of times, each one experimenting with different compilation strategies and collections of primitives. The virtual machine is, in fact, quite simple to implement in its basic form (indeed, one version was written and tested in Scheme in a single day!) This chapter, then, describes the virtual machine and the language that executes upon it. The issue of reflection is not particularly relevant to this book, so detailed consideration is omitted.

The aim of this chapter is to show how a virtual machine for a language that has fairly unconventional semantics can be constructed. In order to do this, the virtual machine is described and then formalised using transition rules. A compilation scheme for the language that executes on this virtual machine is also provided (however, it should be noted that only the *core* schemes are given).

The schemes also include a simple scheme for compiling patterns to virtual machine code. As will be seen, pattern compilation involves nothing unusual; it does not require unification primitives or special variable-binding methods.

Appendix B contains a set of rules that describe the compilation of Harrison Machine rules. The target of this compiler is the virtual machine described in this chapter.

Section 6.7 is not strictly germane to the central theme of this book. It is concerned with the optimisation of rule compilation by means of source-to-source translation of derived rule forms to primitive ones.

6.2 The Structure of Rules

Here, the forms taken by the system's rules are described in an informal fashion.

The following rule classes are supported by the system:

- always.

- when.
- unless.
- since.
- until.
- next.
- alt.

The classes are interpreted informally as follows. The initial keyword denotes the temporal operator (or simply "operator") for the rule. The operator has a scope that extends to the end of the rule.

In all cases except the first and last, the parameter p occurring immediately after the operator is an expression representing an event predicate. The predicate is implemented as a simple pattern, so rule classes with this parameter are referred to as *pattern* rules. When the class of rule is not at issue, the term "rule" is used to refer to rules of any of the above classes.

In all cases except the last (alt), the *Body* denotes a sequential program. This program can contain occurrences of rules. In such cases, the term "nested rule" is employed to denote those rules inside the scope of an operator.

always do(*Body*). The body of the rule is executed on every cycle of the Virtual Machine unless a command in the body causes the rule to terminate.

when(p) do(*Body*): When an event occurs that satisfies the pattern p, the body is executed.

unless(p) do(*Body*): If an event occurs that *does not* satisfy the pattern, the body is executed. (An unless rule can be interpreted as when(not p) do(*Body*).)

since(p) do(*Body*): If an event occurs that satisfies p, repeatedly execute body. A since rule can be interpreted as the nested rule when(p) do(always do(*Body*)): (In some ways, the name "since" is a little misleading, for its intended interpretation is "henceforth"; that this is the correct interpretation will become clear below. The name "since" was chosen simply because it reads as better English.)

until(p) do(*Body*): Repeatedly execute body until an event occurs that satisfies p. An until rule can be interpreted as the nested rule always do(*Body*; when(p) do(*Abort*)), where *Abort* is a system operation that terminates the rule and causes it to be deleted from the system.

The next operator, if included, will have the form:

next do(*Body*): This operator cannot occur first in a rule. It is executed in response to the event that caused the immediately preceding rule to execute. The interpretation of a next rule is equivalent to when(true) do(*Body*). When proceded by since or until, next operators are executed on the event immediately following the termination of these iterative constructs, if they terminate.

As an example of the complex behaviours that can be obtained by nesting rules, the following is offered. If one wanted to represent the proposition that

```
always do(
    when ($day = TUESDAY )do(
        when ( $time = 2pm )do(
            teach(CS330);
          ) -- end innermost when
      ) -- end when
  ) -- end always
```

Fig. 6.1. *A rule for "I always teach CS330 on Tuesdays at 2pm".*

"I always teach CS330 on Tuesdays at 2pm", a rule like that shown in Figure 6.1 might be written (the rule in the figure is written in pseudocode).

A further form could be defined that consists of a since rule with an until rule nested within it. Such a rule would be triggered by one event and would continue until an event caused it to terminate. This form would be associated with the during operator. This form was not employed in the systems described here. Its implementation is a simple source-to-source transformation.

$\mathsf{alt}(R_1,R_2,\ldots,R_n)$, where R_i, $1 \le i \le n$ is a pattern rule (always, next, since and until rules are not permitted). Rules of this form are interpreted as follows. The pattern of each rule is evaluated in turn. The first rule whose pattern to be satisfied is executed. In other words, a rule

$$\mathsf{alt}(R_1, \ldots, R_n)$$

is equivalent to:

$$R_1 \vee \ldots \vee R_n$$

where the R_i are, in this, case rules of any kind except next. Given this equivalence, rules of this form are not strictly necessary because they can be written as a set of separate rules; they turn out, however, to be useful when writing rule programs.

The *Body* of a rule is either one or more nested rules (rules can be nested to an arbitrary depth) or a simple imperative program that can also contain rules. In addition to rules, bodies contain the following principal commands:

- Assignment (of the usual form);
- Procedure call;
- The *Cause* operation to cause events;
- The McCarthy/Dijkstra conditional (**if**);
- Dijkstra's **do** command;
- **let** bindings to introduce local variables.

At present, it is not possible to define routines using the internal language for rules. This might be considered in a later version of the system.

6.3 Events

The Harrison Machine is based on events. Events are used to trigger the execution of rules and are caused by rules; events cause rules to perform their actions. Rules containing the when operator wait for events to occur. Other operators are concerned with repetitive performance of actions either after an event has occurred or until an event occurs. The execution of a rule's action can cause one or more events. Usually, these events are stored in the global Event Queue. Some rules have actions that do not cause further events.

The events in the Harrison Machine act in ways that are similar to continuations in more conventional programming languages. In denotational semantics, a distinction is made between "pure" and "impure" continuations. The former merely represent the rest of the program, specifically the next statement or command to be executed. The latter have this purpose but they also convey additional information.

This distinction is carried over to the events in the Harrison Machine. It is possible to have "pure" events that just indicate that something has happened (for example, the *$start* event that conventionally initiates execution of rules). It is also possible to have "impure" events. These are events that also convey data to the rules that trigger on them. Impure events are similar to structures in LISP or C and can contain data of any legal type. When a rule triggers on an impure event, it can extract some or all of the data the event's structure contains and use it in the performance of their actions. It must be remembered that impure events also denote that something has happened. Events of both kinds are usually caused by a primitive command that is executed by rule actions.

Events of both kinds are associated with a type. All events of the same type have identical structure. Pure events have only a type (they are implemented as a type field and an empty structure). Impure events have a type and a data-containing structure. The structure holds the values that are communicated by impure events.

The triggering process is based upon matching the rule's pattern against the current event. The matching operation is divided into two phases. First, the type of the event is tested. If it is the desired type, the second phase is invoked; otherwise, the match fails and the rule cannot trigger. The second phase consists of either the extraction or testing of component values from the event structure. Value extraction always succeeds. Rule patterns are conventionally interpreted as conjunctions. A rule whose pattern matches the current event is said to be triggered and its action can then be executed.

6.4 Execution Cycle

The Virtual Machine's execution cycle operates on the following objects:

- A queue of events awaiting processing;

- The event that is currently being processed by rules (the *Current Event*);
- A set of rules that have executed and are waiting for another event (the *Waiting Set*);
- A set of rules that are ready to execute their bodies (the *Ready Set*);
- A library of routines that operate on the VM state.

The execution cycle is driven by the successive events generated by its rules. These events are stored in a globally accessible queue. When rules can produce no more events and the queue is empty, the system must halt; usually, however, a special event type, called *HALT*, is used to halt execution of the system. The central event queue is a DEQueue so that events can be added to the front and to back. This will be justified below; for now, it should be noted that the event queue usually operates in the standard FIFO regime, so events are handled in time order with the oldest being handled first.

On each cycle, the first event in the event queue is removed. It is made the *Current Event*. The patterns in rules are matched against the current event to determine whether the rule should be executed in the current cycle. The exception to this is the always rule class, whose members execute on every VM cycle.

When a new cycle begins, the first event is usually removed from the event queue to become the Current Event (exceptions to this will be discussed below). The rules in the *Waiting Set* are executed. Execution causes the event predicates in each rule to be executed, performing a matching operation against the current event. If a predicate is not satisfied by the current event, its rule executes a suspend instruction and is returned to the Waiting Set. Otherwise, the rule is added to the *Ready Set*.

Once the event predicates of all the rules in the VM have been executed, the Ready Set is either empty or it contains a set of rules to be run. If the Ready Set is not empty, the body of each rule is executed in turn. Execution of a rule body usually produces events that are added to the Event Queue in FIFO order. When executing the Ready Set, each rule is first removed from it, so that, at the end of this part of the cycle, the Ready Set is empty. If the Ready Set is empty at the start of this sub-cycle, the next event is removed from the Event Queue and the operations of the cycle are repeated.

On initialisation, compiled rules are loaded into the Waiting Set and at least one event is added to the Event Queue. The first event is usually the special event called *START* and one of the rules in the Waiting Set has an outermost event predicate that matches *START*.

The Virtual Machine's operating cycle can be summarised as follows. Let E_q be the Event Queue and c be the Current Event; the empty queue is denoted by $\langle \rangle$ and the operation of removing the first element of a queue is denoted by the function $hd(E_q)$. Let S_w be the Waiting Set and S_r be the Ready Set. Let r_e be the rule to be executed (current rule) and let $p(r_e, c)$ denote the execution of the current rule's event predicate with the Current Event and let $b(r_e)$ be the body of the current rule. The assignment operation is denoted by $\leftarrow$. Before the cycle starts, S_r should be empty. The operation of the cycle is then:

1. If $E_q = \langle\rangle$, go to 8.
2. $c \leftarrow hd(E_q)$.
3. $S_m \leftarrow S_w$, $S_w \leftarrow \emptyset$.
4. For each $r \in S_w$, set $r_e \leftarrow r$ making $S_m \leftarrow S_m\backslash\{r_e\}$. Execute $p(r_e, c)$.
   a) If $p(r_e, c)$ is satisfied, $S_r \leftarrow S_r \cup \{r_e\}$.
   b) Otherwise $S_w \leftarrow S_w \cup \{r_e\}$.
5. If $S_r = \{\}$, go to 1. Otherwise, continue at the next step.
6. For each $r \in S_r$, set $r_e \leftarrow r$ making $S_r \leftarrow S_r\backslash\{r_e\}$. Execute $b(r_e)$.
   a) If r_e executes a **suspend** instruction, $S_w \leftarrow S_w \cup \{r_e\}$.
   b) If r_e executes a **term** instruction, it is deleted completely.
7. Go to 1.
8. Set VM termination flag.
9. Stop.

There are some observations that must be made about the cycle.

- On the very first cycle, all **always** rules are executed and are added to S_r. This is because their code always places them in the Ready Queue when they are first executed.
- The functions $p(r, e)$ and $b(r)$ denote the current event predicate and current body of the current rule, r_e. If the rule being executed contains nested rules, the current event predicate and current body functions denote the predicate and body of the nested rule that is to be executed. In machine terms, the values of these functions depend upon the rule's instruction pointer.
- The cycle can also be halted if a rule executes the **haltvm** instruction. This immediately terminates execution of the VM.

The cycle is initialised as follows. Let R be a set of rules in compiled form, let e_s be the $START$ event.

1. $S_w \leftarrow R$.
2. $E_q \leftarrow \langle\rangle$.
3. $c \leftarrow e_s$.
4. $S_r \leftarrow \{\}$.

6.5 Interpretation Rules

In this section, it is shown how Harrison Machine rules can be used to implement the basic operations of the system. These rules must be able to execute rules whose patterns have been satisfied by the current event. This entails that they must have access to the current event, the Event Queue and the Waiting Set. This causes a slight problem because the underlying architecture must use these structures in order to run the interpretative rules.

One solution is to search the Waiting Set so that the interpretative rules are retrieved. This is a non-solution because it requires a fundamental modification to the architecture to support the search. Furthermore, there would have to be some way to communicate the means by which the interpretative rules are to be identified with the architecture's search operation. The final problem for this approach is that, in the context of a reflective tower model, it would be necessary to have an unrestricted number of interpretative rules divided into levels and each level would have to communicate with the search operation so that the right rules can be selected.

In this architecture, there is *no* distinction between fundamental and other rules. First, an unrestricted number of levels in the reflective organisation is permitted; this is a property that we see as valuable because it preserves referential relations in a relatively clean fashion (references are either strictly "up" or strictly "down"). If the special rules model were adopted, this would mean communicating with the architecture so that it was aware of which rules to treat as special and which to treat as ordinary. Secondly, the right is reserved to alter the interpretative rules *at runtime*, thereby allowing different behaviours. For example, the FIFO Event Queue discipline might be replaced by a LIFO (or stack-like) discipline for a short period of time in response to something that has been detected in the environment. Thirdly, it is desirable to be able to add and remove rules at runtime without regard to their status. Addition and removal are important operations in the dynamic configuration of systems.

As a result of these conditions, it was decided not to introduce special mechanisms for the manipulation of interpretative rules. All rules are, therefore, treated as equals in this system while allowing some to be more equal than others.

The solution to the problem was to permit rules to operate on the fundamental structures of the architecture. Rules can access and update the Event Queue and the Current Event; they can also access and update the Waiting Set and the Ready Set. The **cause** operation that rules normally use to add events to the Event Queue constructs an event object, so it was an easy step to add operations to treat events as first-class entities; events can be constructed and inspected as if they were record structures and they can be assigned just like any other data object. The queue and rule set types were also made first class so that interpreter state could be maintained by rules.

This is done by providing procedures and functions in the runtime library that can be called from rules. Any rule can access these routines so, potentially, any rule can participate in reflective processing.

It is possible to define the architecture's basic operation in a single rule. For ease of presentation, and to better illustrate the process, a three-rule interpreter is described in some detail below. This is the original model for the system. Indeed, before any design was undertaken, the architecture was described in terms of rules, specifically the rules that are presented below. The rules are shown in a tidied-up form for ease of presentation. In each case, the rules are when rules, triggered by the occurrence of an event which is specified as a tuple appearing after the temporal operator. The type of the event is always the first element of the tuple and has the prefix "$".

The rules that are shown in this section run on the basic architecture and employ the data structures (Event Queue, Current Event, Waiting Set and Ready Set) provided by it. The rules provide the queues, current events and rule sets required to execute the rules at the next level above in the reflective tower.

```
when ( $start, rules ) do(
   if empty-set(rules) -> cause( $stop );
   || true -> cause( $next-cycle, rules, emptyqueue );
   ) -- end rule
```

Fig. 6.2. *The application-specific start rule.*

The rule to start the system is shown in Figure 6.2. It should be noted that, in order to make rules easier to read, a little syntactic sugar has been employed. The rule is triggered when a special start event is removed from the Event Queue. This event is usually the only event in the queue at the start of execution.

In addition, there is a standard rule for halting the system (shown in Figure 6.5). This rule is provided so that an application can perform clean-up operations before instructing the system to stop. The event that causes this rule to execute is used in the interpretive rules shown in figures 6.2, 6.3 and 6.4. For the purposes of exposition, the clean-up code and display of informative messages has been removed from the examples.

The rules shown in Figures 6.3 to 6.5 could be conflated into a single rule of the form shown in Figure 6.6.

These rules show that the system is capable of controlling the execution of its own rules. The rules shown in the figures are able to control the execution of themselves at any level of the reflective tower. For expository purposes, the rules in this section were written in a way that completely implements the architecture in rules; this requires a set of additional primitive operations that duplicate the operations of the architecture. It is also possible to manipulate the architecture's structures directly and this is the way in which the actual implementations have operated (although they also contain the duplicate primitives to allow flexibility). The "direct access" method requires the swapping of the current event, the event queue and the rule sets between rules and the architecture. Figure 6.7 shows, for example, how the body-executing rule can be implemented using the "direct access" method:

The operation **execute-rule** locally saves the Current Rule, its associated stack, environment and instruction pointer and replaces them by the corresponding elements of the parameter **rule**. The virtual machine then ex-

```
when( $next-cycle, waiting-rules, event-queue ) do(
    let [ local-current-event = next-front(event-queue);
          local-ready-rules   = emptyset ]
    in
      if empty-queue( event-queue ) -> cause( $stop );
      || empty-set
      fi;
      foreach rule in waiting-rules do
        execute0( rule,
                  local-current-event,
                  waiting-rules,
                  local-ready-rules );
      od;
      if not(empty-set(local-ready-rules)) ->
        cause( $runnable-rules,
               local-ready-rules,
               waiting-rules,
               event-queue );
      || true -> cause( $next-cycle,
                        waiting-rules,
                        event-queue );
      fi
    endlet;
) -- end rule
```

Fig. 6.3. *The triggering rule.*

ecutes the rule until either it terminates completely, suspends (thus returning
to the Waiting Set) or aborts. In the first and third cases, the rule is garbage-
collected. Note that the operations performed by **execute-rule** can be performed by any rule in the system provided that it executes the appropriate
primitives from the runtime library. The **execute-rule** library operation is
provided for safety.

The other rules can be written in a similar fashion.

6.6 VM Specification

In this section, the Harrison Machine's virtual machine is specified as a collection of state transitions. The specification is complicated slightly by the fact
that some transitions involve the internal state of the rules executed by the
virtual machine in the sense that some instructions executed by individual
rules, for example rule termination and matching, affect the operation of the
virtual machine as a whole.

There is somewhat more description in this section for the reason that the
operation of the Harrison Machine is somewhat unusual.

```
when ( $runnable-rules, ready-rules,
        waiting-rules, event-queue )
  do(
    let [ locally-executed = emptyset ]
    in
      foreach rule in ready-rules do
        execute1( rule,
                    locally-executed,
                    event-queue );
      od;
      if empty-set(locally-executed) -> syserror( ... );
      || true ->
          waiting-rules :=
              setunion( waiting-rules, locally-executed );
          cause( $next-cycle, waiting-rules, event-queue );
      fi;
    endlet;
  ) -- end rule
```

Fig. 6.4. *The body execution rule.*

```
when ( $stop ) do(
    syshalt();
  ) -- end rule
```

Fig. 6.5. *The stop rule.*

```
when ( $start, waiting-rules ) do (
  until ( $stop ) do (
      when ( $next-cycle, ... ) do (
        ) -- end rule 1
      when ( $runnable-rules, ... ) do (
        ) -- end rule 2
    ) -- end until rule
  when ( $stop ) do (
      -- perform application-specific cleanup
      syshalt();
    ) -- end stop rule
  ) -- end outer rule
```

Fig. 6.6. *The form of a single rule interpreter.*

6.6.1 States and Notational Conventions

The state of the entire virtual machine is described by tuples:

$$S_M = \langle m, w, a, r, e, q, h, h_r \rangle$$

where:

```
when ( $runnable-rules, rules-to-run,
       waiting-queue, event-queue)
do (
  let [ saved-event   = get-currentevent();
        saved-events  = get-eventqueue();
        saved-waiting = get-waiting-rules();
        saved-ready   = get-ready-rules();
        eventq        = emptyqueue;
        waiters       = emptyset;
      ]
  in
    set-eventqueue( event-queue );
    set-waiting( waiting-queue );
    set-ready( rules-to-run );
    clear-executed-rules();
    next-event();
    foreach rule in waiting-rules() do
        execute-rule(rule);
    od;
    if empty-executed-rules() -> syserror( ... );
    || true -> make-executed-waiting()
    fi;
    eventq  := get-eventqueue();
    waiters := get-waitingrules();
    set-currentevent( saved-event );
    set-eventqueue( saved-events );
    set-waitingrules( saved-waiting );
    set-readyrules( saved-ready );
    cause( $next-cycle, waiters, eventq );
  endlet;
) -- end rule
```

Fig. 6.7. *Direct access version of the body rule.*

- m is a set of rules. It is used only during matching. Usually it is empty.
- w is the set of rules that are not to be executed on this event (the Waiting Set).
- a is the set of rules to be executed on this event (the Ready Set).
- r is the currently executing rule.
- e is the current event.
- q is the event queue.
- h is a flag. When true, it indicates that the entire VM should halt
- h_r is a flag. When set, it indicates that the current rule is to be suspended (returned to the Waiting Set).

Individual rules will be denoted by the letter r (with or without decoration). The null rule is written $r_\perp$ (it is used as a placeholder in some transitions). The symbol R is used to denote the set of rules, E the set of events, with $E_\perp$ denoting the empty event; Q denotes the set of queues and $\mathbb{B}$ truth values ($\mathbb{B} = \{ff, tt\}$). Unless stated otherwise, $\mathbb{N}$ is the naturals *plus* zero and $\mathbb{Z}$ denotes the integers.

It is assumed that there is a set D of *denotable* values (i.e., values that can be represented by a valid Harrison Machine program). There is a special element, written $d_\perp$, that denotes the undefined element of D (it serves as a "don't care" or "don't know" element). For reasons that will become clearer towards the end of this section, it will be required that D will include in D such entities as $\mathbb{Z}$, truth values ($\mathbb{B}$), event type names (T), event type structures (defined as $E_S = T \times D^*$, where D^* is the set of all sequences over D) and rules.

It should be noted that, for the purposes of the specification of the VM's transitions and the compilation schemes, only event structures to consist of sequences of elements of D prefixed by an element of E_T will be permitted. In a real implementation, event structures can have a richer structure: an element of E_T followed by a (possibly empty) sequence of values or trees of elements of D.

The value-binding environment, or environment, is defined as $\rho : \mathbb{N} \to \mathbb{N} \to D$, i.e., as a sequence of sequences of D. The environment is organised as a stack of binding frames, each frame being a sequence of elements of D (frames are denoted ρ also). The nth element of the environment ρ is written $\rho(n)$. The notation $[v \mapsto n]\rho$ again denotes the replacement of $\rho(n)$ by v. Environments figure in the definition of rule states.

Rule states are described by tuples of the form:

$$S_R = \langle c, \sigma, t, i, n, \rho \rangle$$

where:

- $c \in C$ is the code for the rule, where C is the set of Harrison Machine instructions.
- $\sigma \in \Sigma$ is the rule's stack, where Σ is the set of stacks (Σ is a sequence of denotable values, D).
- $t \in \mathbb{B}$ is the termination flag for the rule. When set, it indicates that the rule has terminated and should be returned to the Waiting Set.
- $i \in C$ is the currently executing instruction.
- $n \in \mathbb{N}_0$ is the *instruction pointer*, an index into the rule's code. (Note that $n = 0$ is considered valid.)
- $\rho \in P$ is the rule's environment.

The following notational conventions for the remainder of this section are adopted. The empty sequence is written $\langle \rangle$. The addition of an element, v, to the end of a sequence, s, is written as $s \ddagger \langle v \rangle$. A sequence, s, whose first element is v is written $v.s$. If $v_1, \ldots, v_n$ are the first n elements of a sequence, s is written $v_1.\cdots.v_n.s$. The length of sequence c is written as $|c|$ (this will be used to represent the number of instructions in $c \in C$). The $[v \mapsto i]s$

notation will be used for update (substitution) with the interpretation that $[v \mapsto i]s = s'$ where s' is a sequence that is identical to s except at the ith element $(s'(i) = v)$ (these are the same conventions as in Section 4.2.10).

The event queue, q is a sequence of elements $e \in E$.

Rule stacks are denoted by $\sigma \in \Sigma$; the elements of Σ are sequences of elements of D.

The number of instructions in the code segment for a rule is written $|c|$.

A set of *event type* names must be defined T_e and its elements are denoted by τ. There are two distinguished values in T_e: τ_s and τ_h denoting the *start* and *halt* events, respectively. The former is used to start the VM and the latter to halt it. The τ_h event is used *only* to cause normal termination of the VM. Error terminations are handled by transitions.

For the time being, it will be assumed that $D = \mathbb{Z} \cup \{d_\perp\}$, with $d_\perp$ representing an undefined value. It will also be assumed that events are composed of a type tag and a vector of elements of D. These assumptions permit the simplification of the presentation without losing too much in the way of accuracy or generality.

The reader should note that side conditions will often be written above transitions with a horizontal line separating the two. This makes the rules resemble those of Kahn's Natural Semantics [27] and Plotkin's Simple Operational Semantics [41].

6.6.2 Infra-Rule Transitions

This subsection contains the transitions that deal *only* with rule states.

First, there are the jump instructions. The Harrison Machine VM supports three kinds of jump: one unconditional (jmp), the other two conditional (jeq and jne). The conditional jumps first examine the top element of the stack. For jeq, the jump is taken if the top element is 1, while jne performs the jump if the top element is 0. In both cases, the top stack element is popped before the jump is taken.

The transitions for each of these jumps is as follows. In each case, the code component (C) is unaffected. The instruction pointer (n) is updated by the jump to another value (n'). In each case, the destination address of the jump is tested to determine whether it is in the code segment $(n' \leq |c|)$. Finally, the instruction at offset n' in the code segment is referred to as o. The transition for the unconditional jump is given first.

$$\frac{\ell' \leq |c|, o = c(\ell')}{\langle c, \sigma, f\!f, \mathtt{jmp}\ \ell', \ell, \rho \rangle \rightarrow \langle c, \sigma, f\!f, o, \ell', \rho \rangle}$$

For the conditional jumps, the transitions for the case in which the jump is taken and for the case in which it is not are given:

$$\frac{d = t\!t, \ell' \leq |c|, o = c(\ell)}{\langle c,\ d \cdot \sigma, f\!f, \mathtt{jeq}\ \ell', \ell, \rho \rangle \rightarrow \langle c, \sigma, f\!f, o, \ell', \rho \rangle}$$

$$\frac{d = ff, \ell + 1 \leq |c|, o = c(\ell + 1)}{\langle c,\ d \cdot \sigma,\ ff, \mathtt{jeq}\ \ell', \ell, \rho \rangle \rightarrow \langle c, \sigma, ff, o, \ell + 1, \rho \rangle}$$

$$\frac{d = ff, \ell' \leq |c|, o = c(\ell')}{\langle c,\ d \cdot \sigma,\ ff, \mathtt{jne}\ \ell', \ell, \rho \rangle \rightarrow \langle c, \sigma, ff, o, \ell', \rho \rangle}$$

$$\frac{d = ff, \ell' \leq |c|, o = c(\ell)}{\langle c,\ d \cdot \sigma,\ ff, \mathtt{jne}\ \ell', \ell, \rho \rangle \rightarrow \langle c, \sigma, ff, o, \ell + 1, \rho \rangle}$$

The case in which $n > |c|$ is not represented as a transition. The reason for this is that it is a condition that should be detected by the compiler or the assembler.

The conditions $\ell' \leq |c|$ and $o = c(\ell)$ are so common that they are henceforth omitted.

The following transitions define the stack operations that can be performed by a valid Harrison Machine program. In each case, the instruction pointer is incremented by one and the next instruction (o) is fetched; it is assumed that $o = c(n + 1)$ and that the new instruction pointer value is valid.

The push0 instruction pushes zero onto the stack:

$$\langle c, \sigma, ff, \mathtt{push0}, n, \rho \rangle \rightarrow \langle c, 0 \cdot \sigma, ff, o, n + 1, \rho \rangle$$

The push1 instruction pushes one onto the stack.

$$\langle c, \sigma, ff, \mathtt{push1}, n, \rho \rangle \rightarrow \langle c, 1 \cdot \sigma, ff, o, n + 1, \rho \rangle$$

These two transitions describe instructions that are used in a number of contexts. First, 0 and 1 are common values in programs, so the provision of instructions to handle them is a simple optimisation that affects program size. Secondly, 0 represents *false* and 1 represents *true* by convention, so these instructions are used when pushing boolean values onto the stack.

The general **push** instruction is given by the following transition. The instruction has one operand, the value to be pushed; this value is denoted by d.

$$\langle c, \sigma, ff, \mathtt{push}\ d, n, \rho \rangle \rightarrow \langle c, d \cdot \sigma, ff, o, n + 1, \rho \rangle$$

Next, there is the **pop** operation. The error transition for the case in which $\sigma = \langle \rangle$ (i.e., the empty stack) is omitted.

$$\langle c, d \cdot \sigma, ff, \mathtt{pop}, n, \rho \rangle \rightarrow \langle c, \sigma, ff, o, n + 1, \rho \rangle$$

The **dup** and **swap** operations are the usual ones.

$$\langle c, d \cdot \sigma, ff, \mathtt{dup}, n, \rho \rangle \rightarrow \langle c, d \cdot d \cdot \sigma, ff, o, n + 1, \rho \rangle$$

and:

$$\langle c, d_1 \cdot d_2 \cdot \sigma, ff, \mathtt{swap}, n, \rho \rangle \rightarrow \langle c, d_2 \cdot d_1 \cdot \sigma, ff, o, n + 1, \rho \rangle$$

The last stack operation is `clear`, which empties the stack:

$$\langle c, \sigma, ff, \mathtt{clear}, n, \rho \rangle \rightarrow \langle c, \langle \rangle, ff, o, n+1, \rho \rangle$$

When a rule starts, it first constructs an empty environment as an initialisation operation. The `arid` instruction does this:

$$\langle c, \langle \rangle, ff, \mathtt{arid}, n, \rho_\perp \rangle \rightarrow \langle c, \langle \rangle, ff, o, n+1, \langle \rangle \rangle$$

The symbol $\rho_\perp$ is used to denote the undefined environment. It can be seen that the stack is already initialised to empty. It would be possible to define an instruction, say `mkstk`, that creates an empty stack. This was not done because, in some versions of the VM, the stack is used to hold data that was passed to the rule before it started.[2]

In source programs, the let construct opens a new lexical scope. It declares and initialises variables that are local to the new scope which is pushed onto the environment. The scope of the variables declared in a let is the body of the let construct. When the body terminates, the scope declared by the let is popped from the environment. The instruction that constructs a new frame and pushes it onto the environment is `newenv` and the one that pops the topmost frame at the end of a scope is `drop`.

A new scope is created by pushing a new environment frame onto the environment. The compiler can easily determine the size of the new frame (it contains only the variables declared in the let): this is the (natural) value k that appears as the operand to the `newenv` instruction. The transition is:

$$\frac{\rho' = \langle \overbrace{d_\perp, \ldots, d_\perp}^{k \text{ times}} \rangle \cdot \rho}{\langle c, \sigma, ff, \mathtt{newenv}\, k, n, \rho \rangle \rightarrow \langle c, \sigma, ff, o, n+1, \rho' \rangle}$$

This transition creates a new frame of k elements and pushes it onto the environment.

The `drop` instruction is defined by the following transition:

$$\langle c, \sigma, ff, \mathtt{drop}, n, \rho_1 \cdot \rho \rangle \rightarrow \langle c, \sigma, ff, o, n+1, \rho \rangle$$

The `drop` instruction just removes the topmost frame from the environment. The error transition for the case in which $\rho = \langle \rangle$ (i.e., an empty environment) is omitted.

The next two transitions define the `getvar` and `setvar` instructions. The `getvar` instruction extracts the current value of a variable from the environment, while `setvar` assigns a new value to it. Both instructions have two operands: the first is the offset of the frame in which the variable occurs and the second is the offset of the variable within that frame.

In these transitions, some runtime tests are represented, in particular $i \in \rho$ and $j \in \rho(i)$. The first is to determine whether the environment stack contains

---

[2] It is a case of "historical reasons".

the anticipated number of frames; the second determines whether the frame at $\rho(i)$ is of the correct length. The error transitions are omitted (again, they are simple to define but only serve to clutter this description).

$$\langle c, \sigma, \mathit{ff}, \mathtt{getvar}(i,j), n, \rho_0 \cdot \ldots \cdot \rho_i \cdot \rho_r \rangle \rightarrow \langle c, d \cdot \sigma, \mathit{ff}, o, n+1, \rho_0 \cdot \ldots \cdot \rho_i \cdot \rho_r \rangle$$

where $d = \rho_i(j)$.

$$\langle c, \ d \cdot \sigma, \mathit{ff}, \mathtt{setvar}(i,j), n, \rho_0 \cdot \ldots \cdot \rho_{i-1} \cdot \rho_i \cdot \rho_r \rangle$$
$$\rightarrow \langle c, \sigma, \mathit{ff}, o, n+1, \rho_0 \cdot \ldots \cdot \rho_{i-1} \cdot \rho'_i \cdot \rho_r \rangle$$

where: $\rho'_i = [v \mapsto j]\rho_i$.

In this description, the transitions for arithmetic and logical instructions are mostly omitted for the reason that they are all very much alike. First, there is logical negation, lnot. It expects its operand to be on the top of the value stack, σ. Its two transitions are:

$$\langle c, \mathit{tt} \cdot \sigma, \mathit{ff}, \mathtt{lnot}, n, \rho \rangle \rightarrow \langle c, \mathit{ff} \cdot \sigma, \mathit{ff}, o, n+1, \rho \rangle$$

and:

$$\langle c, \mathit{ff} \cdot \sigma, \mathit{ff}, \mathtt{lnot}, n, \rho \rangle \rightarrow \langle c, \mathit{tt} \cdot \sigma, \mathit{ff}, o, n+1, \rho \rangle$$

The transition for iminus (unary minus) is defined by:

$$\langle c, \ d \cdot \sigma, \mathit{ff}, \mathtt{iminus}, n, \rho \rangle \rightarrow \langle c, (-d) \cdot \sigma, \mathit{ff}, o, n+1, \rho \rangle$$

The addition instruction, iadd, is defined by:

$$\frac{d = d_1 + d_2}{\langle c, \ d_1 \cdot d_2 \cdot \sigma, \mathit{ff}, \mathtt{iadd}, n, \rho \rangle \rightarrow \langle c, \ d \cdot \sigma, \mathit{ff}, o, n+1, \rho \rangle}$$

Other binary operators are defined similarly.

Integer equality is similarly defined by the following transition:

$$\frac{d_1 = d_2}{\langle c, \ d_1 \cdot d_2 \cdot \sigma, \mathit{ff}, \mathtt{ieq}, n, \rho \rangle \rightarrow \langle c, \ \mathit{tt} \cdot \sigma, \mathit{ff}, o, n+1, \rho \rangle}$$

and:

$$\frac{d_1 \neq d_2}{\langle c, \ d_1 \cdot d_2 \cdot \sigma, \mathit{ff}, \mathtt{ieq}, n, \rho \rangle \rightarrow \langle c, \ \mathit{ff} \cdot \sigma, \mathit{ff}, o, n+1, \rho \rangle}$$

6.6.3 Extra-Rule Transitions

These transitions define rule operations that affect the entire VM state.

Although, strictly speaking, the mkevent instruction is purely local to the rule that executes it, it is included in this subsection because it is frequently followed by the cause instruction (the cause standard procedure compiles into the sequence . . . mkev cause).

$$\frac{e = \texttt{mkev}(\tau, d_1, \ldots, d_n)}{\langle c,\ \tau \cdot d_1, \cdots, d_n \cdot \sigma,\ \mathit{ff}, \texttt{mkevent}, n, \rho \rangle \to \langle c, e \cdot \sigma, \mathit{ff}, o, n+1, \rho \rangle}$$

This instruction expects an *event type*, τ, to be on the top of the stack, followed by zero or more values (event operands). The $\texttt{mkevent}$ instruction constructs an event structure and pushes it onto the stack. The transitions dealing with invalid event types and incorrect numbers of operands to the event are omitted.

Next, we have the $\texttt{cause}$ primitive:

$$\langle \emptyset, w, a, \langle c, e_c \cdot \sigma, \mathit{ff}, \texttt{cause}, n, \rho \rangle, e, q, \mathit{ff}, \mathit{ff} \rangle \to$$
$$\langle \emptyset, w, a, \langle c, \sigma, \mathit{ff}, o, n+1, \rho, \rangle, e, q \ddagger \langle e_c \rangle, \mathit{ff}, \mathit{ff} \rangle$$

This operation is a little more interesting. First, note that the current rule's state appears as part of the transition. Second, note that the entire VM state is represented in the transition, as it is in all of the transitions that follow. It should be noted that the first component of the VM state is usually $\emptyset$. This is because the first component is used only during the matching of rule patterns. The effect of the transition for $\texttt{cause}$ is to pop the top of the stack (an event structure) and to append it to the event queue, q.

Rule termination and suspension are described by the following transitions. Rules terminate in one of two ways: either they executed the $\texttt{term}$ instruction (into which the **abort** command compiles):

$$\langle \emptyset, w, a, \langle c, \sigma, \mathit{ff}, \texttt{term}, n, \rho \rangle, e, q, \mathit{ff}, \mathit{ff} \rangle \to \langle \emptyset, w, a, r_\perp, e, q, \mathit{ff}, \mathit{tt} \rangle$$

or they set their termination flag:

$$\langle \emptyset, w, a, \langle c, \sigma, \mathit{tt}, o, n, \rho \rangle, e, q, \mathit{ff}, \mathit{ff} \rangle \to$$
$$\langle \emptyset, w \cup \{\langle c, \sigma, \mathit{tt}, o_1, n+1, \rho \rangle\}, a, r_\perp, e, q, \mathit{ff}, \mathit{tt} \rangle$$

The second transition does not correspond to any instruction. It is, however, required by many of the error transitions that have been omitted from this description.

When a rule such as a **when**, **unless**, **next**, **since** or **until** reaches the end of its body, it executes a **suspend** instruction. It is defined by the following transition:

$$\langle \emptyset, w, a, \langle c, \sigma, \mathit{ff}, \texttt{suspend}, n, \rho \rangle, e, q, \mathit{ff}, \mathit{ff} \rangle \to$$
$$\langle \emptyset, w \cup \{\langle c, \sigma, \mathit{ff}, o_1, n+1, \rho \rangle\}, a, r_\perp, e, q, \mathit{ff}, \mathit{ff} \rangle$$

The effect of executing a **suspend** is to transfer the currently executing rule to the Waiting Set. The current rule is then set to the null rule. (The null rule is strictly not necessary, as far as an implementation is concerned; it makes the formal specification of the VM somewhat easier, however.)

When all rules in the Ready Set have been executed and all have either suspended or terminated, the VM implicitly executes an operation that starts the process of matching rule patterns. It is described by the following transition:

$$\langle \emptyset, w, \emptyset, r_\perp, e, q, \mathit{ff}, \mathit{ff} \rangle \rightarrow \langle w, \emptyset, \emptyset, r_\perp, e, q, \mathit{ff}, \mathit{ff} \rangle$$

(i.e., $m = w$).

When a rule executes its pattern code, it must obtain the current event. It does this by executing the getev instruction. The instruction merely pushes the current event onto the rule's local stack.

$$\langle m, w, a, \langle c, \sigma, \mathit{ff}, \mathtt{getev}, n, \rho \rangle, e, q, \mathit{ff}, \mathit{ff} \rangle \rightarrow$$
$$\langle m, w, a, \langle c, e \cdot \sigma, \mathit{ff}, o, n, \rho \rangle, e, q, \mathit{ff}, \mathit{ff} \rangle$$

When a rule's pattern code succeeds, it executes a mkrdy instruction. This instruction adds the calling rule to the ready set and sets the current rule to the null rule:

$$\langle m, w, a, \langle c, \sigma, \mathit{tt}, \mathtt{mkrdy}, n, \rho \rangle, e, q, \mathit{ff}, \mathit{ff} \rangle \rightarrow \langle m, w, a \cup \{r_r\}, r_\perp, e, q, \mathit{ff}, \mathit{ff} \rangle$$

where $r_r = \langle c, \sigma, \mathit{tt}, o, n + 1, \rho \rangle$

Conversely, when a rule's pattern fails to match the current event, the rule is suspended until the next match cycle.

$$\langle m, w, a, \langle c, \sigma, \mathit{ff}, \mathtt{notrdy}, n, \rho \rangle, e, q, \mathit{ff}, \mathit{ff} \rangle \rightarrow$$
$$\langle m, w \cup \{ \langle c, \sigma, \mathit{ff}, o, n + 1, \rho \rangle \}, a, r_\perp, e, q, \mathit{ff}, \mathit{ff} \rangle$$

Next rule to match:

$$\langle m \cup \{r_m\}, w, \emptyset, r_\perp, e, q, \mathit{ff}, \mathit{ff} \rangle \rightarrow \langle m, w, \emptyset, r_m, e, q, \mathit{ff}, \mathit{ff} \rangle$$

Matching ends when:

$$\langle \emptyset, w, a, r_\perp, e, q, \mathit{ff}, \mathit{ff} \rangle$$

6.6.4 VM-Only Transitions

Each time rules are to be matched, the next event must be removed from the event queue. This operation is described by the transition:

$$\langle \emptyset, w, \emptyset, r_\perp, e, e_n \cdot q, \mathit{ff}, \mathit{ff} \rangle \rightarrow \langle \emptyset, w, \emptyset, r_\perp, e_n, q, \mathit{ff}, \mathit{ff} \rangle$$

The case in which $q = \langle \rangle$ is handled by the next transtion. It is an error condition that causes the VM to halt:

$$\langle \emptyset, w, a, r_e, e, \langle \rangle, \mathit{ff}, \mathit{ff} \rangle \rightarrow \langle \emptyset, w, a, r_e, e_n, \langle \rangle, \mathit{tt}, \mathit{ff} \rangle$$

The VM transition that describes the situation in which the next rule is made current is the following:

$$\langle \emptyset, w, a \cup \{r_n\}, r_\perp, e, q, \textit{ff}, \textit{ff} \rangle \rightarrow \langle \emptyset, w, a, r_n, e, q, \textit{ff}, \textit{ff} \rangle$$

A rule is removed from the Ready Set and made the current rule. The configuration:

$$\langle \emptyset, w, \emptyset, r_\perp, e, \langle \rangle, \textit{tt}, b \rangle$$

for $b = \textit{tt}$ or $b = \textit{ff}$, denotes the state in which there is nothing more to do. Finally, the system terminates normally when the halt event is current:

$$\langle \emptyset, w, a, r, e_h, q, \textit{ff}, \textit{ff} \rangle \rightarrow \langle \emptyset, w, a, r, e_h, q, \textit{tt}, b \rangle$$

for $b = \textit{tt}$ or $b = \textit{ff}$ (it does not matter what the termination status of the current rule is).

Equally, the starting state for the system is described by:

$$\langle \emptyset, w, \emptyset, r_\perp, e_\perp, \langle e_s \rangle, \textit{tt}, \textit{ff} \rangle \rightarrow \langle \emptyset, w, \emptyset, r_\perp, e_s, \langle \rangle, \textit{ff}, \textit{ff} \rangle$$

Initially, the VM termination flag is set and the event queue contains (minimally) the start event, e_s. The system is started by altering the state of the VM termination flag and making the start event the current one.

The clone instruction must be defined. This instruction creates a complete copy of the current rule. It leaves the stack and environment intact (they can be cleared using arid and clear):

$$\langle \emptyset, w, a, \langle c, \sigma, \textit{ff}, \texttt{clone}, n, \rho \rangle, e, q, \textit{ff}, \textit{ff} \rangle \rightarrow$$
$$\langle \emptyset, w, a \cup \{\langle c, \sigma, \textit{ff}, o, n+1, \rho \rangle\}, \langle c, \sigma, \textit{ff}, o, n+1, \rho \rangle, e, q, \textit{ff}, \textit{ff} \rangle$$

Cloning is useful when writing alt rules. Generally, though, it is dangerous because there is no way at present to name rules, thus there is no way to distinguish between instances of a rule at runtime. For alt, this appears not to be as important an issue, however.

Finally, the clear instruction is useful when creating new instances of alt rules. It can be used with the reset instruction to reset the entire rule's instruction pointer:

$$\langle \emptyset, w, a, \langle c, \sigma, \textit{ff}, \texttt{reset}, n, \rho \rangle, e, q, \textit{ff}, \textit{ff} \rangle \rightarrow$$
$$\langle \emptyset, w, a \cup \{\langle c, \sigma, \textit{ff}, c(0), 0, \rho \rangle\}, e, q, \textit{ff}, \textit{ff} \rangle$$

The reset and clone instructions can be used in introspective routines to copy rules entirely and to clone them on demand.

6.6.5 Introspective Operations

In this subsection, a few operations that support the introspective behaviour of Harrison Machine rules are defined. The transitions defined here are not implemented as VM instructions; instead, they define routines that can be used as part of the runtime library. The fact that the subject, here, is routines and not VM instructions is emphasised by the use of a sans font.

The reader should note that the operations specified below are not the only ones that can be defined, given the architecture. They are included only as a sample of what can be done.

The first operation employs the `getev` instruction that has already been encountered. It pushes the current event onto the local stack to make it available for manipulation by other operations within a rule:

$$\langle \emptyset, w, a, \langle c, \sigma, ff, \text{next-event}, n, \rho \rangle, e, q, ff, ff \rangle \rightarrow$$
$$\langle \emptyset, w, a, \langle c, \ e \cdot \sigma, ff, o, n+1, \rho \rangle, e, q, ff, ff \rangle$$

Conversely, the `setev` routine takes an event structure from the current rule's stack and sets the current event to that event:

$$\langle \emptyset, w, a, \langle c, \ e_1 \cdot \sigma, ff, \text{set-currentevent}, n, \rho \rangle, e, q, ff, ff \rangle \rightarrow$$
$$\langle \emptyset, w, a, \langle c, \ e_1 \cdot \sigma, ff, \text{setev}, n, \rho \rangle, e_1, q, ff, ff \rangle$$

The manipulation of the event queue as a first-class entity is often of use to introspective Harrison Machine programs. This confers upon programs the ability to change the events that trigger rules. The routines specified below are: `evqueue`, which returns the *entire* current event queue, and `setevqueue`, which sets the current event queue to another queue of events.

$$\langle \emptyset, w, a, \langle c, \sigma, ff, \text{get-eventqueue}, n, \rho \rangle, e, q, ff, ff \rangle \rightarrow$$
$$\langle \emptyset, w, a, \langle c, q \cdot \sigma, ff, o, n+1, \rho \rangle, e, q, ff, ff \rangle$$

$$\langle \emptyset, w, a, \langle c, q_1 \cdot \sigma, ff, \text{set-eventqueue}, n, \rho \rangle, e, q, ff, ff \rangle \rightarrow$$
$$\langle \emptyset, w, a, \langle c, \sigma, ff, o, n+1, \rho \rangle, e, q_1, ff, ff \rangle$$

The queue of events that is to be made current is first loaded onto the stack. The operation transfers the stacked event queue to the one in the VM.

It is also easy to define operations for manipulating the event queue from rules. The following have been implemented: `addevent-back` (add an event to the back of the event queue), `addevent-front` (add an event to the front of the event queue—the event queue is a DEQueue) and the corresponding dequeueing operations, `popevent-front` and `popevent-back`.

$$\langle \emptyset, w, a, \langle c, \ e_1 \cdot \sigma, ff, \text{addevent-back}, n, \rho \rangle, e, q, ff, ff \rangle \rightarrow$$
$$\langle \emptyset, w, a, \langle c, \ \sigma, ff, o, n+1, \rho \rangle, e, \ q \ddagger \langle e_1 \rangle, ff, ff \rangle$$

$$\langle \emptyset, w, a, \langle c, \ e_1 \cdot \sigma, ff, \text{addevent-front}, n, \rho \rangle, e, q, ff, ff \rangle \rightarrow$$
$$\langle \emptyset, w, a, \langle c, \ \sigma, ff, o, n+1, \rho \rangle, e, \ \langle e_1 \rangle \ddagger q, ff, ff \rangle$$

$$\langle \emptyset, w, a, \langle c, \ \sigma, ff, \text{popevent-front}, n, \rho \rangle, e, \ e_1 \cdot q, ff, ff \rangle \rightarrow$$
$$\langle \emptyset, w, a, \langle c, \ \sigma, ff, o, n+1, \rho \rangle, e, q, ff, ff \rangle$$

$$\langle \emptyset, w, a, \langle c, \ \sigma, ff, \text{popevent-back}, n, \rho \rangle, e, q \ddagger \langle e_1 \rangle, ff, ff \rangle \rightarrow$$
$$\langle \emptyset, w, a, \langle c, \ \sigma, ff, o, n+1, \rho \rangle, e, q, ff, ff \rangle$$

In neither of the two last transitions are errors considered. An empty event queue, clearly, should cause an error. However, a routine to test the event queue can be defined:

$$\langle \emptyset, w, a, \langle c, \sigma, \text{is-empty-evqueue}, n, \rho \rangle, e, \langle \rangle, ff, ff \rangle \rightarrow$$
$$\langle \emptyset, w, a, \langle c, \ t\!t \cdot \sigma, o, n+1, \rho \rangle, e, \langle \rangle, ff, ff \rangle$$

and, for $q \neq \langle \rangle$:

$$\langle \emptyset, w, a, \langle c, \sigma, \text{is-empty-evqueue}, n, \rho \rangle, e, q, ff, ff \rangle \rightarrow$$
$$\langle \emptyset, w, a, \langle c, \ ff \cdot \sigma, o, n+1, \rho \rangle, e, q, ff, ff \rangle$$

It is possible to load and unload rules dynamically (unloading is not always a good idea!) This is made possible by the representation of rules as independent stateful entities. The following transition defines one possible addrule operation. In order to make proper sense of it, rules must be included in D, the set of denotable values.

$$\langle \emptyset, w, a, \langle c, r \cdot \sigma, ff, \text{addrule}, n, \rho \rangle, e, q, ff, ff \rangle \rightarrow$$
$$\langle \emptyset, w \cup \{r\}, a, \langle c, \sigma, ff, o, n+1, \rho \rangle, e, q, ff, ff \rangle$$

The new rule first occurs on the top of the stack. It is then added to the Waiting Set. The rule might be read from disk or dynamically constructed and then compiled (many versions of the Harrison Machine have included abstract syntax constructors and the rule compiler as library routines).

These routines can be implemented as runtime library routines. They are called as pre-defined routines by rules.

6.7 Rule Equivalences

The attentive reader will, at this stage, be asking why all of the above schemes have been presented when there are some simplifications that can be made.

The clearest simplifications concern since and until rules. Given the intended interpretations, they can be rewritten in terms of rules with simpler semantics, as follows.

Rules of the form since (t, p) do s can be written as:

$$\text{when (t, p) do (always do s)}$$

Rules of the form until (t, p) do s can be written as:

$$\text{always do(s; when(t, p) do (term))}$$

These transformations can also be employed when since and until rules are wrapped inside declarations.

Unfortunately, because negation in pattern expressions is not permitted, it is impossible to express unless in terms of when. Similarly, given the current apparatus, it is impossible to re-write alt in a simpler form.

6.8 Concluding Remarks

The Harrison Machine is an example of an architecture that extends the stack-based machine architecture in a number of ways:

- The main control structure is represented by a queue of objects.
- There are multiple stacks, one for each active rule. This is similar to the pseudo-concurrent stack-machine architecture described in Chapter 5.
- Each rule, like a process, has its own code pointer and its own instruction pointer. Code is distributed in the implementation: each rule points to its own code block; code blocks can be shared between rules with identical behaviours. Rules sharing code will, typically, have different instruction pointer values at any particular time.
- The main execution loop for the Harrison Machine is somewhat more complex than that in the other machines so far examined: it must manipulate the various queues, not just test the instruction pointer for validity and test the halt flag to detect termination.

In the Smalltalk VM [21], the code for each method is stored in a separate vector. The code vector is stored in the method table associated with the class in which the method is defined. In a similar fashion, the Harrison Machine allocates the code for a rule in a byte vector that is pointed to by the rule; any other rule with an identical set of behaviours can share the code.

Despite these differences, the Harrison Machine is conventional in a number of ways:

- A stack is used as the primary evaluation mechanism.
- A set of registers is used as well as the stack. In particular, the full Harrison Machine contains two registers, the A and S registers. These two registers are used to optimize vector and string accesss. The A register is an accumulator, used to index vectors and strings, while the S register holds pointers to vectors and strings.

The Harrison Machine has been implemented a number of times, each with subtly different semantics. The overall architecture has been found to be quite rugged, even if it is a little difficult to control. Various implementation techniques have been employed, including an object-oriented one and a register-transfer machine has been designed for it (see Chapter 7). The object-oriented version suggested that the virtual machine could be represented as a data structure to be manipulated by the runtime primitives of the system—this is an extremely interesting possibility (see Chapter 9).

One version of the Harrison Machine was written in Ocaml. The intermediate language was implemented as an algebraic type. As such, it contained type information that would be lost in the final instruction set (which was as implemented above plus the string and vector operations that were omitted there). It was clear that the intermediate code could be executed directly if an appropriate virtual machine were constructed. A switch was added to the directives in the output of the compiler to indicate whether the intermediate code or the instruction set was to be executed. The virtual machine was also modified to execute the intermediate code using a separate module. The result ran somewhat slower than fully compiled code but was useful as a debugging aid. However, not much use was made of the type information that was associated with the intermediate code.

Register-Based Machines

7.1 Introduction

The virtual machines described so far have all had the same property: they use at least one stack and a collection of special-purpose registers. This has been taken as *the* way to construct virtual machines. It is certainly a relatively quick and easy way to do it and it is a target machine for which it is particularly easy to generate code. There are, however, alternatives, the primary being that based on the *Register-Transfer Model* (RTM). This is the model upon which most hardware processors are based.

There have been many machine simulators over the years and there are programming environments, particularly for real-time and embedded systems, that allow programs for one processor to be executed using a simulated processor. However, the use of the RTM for virtual machines is relatively new; the largest implementation to date (2004) is the Parrot virtual machine for Perl6.

This chapter is concerned with this alternative organisation for virtual machines. Section 7.2 is concerned with the arguments surrounding register-based machines, both *pro* and *con*. Section 7.3 contains a description of one way to organise a register-based virtual machine. Since the only really public register-based virtual machine of any strength is that for Parrot, Section 7.4 is a description of Parrot's general organisation, while Section 7.5 contains a description of Parrot's instruction set (the description is only partial because the published documentation is, as yet, incomplete—the best way to *understand* the Parrot VM is to read its code). In Section 7.6, a DIY register machine is presented. In Section 7.7, it is shown how the two-stack code for the simple ALEX programming language can be converted (macro processed, in essence) into code for the DIY register-transfer machine. The following section contains examples of such translations using a simple function. The correctness of the translation from two-stack to register-machine code is the subject of Section 7.9 In Section 7.10 a more natural compilation of ALEX to register-machine code is presented. In the last section, Section 7.11 some extensions to the register machine are considered.

7.2 The Register-Transfer Model

Almost all work on abstract machines has concentrated on stack-based architectures. The SECD machine is the classic of this form, of course. The Pascal-S, Pascal P4, UCSD Pascal, Smalltalk and Java abstract machines are also stack-based. One good reason for constructing stack-based machines is that expressions can be directly evaluated on the stack. Stacks are also used to represent scope, thus making procedures and block structures easy to implement. Stacks are required to implement recursion, a feature of ISWIM, Algol60 and most modern programming languages. Stack-based architectures are good for compiler writers, therefore.

It is interesting to note that in the 1960s, the Burroughs Corporation developed two series of mainframe computers, the B6600 and B7700 series, both of which used Algol60 as their systems programming language. These machines introduced a hardware stack and a specialised instruction set to support the execution of an Extended Algol60 that was designed for these machines. In the middle of the 1960s, The English Electric Company (which merged with other British manufacturers to form ICL) introduced the KDF9 computer, another Algol-based machine. It was one of the supercomputers of that age. A feature of the earliest microprocessors, such as the Intel 8080, Intel 8086 and the Motorola 6800, was a hardware stack. Most modern processors still have hardware stacks. A more recent example is the ICL 2900 range of the late-1970s/early 1980s.

Stack-based architectures are also called *zero-address architectures*. The reason for this is that the location of the result of the last expression to be evaluated need not be directly addressed. It is always at the top of the stack and is pointed to by the stack pointer, not by a general address. More generally, expression evaluation does not require any addresses because operands are always located on the stack.

The primary competitor to the zero-addressed architecture is the *Register-Transfer Machine*. In this architecture, there are many high-speed registers in the processor. Operands are loaded into registers. Instructions specify the registers upon which they operate. Operands can also reside in memory and are fetched and stored by explicit instructions and by means of addressing modes of greater or lesser complexity. Many processors have been constructed using this model: the IBM mainframe series following the S360, the Digital PDP-11 and VAX-11 machines, are examples.

Hybrid architectures are also possible. The most popular example at present is the Intel X86 range. This processor range has a hardware stack and a relatively few registers. It has a large set of instructions. Pipelines are used to increase the throughput of these processors.

A more recent idea has been to construct processors using the Register-Transfer model but to reduce the complexity of the instruction set and the addressing modes that they employ. This is the *RISC* or *Reduced Instruction Set Computer* architecture. It is characterised by a large number of general-purpose registers, relatively large instruction set and a relatively few addressing modes. The instructions are designed to execute rapidly, typically requiring one CPU cycle to complete. In addition, RISC machines typically have explicit *load* and *store* instructions to load data into registers and store it in main memory. The MIPS and SPARC processors are examples of RISC machines.

Software abstract machines have not often been constructed using a register-transfer model. The Scheme abstract machine (for example, the one described in [1]) has registers but they are dedicated to special purposes. The Java and Smalltalk VMs, like those for ALEX, OCODE, the Harrison Machine and many others, do have registers but, again, they are reserved for special purposes.

One advantage register-transfer architectures have is that the transfer of data between processor registers is much faster than transfers to and from a hardware stack. The reason for this is that the stack is too large to store in the processor, so it usually resides in main memory. This means that two memory fetches are required to load the top two elements of the stack in central processor registers when performing an instruction that implements a binary operation. The stack must be adjusted when pushing or popping operands, operations that also take time to perform. In pure zero-addressed architectures, the processor registers are not visible to user programs and are purely internal to the processor, so only microcode, if used, can access them. Normal instructions operate on the stack (and possibly the instruction counter) as far as the assembly programmer is concerned. However, instructions must load the stack's data into invisible processor registers when an operation is performed.

Using a register-transfer model, when performing a binary operation, it is necessary to load two (often adjacent) registers with data and then execute the instruction. This requires two external memory fetches but requires no stack adjustment. The value yielded remains in a register and can be employed directly without the need for a further memory fetch. Of course, optimal use of registers requires that operands be in registers when they are required; it also requires that operands are not moved between registers. The latter might be required when an operation is followed by another operation that is not commutative and the result of the previous operation is in the wrong register; often multiplication and division require register pairs to be allocated for their results. Compilers can perform register allocation very well but optimal performance in all cases cannot be guaranteed for the reason that the problem is an instance of the Knapsack or the Bin-Packing Problem. Nevertheless, there are very high-performance algorithms in the literature.

In software abstract machines, the stack is also a bottleneck as far as performance is concerned. This is for reasons similar to those given above: when an operation is performed, the stack must be adjusted either up or down (which can involve range check performance). When an operation is performed, the operands must be loaded into temporary locations allocated by the implementation language's compiler—this is directly analogous to the use of registers internal to the hardware processor. If a register-transfer machine is simulated, operands are loaded into software-specified registers (variables). Transfers between variables is somewhat faster than assignment to array elements or indirect assignment via pointers. In software, of course, it is possible to have as many registers as one desires, thus maximising the number of register register transfers and minimising register-store transfers. The store is often implemented as an array of some kind, so fetching and storing data in an abstract machine requires array indexing (which might involve bounds checking in some programming languages). The use of discrete variables as simulated registers can be optimised if the target hardware is known for it might be possible to arrange that the compiler allocates the variables as machine registers; the number of registers also can be optimised if the size of the hardware cache is known. More generally, software registers can be arranged to have fixed addresses (they can be made global variables in most programming languages) so access to them can be optimised by a good compiler (as can their allocation).

All of this amounts to fairly strong arguments for the construction of abstract machines using the register-transfer architecture. Arguments similar to those given above have been used in support of the new runtime system for the Perl6 language.

The counterarguments to use of a Register-Transfer architecture are relatively simple and clear. First, register-transfer architectures imply that compilers that generate code for them must have more complex code generators than those generating stack machine code. More particularly, such code generators must perform register allocation and management, while a compiler for a stack machine can rely entirely upon the stack. Register-Transfer machines allow some or all routine parameters to be passed in registers ("register spilling"), thus making routine calls much faster; similarly, the results returned by routines can be passed in registers, again making the process faster. However, the compiler must be able to spot this and allocate registers appropriately. Second, it can be argued that, if an abstract machine based on register-transfer is implemented on a processor with relatively few hardware registers, the improvement in performance is considerably reduced. Third, Register-Transfer machines are harder to implement and are larger than stack-based ones. Thus, the runtime code size (the footprint) of a register machine can be greater than the corresponding stack machine. Fourth, register-based machines make routine call and return more constrained by requiring actual parameters and returned values to be passed in registers, unless a stack is also used.

It would appear that the first argument is one for compiler writers. The second argument must be admitted, at least for pure stack machines. However, most common processor architectures have sufficient hardware registers to make a register-based virtual machine a reasonable proposition. What would appear more important is the mapping from implementation code to the hardware cache found on almost all easily available processors. Finally, in our experience, register-based machines are not significantly harder to implement. To us, it appears that the arguments in favour of register-based abstract machines appear superior to those against them. The arguments against register-based abstract machine also ignore the fact that a register-based machine will probably employ a stack as a temporary storage area and as a mechanism that supports context saves and restores when calling and returning from routines. When there are insufficient registers available at a call or return, the stack can always be employed to store them. By requiring register transfer, one is not rejecting the stack entirely; what is being proposed is that, as a goal, compilers producing code for register-based abstract machines should, as far as possible, generate code preferring register transfers and direct loads and stores in favour of stack-based operations.

Henceforth, the terms "Register-Transfer Model" and "Register-Transfer Machine" will be abbreviated as RTM; since the two are near cognates, it does not seem to make much difference to the meaning of the result.

7.3 Register Machine Organisation

What are the main components of a virtual machine based on the RTM? This section is intended to be a partial answer to this question.

It is important to stress this point: the answer can only be *partial*. If the stack-based model is re-considered, it specifies that a virtual machine contains at least one stack and that stack is used to evaluate the arguments of functions. It has already been seen that there are variations on this theme: in an earlier section, it was shown how to execute code using two stacks (a VM can use as many stacks as are required). In addition to the stack, a stack-based VM also has a few registers and can have additional storage structures: a code vector is typically required but a heap is also advantageous. With the RTM, the position is the same. There will be a basic organisation and many variations on that theme.

A basic organisation of a RTM is the following:

- At least one set of registers;
- At least one stack;
- At least one (flat) main storage area;
- At least one code vector.

The registers of a machine might be divided by type. As will be seen in the next section, the Parrot machine has register sets for integer, floating point, string and abstract types. Parrot also has a stack for each register set plus an extra one or two, one of which is for control.

There is the requirement that there be additional storage. This might be a managed heap or an unmanged flat area of store. Given current developments in programming languages, it is most likely that the additional storage will be a managed heap. Some machines will require a single area of this kind, while others might require multiple areas.

Finally, there must be a storage area that holds the code to be executed by the RTM. There might be just one storage area that holds code; there might be more than one area. The code storage area might, indeed, turn out to be part of the main storage area (the Pop-11 virtual machine [8], stores its code in the heap).

The above appears to be the minimal RTM organisation. An actual implementation might augment the above with the addition of such things as:

- Exception handlers (Parrot does this);
- Explicit I/O operations and structures (again, Parrot does this);
- Events (e.g., interrupts).

Given this general organisation, questions naturally arise:

- What are the instructions supported by the RTM?
- Are there special control registers or are they taken from one (or more) of the register sets?
- Is evaluation performed *only* on registers or is a stack involved?
- What are the addressing modes available?
- What are the data types that can be supported?
- What is the pressure on instruction representation?

The first question cannot be answered in general. This is clear: a virtual machine is usually constructed for a particular purpose (although Parrot is general). However, some families of operation will (almost always) be supported:

- Instructions to load registers;
- Instructions to store register contents;
- Instructions to implement control. Jumps of various kinds can be expected.

The constraints that are often imposed by hardware machines on some instructions can be relaxed in virtual machines based on the RTM. For example, the constraint is often imposed that multiplication and division can only be performed on adjacent registers. The reasons for this have to do with the size of the result and with data movement. The result of a multiplication can be larger than a single register can contain; a division might result in a quantity that requires a format other than that employed for integers (e.g., the division $1 \div 30$). Data movement within the processor can also cause such constraints. These constraints can be removed in a virtual machine constructed from software. Thus, instructions performing, say arithmetic, might take three operands, not two. A traditional addition instruction (in register mode) might have the form `add r1, r2`, while that in a virtual RTM can take the form: `add r1, r2, dest`, where `dest` is the name of the register into which the result will be placed (the destination can be one of the two source registers, of course).

The second question cannot, in general, be answered. It would appear, given that the specifier of the RTM is free to include as many registers as they wish, a separate set of registers devoted to control can be provided. The use of general-purpose registers for control leads either to a reduction in the number of registers available for expression evaluation and command execution or to a great many register movements (loads, stores and movement of data between registers).

One reason for moving to the RTM is that evaluation can be performed in registers, thus reducing the number of storage accesses *within* the VM. This suggests that evaluations will be performed on registers, with the concomitant requirement that compilers include register allocation and tracking code. It can be objected that the RTM only *appears* to reduce storage access because a register operation really performs a storage access. However, as argued above, registers can be stored in fixed locations within the virtual machine's code; this allows pointers to be used to optimise access. With a stack-based implementation, such an optimisation is rarely an option for intermediate results.

Many hardware processors, particularly CISC machines, have many addressing modes. These modes can include:

- Immediate mode to load and store constant data (often a byte or word).
- Absolute mode. The actual address of a datum or label is used.
- Register mode. The data upon which the instruction operates are located in registers.
- Indirect mode. A pointer is used to access data (rarely code).
- Indexed mode. This is a composite mode in which a pointer is set to some location in store and an offset is used to access the entity to be loaded or stored. Relative jumps (or branches) are an example of indexed mode in which the instruction pointer (program counter) provides the base address.
- Indexed Indirect mode. This is a combination of the other modes.

Many processors permit combinations of these modes. This requires careful encoding of instructions.

RISC machines, on the other hand, tend to have simpler addressing modes and rely, instead, on the manipulation of registers to implement complex addressing modes. It would appear sensible for a RTM virtual machine to follow the RISC example.

Many virtual machines have only a limited repertoire of runtime types. There appears to be a real need to restrict the repertoire of types available in *hardware* but not software. Very often, as in the case of Java, a restricted set of basic types is represented directly with other types being translated into them. One reason to restrict the number of basic types is that it puts pressure on the instruction set.

There are three basic sources of pressure on the instruction set:

1. Minimisation of the storage required for an instruction; the smaller the instruction, the smaller the overall code size;
2. The number of addressing modes supported by the virtual machine;
3. The number of types supported by the virtual machine.

In stack-based virtual machines, there is often the desire to represent instructions as bytecodes. That is, each instruction is encoded as a byte. This implies that there can be at most 256 instructions, assuming an 8-bit byte. This is not a necessary constraint even though it is quite common. With modern storage systems, it seems fairly reasonable to allow opcodes to occupy 16 bits if necessary.

If a virtual machine supports a set of basic types, it is to be expected that there will be a sufficient number of instructions to support them. A typed instruction set also puts pressure on the representation (the JVM is an example of a stack-based VM whose instruction set was designed to encode as much type information as possible). Sometimes, instructions can be overloaded; for example, the **add** instruction might be used to add integers and floating-point numbers. Some types do not naturally fit within a overloading scheme: array and structure operations are cases in point. Clearly, the more types supported, the greater the number of instructions required to support them.

Parrot, as will be seen in the next section, employs a class-based approach together with overloading to extend its set of basic types. This requires additional sophistication from the runtime system. It also requires that additional code be written to support the additional types; this can be done when the compiler is constructed.

The Parrot approach is, in a sense, a generalisation of the approach employed by Python and Forth which use dictionaries to store code segments. In both languages, native code can be stored in dictionary entries.[1] The dictionary approach makes a language extensible but does so at the cost of execution speed—a dictionary lookup is required when code for an operation is called. This can, however, be optimised by caching code once it has been accessed. The dictionary approach permits the dynamic loading of new types in a fashion similar to the JVM's class loader.

With dictionaries, the main issue is how can completely new types can be introduced into the virtual machine without the introduction of new instructions. In Parrot, opcodes are represented as 32-bit integers, thus providing lots of space into which new opcodes can be loaded. Indeed, Parrot permits instruction sets to be loaded dynamically.

---

[1] Smalltalk also employs dictionaries for its code but it would appear from [21] that native code is not directly stored.

7.4 Parrot—General Organisation

The complete Parrot system is comprised of:

- A parser;
- A compiler;
- An optimiser (currently on the website, there is little information on the Parrot optimiser);
- An interpreter.

The parser and compiler support the Parrot Assembly Language. The parser transforms the input into an Abstract Syntax Tree (*AST*). The compiler walks the AST generating bytecodes as it goes. The compiler does not perform any optimisations. The purpose of the optimiser is to produce better code but might not be able to do everything that a special-purpose optimiser could. For example, when the complete source of a program is presented, an optimiser can produce much better code than is the case when the source is presented one routine or object at a time. Thus, optimisation for Java is expected to be of a local nature.

The parser and compiler can be overridden by special-purpose code that performs the same functions, as can the optimiser.

For the purposes of this chapter, the input syntax and semantics, as well as the interpreter and its supporting structures will be presented.

The interpreter is the ultimate destination of all bytecodes. Bytecodes are loaded into the interpreter in order to cause something to happen; the interpreter is considered a behaviour generator. For Parrot, however, the interpreter need not actually execute the bytecodes that it inputs. It might, for example:

- Save data on disk;
- Transform the input bytecodes to an alternative representation (e.g., JVM or .NET code).

The second case indicates a general point about Parrot: it is intended to be a general-purpose platform that can be integrated with other language systems. Below, it will be seen that the Parrot system has instructions that load new interpreters into the system and execute them.

It is a design goal for the Parrot system to behave as if it were any of:

- Java (JVM);
- .NET;
- Z machine;
- Python;
- Perl5;
- Ruby.

Nothing in the system prevents it from behaving like any other system (the Pascal and OCODE machines appear to be easy to implement, while Smalltalk looks somewhat more difficult).

The interpreter contains a sophisticated memory management system and a Just-In Time (*JIT*) compiler. They will be described below.

The interpreter typically executes bytecodes. In Parrot, the term "byte-code" is a slight misnomer because they are represented as 32-bit integers. These bytecodes are generally directly executed by the interpreter. As usual, bytecodes are the output of a compiler. It is expected that bytecodes will be loaded into the interpreter from disk but loading from other places is also possible (thus allowing Parrot to operate in a fashion similar to the JVM).

Bytecodes are structured as opcodes and operands, as is standard in most bytecode systems and native instruction sets.

The implementation of bytecodes is designed to be extremely flexible. Opcode tables can be loaded on demand and some opcodes can be overridden, thus allowing different operations to be implemented by the same opcode. Dynamic opcodes also allow rarely used functions to be loaded only when they are required, as well as allowing a piecemeal upgrade.

Opcodes can, and often do, throw exceptions to signal abnormal conditions. The bytecode loader can also be overridden so that code can be input from sources other than disks (and can be read in formats other than the default). All opcodes operate on registers.

The interpreter is organised as follows. It has the following register sets:

- 32 integer-valued (IV) registers, named I1 to I32 by the Parrot assembler;
- 32 floating-point (NV) registers, named N1 to N32 by the Parrot assembler;
- 32 string-valued registers, named S1 to S32 by the Parrot assembler;
- 32 registers to hold Perl Magic Cookies (*PMC*s), named P1 to P32 by the Parrot assembler.

Opcodes support type conversion between registers. Thus, it is possible to assign the contents of an integer register to a floating-point register (and vice versa). The interpreter automatically converts from one type to another. It is also possible to convert between string and integer register contents. This is necessary for the execution of Perl5 programs because integers and strings can be freely interchanged (readers who are interested in this should consult a good text on Perl, for example [51]).

In addition, there are storage locations for global and local variables. These locations are designed to permit fast access to the data stored in them.

Parrot's interpreter also contains the following stacks:

- A call stack;
- An integer stack;
- A string stack;
- A floating-point stack;
- A PMC stack;

- A generic stack.

The call stack is used for subroutine call and return. The next four stacks
are intended to support the four register sets (acting as temporary storage).
The integer stack also contains integer values stored there during subroutine
call and return, as well as intermediate results. The string stack is a stack
that holds only strings. It is provided as a support for languages like Perl that
perform extensive string operations. The floating-point stack is provided to
support floating-point operations.

All stacks are segmented, so there is no limit to the size of each one.
Segmented stacks are also used in the JVM and, in a different way, in the
Smalltalk Virtual Machine. Implementing stacks in terms of segments requires
support from a memory manager.

A lot of Parrot's functionality is delegated to PMCs). PMCs are implemented as structures that are opaque to the interpreter. This abstraction
permits the Parrot interpreter to be more powerful and modular than it would
otherwise be. In particular, the engine does not have to distinguish between
scalar, hash and array variables at this level.

PMCs look similar to a form of object orientation. They make available
new data types by providing structures containing data structures and operations on those structures. Both data structures and operations are encapsu-
lated within a single entity, which can be interpreted very much as a class is
in class-based object-oriented languages. The values of the new type bear a
relation to these structures that is quite similar to that between instances and
classes.

The PMC concept is implemented using a structure called a *vtable*. A
vtable is a table of pointers to functions. This allows each variable (or
instance—called a "variable" in Perl parlance) to have its own set of specialised functions, or methods, thus allowing highly customised behaviour to
be supported with little overhead. One nice optimisation performed by vtables is the removal of jumps. On most current processors, jumps are expensive
because they require the pipeline (and possibly the cache) to be flushed and re-
filled. Jump removal is an optimisation that can lead to considerable increases
in execution speed, therefore. Vtables, in essence, allow a type-dependent operation dispatch that is not unlike dynamic method dispatch in class-based
object-oriented programming languages. Vtables support standard (as well as
non-standard) operations on values, for example:

- Name;
- Type;
- Clone (shallow copy);
- Getter function;
- Setter function;
- Addition, subtraction, multiplication and division;
- Call a method;
- Special methods for garbage collection.

PMCs also allow aggregates (arrays and hash tables, for instance) to be handled in a transparent fashion. They do not require Parrot-compiled instructions to index and update them.

The Parrot engine also supports exceptions. Unlike Java exception handlers, exception handlers in Parrot capture closures, thus enabling them to store their state. Like Java exceptions, handlers can target specific classes of exception. Exception handlers are not expected to resume; they halt computation, which is probably a better (and is certainly an easier) option than trying to resume computation from the point at which an exception is raised. An exception handler can be put in place at any time.

Exceptions can be thrown by an opcode that returns a value of zero. They can also be thrown by the throw opcode.

7.5 Parrot Instruction Set

At the time of writing, the Parrot documentation was incomplete, so a more complete description of this project cannot be included (this extends to the instruction set whose documentation is similarly incomplete). The interested reader is directed to the Parrot website at [37]. In this section, a few instructions are described so that the general description can be made a little more concrete.

The instruction set contains operations for control, data management, transcendental operations, register and stack operations, names (identifiers), pads and globals, exceptions, objects, modules, I/O, threading operations, interpreter operations, garbage collection, key operations and symbolic support for high-level languages.

Keys include array and record operations. They use keys to access components of a structured object.

The instructions performing control, data management, stack and register operations are described below. Before describing them, it is necessary, first, to state the notational conventions employed by descriptions (these conventions are identical to those in the Parrot documentation).

All registers can have a type prefix of P, S, I or N. These prefixes stand for PMC, string, integer or floating-point number, respectively.

The opcode format is:

code destination[dest_key], source1[source1_key], ..., sourcek[sourcek_key]

Here, the brackets denote optional arguments and are brackets in the concrete, not meta, syntax (brackets are represented as brackets). If an operand takes a key, the assembler automatically substitutes the null key for any missing keys.

Conditional branches have the form:

code boolean[boolean_key1], true_dest

Again, the key parameters are optional but when present they can be integer- or string-valued. If there are key parameters, they are associated with the parameter to their left and are assumed to be either an array or list index or a hash key. If the source or destination is a PMC, there can be a key. Destinations for conditional branches represent an integer *offset* from the current value of the PC.

7.5.1 Control instructions

if tx, X Test register tx (i.e., Px, Sx, Ix or Nx). If its contents represent the value true, branch by the amount specified by X.

jump tx Unconditionally jump to the address stored in register x (Px, Sx or Ix). The destination is an absolute address.

branch tx Branch (forward or backward) by the amount specified by register x (Ix, Nx or Px). The branch offset can also be an integer constant.

jsr tx Jump unconditionally to the location specified by register x. Push the current location onto the call stack for later return. This is a jump to a subroutine instruction.

bsr tx Branch to the location specified by x (which can be a register or a label). Push the current location onto the call stack for later return. This is an unconditional branch to a subroutine. Presumably (it is not specified in the documentation), the location is relative to the current one.

ret Pop a location from the top of the call stack and and jump unconditionally to that location.

Note that Parrot supports branches or jumps relative to the current instruction pointer. It also supports the basic call and return mechanisms for routine invocation.

7.5.2 Data management instructions

new Px, ly Create a new PMC of class y stored in the PMC register x.

set tx, ty Copy the value in register ty into register tx and make any appropriate conversions.

set Px, Py Copy the PMC pointer in Py into Px. After execution, both registers refer to the *same* PMC.

clone Px, Py Perform a "deeper" copy of Py into Px using the *vtable* appropriate to the class of Py.

tostring Sx, ty, lz Take the value in register y and convert it to a string of type z. Store the result in string register Sx.

add tx, ty, tz* Add the contents of registers y and z, storing the result in register x. The registers must all be of the same type (PMC, integer or floating point).

sub tx, ty, tz* Subtract register z from register y and store the result in register x. The registers must all be of the same type (PMC, integer or floating point).

mul tx, ty, tz* As above but multiplying the values.

div tx, ty, tz* As above but dividing the values.

inc tx, nn* Increment the contents of register x by the amount nn. The value of nn can be an integer constant. If nn is omitted, register x is incremented by one.

dec tx, nn* As for inc but decrementing the value in register x.

length lx, Sy Put the length of string y into register x.

concat Sx, Sy Concatenate string Sy onto string Sx.

repeat Sx, Sy, lz Copy string Sy z times into string Sx.

In addition to the usual instructions (setting registers, arithmetic and register increment and decrement), there are instructions that return the length of strings, concatenate them, copy strings, convert arguments to strings, as well as cloning and copying operands.

This is an interesting set of instructions. It appears to steer a course between representing strings and representing general objects.

7.5.3 Register and stack operations

push_p Push the current frame of PMC registers onto their stack and start a new frame. The new registers are *not* initialised. The frame is the current PMC register set.

push_p_c Push the current frame of PMC registers onto their stack and start a new frame. The new registers are copies of the previous frame.

pop_p Pop the current frame of PMC registers from the stack.

push_i The same as push_p but for integer registers.

push_i_c The same as push_p_c but for integer registers.

pop_i The same as pop_p but for integer registers.

push_s The same as push_p but for string registers.

push_s_c The same as push_p_c but for string registers.

pop_s The same as pop_p but for string registers.

push_n The same as push_p but for floating-point registers.

push_n_c The same as push_p_c but for floating-point registers.

pop_n The same as pop_p but for floating-point registers.

save_i lx Push integer register x onto the generic stack.

save_s Sx Push string register x onto the generic stack.

save_p Px Push PMC register x onto the generic stack.

save_n Nx Push floating-point register x onto the generic stack.

restore_i lx Restore integer register x from the generic stack.

restore_s Sx Restore string register x from the generic stack.

restore_p Px Restore PMC register x from the generic stack.

restore_n Nx Restore floating-point register x from the generic stack.

entrytype lx, iy Put the type of stack entry y into register x.

set_warp string Sets a named marker on the stacks for later use.

warp[string] Reset the current register stacks to the state they were in when the warp was set. It resets only the frame pointers. It does not guarantee the contents of the registers. Users should be careful when modifying the frame pointers by, for example, pushing register frames. If a name is passed, warp back to the named point.

unwarp Reset the current register stacks to the state they were in before the last warp.

These instructions are very much as one would expect. However, the storage of registers in marked areas of the stack is explicitly provided.

Interpreter operations

newinterp Px, flags Create a new interpreter for x using the flags passed in flags.

runinterp Px, iy Jump to the interpreter x and execute the code starting at offset y from the current location.

callout Pw, sy, pz Call routine y in interpreter x, passing it the list of parameters in z. w is a synchronisation object that is returned by the operation. It can be waited on like the synchronisation objects returned by asynchronous I/O operations.

This is a completely new set of instructions that allow multiple interpreters to be present in a system at any one time. This capability implies that, to some extent, at least, an interpreter is a data structure as far as the Parrot system is concerned.

7.6 DIY Register-Based Virtual Machine

In this section, a design for another VM will be presented, this time one based on the RTM. It is clear that a VM on the scale of Parrot is an extremely ambitious project, so the one designed here will, necessarily, be on a smaller scale.

The present exercise will be executed as follows. First, the runtime structures and instruction set will be defined *informally*. Then, a formal specification in terms of transitions will be presented. The rationale for this approach is that the goal is to produce a *correct* implementation of the final product.

Here, there comes a problem: should a general-purpose VM be designed or should it be restricted to a single language. A lot of languages have common properties, so should a VM hard-wire these in, to leave the rest to extension or should it be completely general? This, is a problem with an exercise such as this; no answer is given here.

The reason why this *is* a problem is that it relates to correctness: in relation to what is the final product correct? For a language VM, it should be the semantics of the language; for a general one, the criteria are less clear—some

vague idea of what it should do? It is not possible to construct a VM that
will be adequate for *every* programming language: that would amount to the
software simulation of a conventional CPU, something best done in hardware.
In any case, consider the variations: Prolog and Functional languages at one
end, Java, C++, C#, Python and Ruby in the middle and Perl or BCPL at
the other.

These considerations lead also to design issues. Should the RTM VM be at
a relatively low level; should it, on the other hand, be a high-level construct
that abstracts away from conventional processors? The first route leads to
generality (albeit at the cost of being accused of reinventing the wheel), while
the second leads the way to intermediate code and its direct interpretation.
The intermediate code approach will be specialised and semantically fixed;
the general one will be just that.

One final thing, before continuing, is the following. The reader should be
aware that the design that follows is in no way intended to be optimal; indeed,
it is not really *designed* in the proper sense of the word but just put together in
a few hours using a knowledge of the operations that are typically required by
compilers (e.g., access to stack-allocated parameters and local variables). The
"design" that follows is, after all, just an example to be used in conveying the
fundamental ideas. With more care, and with more time, a better instruction
set could be derived (although experience teaches that it can be very easy of
over-design such an artefact).

With these thoughts in mind, the design continues.

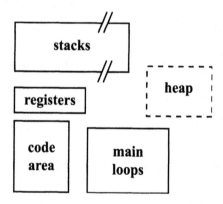

Fig. 7.1. *General organisation of a register-based virtual machine.*

7.6.1 Informal Design

The RTM needs a space in which to store code. It has a heap. Code can be
stored in the heap. It will also have two stacks: one for control and one for

data. Initially, the data stack will be limited to integers and booleans. Two register sets are provided: one for control and one for data.

Figure 7.1 shows the general organisation of this kind of virtual machine. The heap is shown as a dashed box because the other structures (stacks, register sets, code areas and even main loops) might be allocated as heap structures.

There are 32 data registers. Each register is sufficiently wide to hold a pointer or an integer. The data registers are named r0 to r31. Routines rarely have this number of actual parameters, so the opportunity arises of passing parameters in registers.

There are 32 control registers *plus*:

hlt The halt register (when set, halts the VM);

ip The instruction pointer;

err The error register which is set to a numeric code when each instruction completes;

csb A pointer to the base of the control stack;

dsb A pointer to the base of the data stack;

cdr A pointer to the currently executing code vector;

ctop A pointer to the top of the c (control) stack;

itop A pointer to the top of the i (integer) stack.

The remaining control registers are named c0 to c31. (Once again, it is necessary to note that not all of these registers, in particular **csb** and **dsb** are not directly programmable by the machine's instructions. As was the case in Chapter 4, they are included here in order to remind the reader that they are an essential component of the virtual machine.)

It should be noted that, should other stacks be added to the machine, it will be necessary to introduce new base and top pointers. A mechanism is also required for determining when the top of a stack has been reached; the behaviour of the machine in such a circumstance is also left (for reasons of space and avoidance of tedium) undefined in this description.

The usual arithmetic and comparison instructions are included. They are:

add Addition;

sub Subtraction;

mlt Multiplication;

div Division;

mod Modulus;

lt Less than;

gt Greater than;

leq $\leq$;

geq $\geq$;

eq Equality (also used for pointers);

neq Not equal (also used for pointers).

The usual logical operations are provided:

lnot Logical "not";

land Logical "and";

lor Logical "or";

lxor Logical "exclusive or".

Unary arithmetic and logical instructions have the form:

$$< unop > \texttt{srcr destr}$$

where srcr is the *source* register and destr is the *destination* register. Source and destination can be the same register.

Binary arithmetic and logical instructions have the form:

$$< binop > \texttt{srcr1 srcr2 destr}$$

where srcr1 is the first *source* register, srcr2 is the second *source* register and destr is the *destination* register. Source and destination can be the same register.

For the stack operations, the xx prefix denotes the stack upon which the operation is being performed. This prefix will, initially, have the values c or d for control and data stack, respectively. Similarly, the notation xr is used to denote registers, currently control or data registers.

The stack operations are:

xxclear Reset the stack to empty.

xxtopidx xr Store the *index* of the top element in register xr.

xxtaddr n Push the *address* of the nth element from the top of the stack on the same stack.

xxbaddr n Return the *address* of the nth element from the bottom of the stack.

xxpushc c Push the constant c onto the stack.

xxpush xr Push the contents of register xr onto the stack.

xxpop xr Pop the top element of the stack into register xr.

xxdrop Pop the top element of the stack and do not store it.

xxpushn n Push n empty slots onto the stack.

xxdropn n Pop n objects from the stack. Do not store.

xxdup Duplicate the top element.

xxswap Swap the top two elements.

xxtgetnth n Push the nth element from the *top* onto the stack.

xxtsetnth n Set the nth element from the *top* of the stack to the value currently on the top of the stack (pops the stack).

xxbgetnth n Push the nth element from the *start* onto the top of the stack.

xxtsetnthr ro Register ro contains an offset from the *top* of the stack. The value currently on the top of the same stack is stored in that location. The stack is popped.

xxtgetnthr ro Register ro contains an offset from the *top* of the stack. The value stored at that location is pushed onto the same stack.

xxtsetnthrr ro rs Register **ro** contains an offset from the *top* of the stack. The value currently in register **rs** is stored at that location.

xxtgetnthrr ro rd Register **ro** contains an offset from the *top* of the stack. The value stored at that location is stored in register **rd**.

xxbsetnth n Set the *n*th element from the *start* of the stack to the value currently on the top of the same stack. Pop the stack.

xxbsetnth n Set the *n*th element from the *start* of the stack to the value currently on the top of the stack (pops the stack).

xxbgetnthr ro Register **ro** contains an offset from the *start* of the stack. The value at that location is pushed onto the same stack.

xxbsetnthr ro Register **ro** contains an offset from the *start* of the stack. The value currently on the top of the same stack is stored in that location. The stack is popped.

xxbgetnthrr ro rd Register **ro** contains an offset from the *start* of the stack. The value at that location is stored in register **rd**.

xxbsetnthrr ro rs Register **ro** contains an offset from the *start* of the stack. The value currently in register **rs** is stored in that location.

xfer ss sd Transfer the top element of the source stack (**ss**) to the top of the destination stack (**sd**).

xfern n ss sd Transfer the *n* top elements of the source stack (**ss**) to the top of the destination stack (**sd**).

Instructions **xxtgetnth** and **xxtsetnth** are intended to make access and update of local variables and parameters easier. Instructions **xxtaddr** and **xxbaddr** are intended to make reference parameters and global accesses easier and faster.

The general register operations are:

ldc xr c Load constant c into register **xr**.

lda xr ra Load register **xr** from the store at location **ra** where **ra** is a register.

ldm xr a Load register **xr** from the store at the location specified by the constant **a**.

stoa xr a Store register **xr** at location **a** in the store.

stor xsr xdr Store the contents of register **xsr** at the location in the store whose address is in register **xdr**.

pushr xr xx Push register **xr** on to stack **xx**.

popr xx xr Pop stack **xx** to register **xr**.

setr xsr xdr Set the contents of register **xdr** to the contents of register **xsr**.

incr xr Increment the contents of register **xr** by one.

decr xr Decrement the contents of register **xr** by one.

The control instructions are:

stop Halt execution of the VM.

goto l Transfer control to address l.

rgoto xr Transfer control to the address in register **xr** ("Register goto").

sgoto xx Pop the stack xx into register ip ("Stack goto").

if_true xr l If the value of register xr is *true*, transfer control to address l.

if_false xr l If the value of register xr is *false* (not *true*—see below), transfer control to address l.

go_on xr n (l1 ... ln) If register xr has a value in the range 1...n, transfer control to the corresponding label. The operand n is the number of labels to which control can be transferred.

call l Push the current value of the next instruction onto the control stack and transfer control to label l.

calls xx Push the address of the next instruction onto the control stack and transfer control to the address on the top of stack xx. (The stack is popped.)

callr xr Push the address of the next instruction onto the control stack and transfer control to the address in register xr.

ret Pop the control stack to register ip.

error n Set the error register, err, to the literal value n. Continue with the next instruction.

errorr re Move the value in register re into the error register err. Continue with the next instruction.

Instructions goto, if_true and if_false are the usual unconditional and conditional jumps. Instruction go_on is intended to make case or switch commands easier to implement in simple cases. Instructions call and ret are the usual routine call and return instructions; they do very little because they do not make assumptions about stack frame existence and organisation. The remaining instructions (calls and callr) are used to ease the implementation of such things as exception handlers and method lookup.

The instructions listed above are intended to be the start. However, one, so far unstated, aim in the design of the above was to provide instructions that could be of utility in the design of other instructions. For example, if it was desired to add Interrupt Service Routines, it would be useful to store the address of the routine somewhere and the stack is a useful place to do this.

7.6.2 Extensions

The register-based machine can be extended in a variety of ways. Some immediately obvious extensions are the following:

- More data types could be added. For example, floating point numbers and strings could easily be added. This would require the addition of a set of registers and a stack for each new type; some new instructions would have to be added. A decision as to whether integer and floating point instructions are to be overloaded needs to made; if the decision is in the negative, the integer and other instructions must be differentiated.
- Data types could be added by means of an object protocol similar to that used by Parrot; a special set of registers and a special stack, like that

found in Parrot, would be useful for dealing with these entities. In such a scheme, a standard format is used to define the basic operations that can be performed on these entities (the basic operations would provide a minimum functionality—an extension mechanism would be useful, too).

- The addition of instructions to allocate storage would be of use. For example, an instruction to allocate a block of storage of size n could be added, as well, perhaps, as one to deallocate it. Storage allocation and deallocation operations could usefully be associated with new types.

- Additions to implement pseudo-parallel execution of code. This would require the addition of structures similar to those discussed in Section 5.3.

- The addition of an escape mechanism to handle library routines. If the Parrot-like object-based extension is employed, library routines can be related in a natural fashion to the types manipulated by the virtual machine.

Some of the ideas presented in the final chapter of this book can also be applied to register-based virtual machines.

7.6.3 Transition Rules

In this section, the transition rules describing the above instruction set and architecture are presented. The same notation is used as in other transitions.

The two sets of registers will be considered *sequences*, denoted R_C and R_I, respectively. The contents of integer register i will be written as $R_I(i)$, while an update of the contents of integer register i to v will be written $[v \mapsto i]R_I$. The transitions will take the form:

$$\langle R_C, R_I, i, S_C, S_I, instr \rangle$$

where R_C and R_I are the register files, as discussed above, and S_C and S_I are the control and integer stacks respectively; i is the instruction pointer, while *instr* is the current instruction. Code store will be denoted, in this case, by κ (this is to avoid confusion with any *cs* that appear in transitions, so for any label, l, $\kappa(l)$ is an instruction (specifically, the instruction at the address denoted by l). In order to implement some of the instructions listed above, a flat memory for data is also required: this is denoted by M (and is assumed to be a sequence of cells all of which are of the same size).

$$\langle M, R_C, R_I, i, S_C, S_I, \texttt{unop s d} \rangle$$
$$\to \langle M, R_C, [unop(R_I(s)) \mapsto d]R_I, i+1, S_C, S_I, \kappa(i+1) \rangle$$

$$\langle M, R_C, R_I, i, S_C, S_I, \texttt{binop s1 s2 d} \rangle$$
$$\to \langle M, R_C, [binop(R_I(s_1), R_I(s_2)) \mapsto d]R_I, i+1, S_C, S_I, \kappa(i+1) \rangle$$

$$\langle M, R_C, R_I, i, S_C, S_I, \texttt{iclear} \rangle \to \langle M, R_C, R_I, i+1, S_C, \langle \rangle, \kappa(i+1) \rangle$$

$$\langle M, R_C, R_I, i, S_C, S_I, \mathtt{cclear}\rangle \to \langle M, R_C, R_I, i+1, \langle\rangle, S_I, \kappa(i+1)\rangle$$

$$\langle M, R_C, R_I, i, S_C, S_I, \mathtt{itopidx\ r}\rangle$$
$$\to \langle M, R_C, [|S_I| \mapsto r]R_I, i+1, S_C, S_I, \kappa(i+1)\rangle$$

(The index of the top element of a sequence denoting a stack is assumed always ≥ 1; it corresponds to the length of the sequence.)

$$\langle M, R_C, R_I, i, S_C, S_I, \mathtt{ibaddr\ n}\rangle \to \langle M, R_C, R_I, i, S_C, a \cdot S_I, \kappa(i+1)\rangle$$

where $a = addr(S_I(n+1))$. Note that this instruction locates the nth element from the *bottom* of the stack. The stack sequence indices are one-based, while the instruction expects a zero-based offset. If $n + 1 \leq |S_I|$, the operation succeeds; otherwise, it raises an exception.

The instruction to return the address of a stack element indexed relative to the top of the stack ($\mathtt{itaddr}$) is given by:

$$\langle M, R_C, R_I, i, S_C, S_I, \mathtt{itaddr\ n}\rangle \to \langle M, R_C, R_I, i, S_C, a \cdot S_I, \kappa(i+1)\rangle$$

where $a = addr(S_I(|S_I| - n))$. The offset n is, again, zero based. If $n < 0$ or $n > |S_I|$, an error is signalled.

The following transition defines the instruction to push the contents of register $R_I(r)$ onto the stack S_I:

$$\langle M, R_C, R_I, i, S_C, S_I, \mathtt{ipushc\ v}\rangle \to \langle M, R_C, R_I, i+1, S_C, v \cdot S_I, \kappa(i+1)\rangle$$

$$\langle M, R_C, R_I, i, S_C, S_I, \mathtt{ipush\ r}\rangle$$
$$\to \langle M, R_C, R_I, i+1, S_C, R_I(r) \cdot S_I, \kappa(i+1)\rangle$$

$$\langle M, R_C, R_I, i, S_C, v \cdot S_I, \mathtt{ipop\ r}\rangle$$
$$\to \langle M, R_C, [v \mapsto r]R_I, i+1, S_C, S_I, \kappa(i+1)\rangle$$

$$\langle M, R_C, R_I, i, S_C, v \cdot S_I, \mathtt{idrop}\rangle \to \langle M, R_C, R_I, i+1, S_C, S_I, \kappa(i+1)\rangle$$

The $\mathtt{pushn}$ instruction pushes n slots onto the stack, each slot containing zero. There are two versions of this instruction: $\mathtt{cpushn}$ and $\mathtt{ipushn}$ operating, respectively, on the c and i stacks. The version for the c stack is specified by:

$$\langle M, R_C, R_I, i, S_C, S_I, \mathtt{ipushn\ n}\rangle$$
$$\to \langle M, R_C, R_I, i+1, S_C, \overbrace{0 \cdot \ldots \cdot 0}^{n\ \text{times}} \cdot S_I, \kappa(i+1)\rangle$$

The inverse operation (again for the i stack) is defined by:

$$\langle M, R_C, R_I, i, S_C, \overbrace{v_1 \cdot \ldots \cdot v_n}^{n \text{ times}} \cdot S_I, \mathtt{idropn\ n} \rangle$$
$$\rightarrow \langle M, R_C, R_I, i+1, S_C, S_I, \kappa(i+1) \rangle$$

$$\langle M, R_C, R_I, i, S_C, v \cdot S_I, \mathtt{idup} \rangle$$
$$\rightarrow \langle M, R_C, R_I, i+1, S_C, v \cdot v \cdot S_I, \kappa(i+1) \rangle$$

$$\langle M, R_C, R_I, i, S_C, v_1 \cdot v_2 \cdot S_I, \mathtt{iswap} \rangle$$
$$\rightarrow \langle M, R_C, R_I, i+1, S_C, v_2 \cdot v_1 \cdot S_I, \kappa(i+1) \rangle$$

$$\langle M, R_C, R_I, i, S_C, v_1 \cdot \ldots \cdot v_{n-1} \cdot v_n \cdot S_I, \mathtt{itgetnth\ m} \rangle$$
$$\rightarrow \langle M, R_C, R_I, i+1, S_C, v_n \cdot v_1 \cdot \ldots \cdot v_{n-1} \cdot v_n \cdot S_I, \kappa(i+1) \rangle$$

where $m = n - 1$.

$$\langle M, R_C, R_I, i, S_C, v_1 \cdot \ldots \cdot v_{n-1} \cdot v_n \cdot S_I, \mathtt{itgetnthr\ r} \rangle$$
$$\rightarrow \langle M, R_C, R_I, i+1, S_C, v_n \cdot v_1 \cdot \ldots \cdot v_{n-1} \cdot v_n \cdot S_I, \kappa(i+1) \rangle$$

where $R_I(r) = n - 1$.

$$\langle M, R_C, R_I, i, S_C, v \cdot v_1 \cdot \ldots \cdot v_{n-1} \cdot v_n \cdot S_I, \mathtt{itsetnth\ m} \rangle$$
$$\rightarrow \langle M, R_C, R_I, i+1, S_C, v_1 \cdot \ldots \cdot v_{n-1} \cdot v \cdot S_I, \kappa(i+1) \rangle$$

where $m = n - 1$.

$$\langle M, R_C, R_I, i, S_C, v \cdot v_1 \cdot \ldots \cdot v_{n-1} \cdot v_n \cdot S_I, \mathtt{itsetnthr\ r} \rangle$$
$$\rightarrow \langle M, R_C, R_I, i+1, S_C, v \cdot v_1 \cdot \ldots \cdot v_{n-1} \cdot v \cdot S_I, \kappa(i+1) \rangle$$

where $R_I(\mathbf{r}) = n - 1$.

$$\langle M, R_C, R_I, i, S_C, v \cdot S_I, \mathtt{ibsetnth\ m} \rangle$$
$$\rightarrow \langle M, R_C, R_I, i+1, S_C, S_I', \kappa(i+1) \rangle$$

where $m = n-1$, $S_I = v_m \cdot \ldots \cdot v_n \cdot \ldots \cdot v_1$ and $S_I' = v_m \cdot \ldots \cdot v_{n+1} \cdot v \cdot v_{n-1} \cdot \ldots \cdot v_1$.

$$\langle M, R_C, R_I, i, S_C, S_I, \mathtt{ibgetnth\ m} \rangle$$
$$\rightarrow \langle M, R_C, R_I, i+1, S_C, v_n \cdot S_I, \kappa(i+1) \rangle$$

where $m = n - 1$ and $S_I = v_m \cdot \ldots \cdot v_n \cdot \ldots \cdot v_1$.

$$\langle M, R_C, R_I, i, S_C, S_I, \mathtt{ibgetnthr\ r} \rangle$$
$$\rightarrow \langle M, R_C, R_I, i+1, S_C, v_n \cdot S_I, \kappa(i+1) \rangle$$

where $r \in R_I$, $R_I(r) = n - 1$ and $S_I = v_m \cdot \ldots \cdot v_n \cdot \ldots \cdot v_1$ (if $|S_I| < n$ or $n < 0$, an error is signalled). Note there are the following variants of this instruction depending on which register is specified:

- r is in R_I;
- r is in R_C.

There is also a **cbgetnthr r** that operates on stack S_C.

$$\langle M, R_C, R_I, i, S_C, v \cdot S_I, \text{ibsetnthr r} \rangle$$
$$\rightarrow \langle M, R_C, R_I, i+1, S_C, S_I', \kappa(i+1) \rangle$$

where $r \in R_I$, $R_I(\hat{r}) = n-1$, $S_I = v_m \cdot \ldots \cdot v_n \cdot \ldots \cdot v_1$ and $S_I' = v_m \cdot \ldots \cdot v_{n+1} \cdot v \cdot v_{n-1} \cdot \ldots \cdot v_1 = [v \mapsto n]S_I$. The same comments apply with respect to register specification and to contents.

$$\langle M, R_C, R_I, i, S_C, S_I, \text{ibgetnthrr ro rd} \rangle \rightarrow \langle M, R_C, R_I', i+1, S_C, S_I, \kappa(i+1) \rangle$$

where r_o and $r_d \in R_I$, $n = R_I(r_o) + 1$, $[S_C(n)) \mapsto r_d]R_I = R_I'$.

$$\langle M, R_C, R_I, i, S_C, S_I, \text{ibsetnthrr ro rs} \rangle \rightarrow \langle M, R_C, R_I, i+1, S_C, S_I', \kappa(i+1) \rangle$$

where the operands are as for **ibgetnthrr** and $R_I(r_o) = n-1$, $S_I = v_m \cdot \ldots \cdot vn \cdot \ldots$ and $S_I' = v_m \cdot \ldots \cdot v_{n+1} \cdot R_I(r_s) \cdot v_{n-1} \cdot \ldots$.

$$\langle M, R_C, R_I, i, S_C, S_I, \text{itgetnthrr ro rd} \rangle \rightarrow \langle M, R_C, R_I, i+1, S_C, S_I, \kappa(i+1) \rangle$$

where $R_I(r_o) = n-1$, $S_I = v_1 \cdot \ldots \cdot v_n \cdot \ldots$ and $R_I' = [S_I(n) \mapsto r_d]R_I$.

$$\langle M, R_C, R_I, i, S_C, S_I, \text{itsetnthrr ro rs} \rangle \rightarrow \langle M, R_C, R_I, i+1, S_C, S_I, \kappa(i+1) \rangle$$

where $R_I(r_o) = n-1$, $S_I = v_1 \cdot \ldots \cdot v_n \cdot \ldots$ and $S_I' = v_1 \cdot \ldots \cdot v_{n-1} \cdot R_I(r_s) \cdot \ldots$.

$$\langle M, R_C, R_I, i, S_C, S_I, \text{pushr r si} \rangle$$
$$\rightarrow \langle M, R_C, R_I, i+1, S_C, R_I(\text{r}) \cdot S_I, \kappa(i+1) \rangle$$

$$\langle M, R_C, R_I, i, S_C, S_I, \text{ldc r c} \rangle$$
$$\rightarrow \langle M, R_C, [c \mapsto r]R_I, i+1, S_C, S_I, \kappa(i+1) \rangle$$

$$\langle M, R_C, R_I, i, S_C, S_I, \text{lda r a} \rangle$$
$$\rightarrow \langle M, R_C, [M(R_I(a)) \mapsto r]R_I, i+1, S_C, S_I, \kappa(i+1) \rangle$$

$$\langle M, R_C, R_I, i, S_C, S_I, \text{ldm r a} \rangle \rightarrow \langle M, R_C, [M(a) \mapsto r]R_I, i+1, S_C, S_I, \kappa(i+1) \rangle$$

$$\langle M, R_C, R_I, i, S_C, S_I, \text{sto r a} \rangle$$
$$\rightarrow \langle [R_I(r) \mapsto a]M, R_C, R_I, i+1, S_C, S_I, \kappa(i+1) \rangle$$

$$\langle M, R_C, R_I, i, S_C, S_I, \text{stor r a}\rangle$$
$$\rightarrow \langle [R_I(r) \mapsto R_I(a)]M, R_C, R_I, i+1, S_C, S_I, \kappa(i+1)\rangle$$

where r and a denote registers (here assumed to be in R_I).

$$\langle M, R_C, R_I, i, S_I, S_C, \text{incr r}\rangle$$
$$\rightarrow \langle M, R_C, [R_I(r)+1 \mapsto r]R_I, i, S_I, S_C, \kappa(i+1)\rangle$$

for $r \in R_I$, here (r can also be in R_C).

$$\langle M, R_C, R_I, i, S_I, S_C, \text{decr r}\rangle$$
$$\rightarrow \langle M, R_C, [R_I(r)-1 \mapsto r]R_I, i, S_I, S_C, \kappa(i+1)\rangle$$

$$\langle M, R_C, R_I, i, S_C, S_I, \text{setr s d}\rangle$$
$$\rightarrow \quad \langle M, R_C, [R_I(s) \mapsto d]R_I, i+1, S_C, S_I, \kappa(i+1)\rangle$$

$$\langle M, R_C, R_I, i, S_C, S_I, \text{goto } \ell\rangle \rightarrow \langle M, R_C, R_I, \ell, S_C, S_I, \kappa(\ell)\rangle$$

$$\langle M, R_C, R_I, i, S_C, S_I, \text{rgoto r}\rangle$$
$$\rightarrow \langle M, R_C, R_I, R_C(r), S_C, S_I, \kappa(R_C(r))\rangle$$

$$\langle M, R_C, R_I, i, S_C, \ell \cdot S_I, \text{sgoto si}\rangle \rightarrow \langle M, R_C, R_I, \ell, S_C, S_I, \kappa(\ell)\rangle$$

$$\langle M, R_C, R_I, i, \ell \cdot S_C, S_I, \text{sgoto sc}\rangle \rightarrow \langle M, R_C, R_I, \ell, S_C, S_I, \kappa(\ell)\rangle$$

$$\langle M, R_C, R_I, i, S_C, S_I, \text{if\_true r } \ell\rangle$$
$$\rightarrow \langle M, R_C, R_I, \ell, S_C, S_I, \kappa(\ell)\rangle$$

if $R_I(r)$ (or $R_C(r)$) contains the value representing *true*.

$$\langle M, R_C, R_I, i, S_C, S_I, \text{if\_true r } \ell\rangle$$
$$\rightarrow \langle M, R_C, R_I, i+1, S_C, S_I, \kappa(i+1)\rangle$$

if $R_I(r)$ (or $R_C(r)$) does not contain the value representing *true*.

$$\langle M, R_C, R_I, i, S_C, S_I, \text{if\_false r } \ell\rangle$$
$$\rightarrow \langle M, R_C, R_I, i+1, S_C, S_I, \kappa(i+1)\rangle$$

if $R_I(r)$ (or $R_C(r)$) contains the value representing *true*.

$$\langle M, R_C, R_I, i, S_C, S_I, \text{if\_false r } \ell\rangle$$
$$\rightarrow \langle M, R_C, R_I, \ell, S_C, S_I, \kappa(\ell)\rangle$$

if $R_I(r)$ (or $R_C(r)$) does not contain the value representing *true*.

$$\langle M, R_C, R_I, i, S_C, S, \text{go\_on r n } (\ell_1, \ldots, \ell_k)\rangle$$
$$\rightarrow \langle M, R_C, R_I, \ell_r, S_C, S_I, \kappa(\ell_r)\rangle$$

if $r \in R_C$, $R_C(r) \in \{\ell_1, \ldots, \ell_n\}$ and $R_C(r) = \ell_r$. If $n \neq k$, an error is signalled; the value of n is also be used to calculate the storage required for the instruction.

Otherwise:

$$\langle M, R_C, R_I, i, S_C, S, \text{go\_on } \mathbf{r} \ \mathbf{n} \ (\ell_1, \ldots, \ell_n) \rangle$$
$$\rightarrow \langle M, R_C, R_I, i+1, S_C, S_I, \kappa(i+1) \rangle$$

For the call instructions, the convention is adopted that the return address is computed by adding 1 to the current instruction pointer (i.e., it is assumed that `call` instructions have a length of 1). In an actual implementation, the instruction pointer will be incremented by some other value depending upon the length of the `call` instruction and the units in which this length is expressed (bytes, words, half words, etc.).

$$\langle M, R_C, R_I, i, S_C, S_I, \text{call } \ell \rangle \rightarrow \langle M, R_C, R_I, \ell, (i+1) \cdot S_C, S_I, \kappa(\ell) \rangle$$

$$\langle M, R_C, R_I, i, \ell.S_C, S_I, \text{calls } \mathbf{c} \rangle \rightarrow \langle M, R_C, R_I, \ell, (i+1) \cdot S_C, S_I, \kappa(\ell) \rangle$$

and:

$$\langle M, R_C, R_I, i, S_C, \ell.S_I, \text{calls } \mathbf{i} \rangle \rightarrow \langle M, R_C, R_I, \ell, (i+1) \cdot S_C, S_I, \kappa(\ell) \rangle$$

(here the operand to `calls` is the *name* of the stack on which the destination address is to be found).

$$\langle M, R_C, R_I, i, S_C, S_I, \text{callr } \mathbf{r} \rangle \rightarrow$$
$$\langle M, R_C, R_I, R_C(\mathbf{r}), (R_C(\mathbf{r})+1) \cdot S_C, S_I, \kappa(R_C(\mathbf{r})) \rangle$$

for $\mathbf{r} \in R_C$.

In the following, `hlt` and `err` denote control register names (indices) that are pre-defined. It is expected that these registers are not used for general computation.

$$\langle M, R_C, R_I, i, \ell \cdot S_C, S_I, \text{ret} \rangle \rightarrow \langle M, R_C, R_I, \ell, S_C, S_I, \kappa(\ell) \rangle$$

$$\langle M, R_C, R_I, i, S_C, S_I, \text{stop} \rangle$$
$$\rightarrow \langle M, [true \mapsto R_C(\text{hlt})]R_C, R_I, i+1, S_C, S_I, \kappa(i+1) \rangle$$

$$\langle M, R_C, R_I, i, S_C, S_I, \text{error } \mathbf{n} \rangle$$
$$\rightarrow \langle M, [\mathbf{n} \mapsto R_C(\text{err})]R_C, R_I, i+1, S_C, S_I, \kappa(i+1) \rangle$$

$$\langle M, R_C, R_I, i, S_C, S_I, \text{error } \mathbf{r} \rangle$$
$$\rightarrow \langle M, [R_I(r) \mapsto R_C(\text{err})]R_C, R_I, i+1, S_C, S_I, \kappa(i+1) \rangle$$

7.7 Translating ALEXVM into RTM

In this section, the translation between the ALEX two-stack virtual machine instructions and the instructions of the register machine are presented.

It is initially necessary to introduce some register conventions:

rg is a control register that *always* points to the start of the globals area. This register is initialised when program execution starts and should *never* be altered.

rp is a control register that points to the parameter area of the *current* routine.

rl is a control register that points to the local variables of the *current* routine.

The **rp** and **rl** registers must be saved before a routine call and restored immediately upon return.

It is assumed that the control stack can be used as scratch storage when calling a routine. The values to be assigned to the **rp** and **rl** in the called routines are stored there by the translation of the **frame** instruction.

Next, it is essential to observe that the ALEX VM operates entirely on its stacks while the RTM operates principally on registers. This causes problems because a register-allocation algorithm is required. For the purposes of the translation exercise, it implies that the translation must choose the registers into which the results of execution (mostly expression evaluation) are dumped. For the time being, it will be assumed that the translation scheme, denoted $\mathcal{T}$, does this. Register allocation is not a trivial topic (indeed, the problem of finding an *optimal* allocation is *NP*-complete).

First, there are some relatively simple instructions. ALEX VM instructions will appear in this font, while RTM instructions will appear in *this* font. The symbols r_{s_i} and r_d will be used to denote the source and destination registers for expressions.

It is necessary to make two observations about the translation:

1. All parameters are passed on the stack.
2. Registers are considered to hold nothing of importance during routine calls.

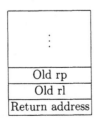

Fig. 7.2. *The c stack organisation.*

Fig. 7.3. *The i stack organisation.*

The organisation of the c stack is shown in Figure 7.2, while that of the i stack is shown in Figure 7.3. If other stacks were required, the parameters and locals would be distributed among them. The scheme depicted in the two figures can be applied to multiple control and data stacks, however. In both figures, the stacks grow downwards.

[e unop]:

$$\mathcal{T}(e) \rightarrow r_s$$
$$(\text{unop}) \; r_s \; r_d$$

[e2 e1 binop]:

$$\mathcal{T}(e2) \rightarrow r_{s_2}$$
$$\mathcal{T}(e2) \rightarrow r_{s_1}$$
$$(\text{binop}) \; r_{s_1} \; r_{s_2} \; r_d$$

[jmp l]:

$$\text{goto } l$$

[jeq l]:

$$\mathcal{T}(e) \rightarrow r_s$$
$$\text{if\_true } r_s \; l$$

[jne l]:

$$\mathcal{T}(e) \rightarrow r_s$$
$$\text{if\_false } r_s \; l$$

In the following instructions, the operand to the dual-stack instruction is specified by an upper-case letter "N". In addition, the destination register (typically, rv) is specified as an extra (parenthesised) operand. This is intended to make the register-machine code clearer.

[getlocal N (rv)]:

$$\text{add r1 N r0}$$
$$\text{ibgetnthrr r0 rv}$$

[setlocal N (rv)]:

$$\text{add r1 N r0}$$
$$\text{ibsetnthrr r0 rv}$$

[getparam N (rv)]:

```
add rp N r0
ibgetnthrr r0 rv
```

[getglob N (rv)]:

```
add rg N ra
lda rv ra
```

[setglob N (rv)]:

```
add rg N ra
stor ra rv
```

[frame L P]:

```
cpush rp
cpush rl
cpushc L
cpushc P
```

[call $P]:

```
cpop r0 % r0 = P
sub itop r0 rp
cpop r0 % r0 = L
add rp r0 rl
call $P
```

[ret]:

```
cpop r0 % r0 := return address
cpop rl
cpop rp
setr rp itop % return the data frame pointer
cpush r0 % replace return address on c stack
ret
```

[retval]:

```
ipop r1 % r1 := return value
cpop r0 % r0 := return address
cpop rl
cpop rp
setr rp itop % return the data frame pointer
cpush r0 % replace return address on c stack
ipush r1 % replace return value on i stack
ret
```

The switch instruction in the ALEX instruction set is easily translated. It does, though, involve a little transformation of the ALEX code. Consider the ALEX stack machine code:

```
          -- Code for Exp
          switch
          jmp $L1
          ...
          jmp $Ln
$L1:  -- Code for case 1
          jmp $end
$Ln:  -- Code for case n
          jmp $end
$end:  ...
```

For the register-based virtual machine, this must be translated into:

```
          -- Code for exp, leaving result in register rv
          go_on rv n ($L1, ..., $Ln)
$L1:     -- Code for case 1
          jmp $end
          ...
$Ln:     -- Code for case n
$end:
```

7.8 Example Code

In this section, the ALEX *add2* virtual machine code is again presented, as is the code for a call to *add2(1,2)*. The virtual machine code presented below is that obtained by translating the instruction sequence shown in Figure 4.9 in Section 4.2.9 (where the two-stack virtual machine for ALEX was first defined).

The result of the translation is shown in Figure 7.4. In the figure, the corresponding stack-based instructions (using the two-stack virtual machine for ALEX) are shown as comments. The following register assignments are assumed: rc is c0, rp is c1 and rl is c2.

The code for calling *add2* is shown in Figure 7.5.

As can be seen from the figures, a reasonable translation between the stack and register machines is obtained. For comparison, the same pieces of code have been re-written using what is hoped to be a more idiomatic translation for the register machine; these alternative pieces of code are shown and discussed in the next section.

7.9 Correctness of the Translation

The translation given in Section 7.7 seems to give the right answers. It is necessary to be a little more careful and justify the translation of each two-stack instruction into register machine instructions. The justification will be as rigorous as possible and will amount to an informal proof.

```
%$add2:
ldc r15 0
% setlocal 0 % z := 0
add r1 0 r0
ibsetnthrr r0 r15
% getparam 1
add rp 1 r0
ibgetnthrr r0 r16
% getparam 0
add rp 0 r0
ibgetnthrr r0 r17
% add -- x + y
add r17 r16 r18
% setlocal 0 % z := x + y
add r1 0 r0
ibsetnthrr r0 r18
% getlocal 0 % get z for return
add r1 0 r0
ibgetnthrr r0 r15
ipush r15
% reti
ipop r15       % r1 := return value
cpop r16       % r0 := return address
cpop c2
cpop c1
setr c1 itop   % return the data frame pointer
cpop c0
cpush r16      % replace return address on c stack
ipush r15      % replace return value on i stack
ret
```

Fig. 7.4. *Stack VM code for add2 translated to RTM code.*

The correctness criterion is relatively weak. It is required only that:

> *the state before the execution of a two-stack instruction corresponds to the register machine state before the execution of the instructions comprising the translation; the state of the two-stack machine after the execution of the instruction corresponds to the state of the register machine after the execution of the translation.*

Because this condition is relatively weak, it is clear that is permits redundant instructions to appear within the translation of a two-stack instruction. Such code would not be optimal, even though it might be correct according to the condition stated above. Translations consisting of too many instructions such as the following should be avoided:

```
ldc  r0 1
setr r0 r1
```

```
% frame 1 2
cpush c0
cpush c1
cpush c2
cpushc 1   % L
cpushc 2   % P
% pushc 2
ipushc 2
% pushc 1
ipushc 1
% call $add2
setr itop rc0
cpop r0          % r0 = P
sub  itop r0 c1
cpop r0          % r0 = L
add  c1 r0 c2
call $add2
```

Fig. 7.5. *Stack VM code for calling add2 translated to RTM code.*

```
incr r1
add  r0 r1 r2
ldc  r1 1
incr r1
setr r1 r0
add  r2 r0 r0
```

Here, the first three instructions implement the same result as would `ldc r1 2`, while the instructions between the two `add` instructions could be replaced by:

```
ldc  r0 2
```

Equally, translations consisting of sequences of instructions adding up to a *no-op* should also be avoided, for example:

```
ldc  r0 0
setr r0 r0
setr r0 r0
setr r0 r0
setr r0 r0
```

It is desirable for the translation not to contain redundant sequences such as these.

In order to avoid redundant instructions, it is necessary to strengthen the condition to include the injection that:

The translation of each two-stack instruction should consist of the least number of register machine instructions.

It would be highly desirable to include a clause to the effect that the translation consists of an *optimal* selection of register-machine instructions. For a variety of reasons (including that the register machine has not been implemented so there is no information on the performance of its instructions and that there are different organisations for the translation, so the one given here might be sub-optimal) optimality cannot be imposed here. Nevertheless, the strengthened condition can be used to justify the translation.

The translation is, in essence, a mapping from the two-stack to the register machine; the register machine simulates, or emulates, the two-stack machine. To do this, some conventions were imposed that comprise part of the mapping.

It is necessary to make all the conventions explicit before moving one. To do this, the state of the two-stack machine can be compared with that of the register machine. The two-stack state is described (adding subscripts as necessary to identify components) by:

$$\langle g, d, c, p, \sigma_c, \sigma_d, i_2, \kappa_2(i) \rangle$$

The state of the register machine is described (adding subscripts as necessary to identify components) by:

$$\langle M, R_C, R_I, i_r, S_C, S_I, \kappa_r(i) \rangle$$

Immediately, the following can be noted:

$g \mapsto M$ The two-stack machine globals are implemented by the register-machine's general (non-stack or flat) store.

$\sigma_c \mapsto S_C$ The control stack of the two-stack machine is implemented by the control stack in the register machine.

$\sigma_i \mapsto S_I$ The data stack of the two-stack machine is implemented by the integer stack of the register machine (ALEX only supports integer variables and vectors of integers, remember). If ALEX supported more types, the mapping would be between σ_i and a collection of register-machine data stacks.

There are additional correspondences. These are between two-stack machine components and register-machine registers. In particular:

$d \mapsto \text{r1}$ The data frame pointer of the two-stack machine corresponds to the r1 register (one of the register machine's control registers).

$p \mapsto \text{rp}$ The parameter start pointer of the two-stack machine corresponds to the rp register (one of the register machine's control registers).

The following observations are required:

- The instruction pointers correspond in only an inexact sense. Clearly, the register machine translation consists of more instructions than the two-stack code. What is required is only that the value of i_2 be equivalent to the value of i_r when the translation of each instruction starts. At the end of the instruction sequence translating a two-stack instruction, the value of i_2 points to the next instruction; at the same point in the translation, i_r must point to the instruction immediately after the last instruction of the translation.

- The instructions denoted by κ_2 and κ_r are similar.
- The c register in the two-stack machine points to the current control frame. The translation does not require such a register. (Actually, the c register's use could be reduced if the two-stack instructions were defined in a slightly different fashion.)

Finally, it is necessary to relate the two-stack machine's data stack and the i-registers of the register machine. In general, the top few locations of σ_d will be represented by i registers. The details will be explained below.

With these conventions in mind, it is now possible to move on to the justification of each translation. The two-stack instructions will be considered in the same order in which they were presented (in Section 7.7). Naturally, the same notational conventions will be employed. The translation of each two-stack instruction is repeated so that the reader does not have to flip back and forth between this section and Section 7.7. It should be remembered that $\mathcal{T}(x)$ is the translation of an expression into register-machine code.

The translation of literal constants needs to be defined so that the translation can be completed.

[pushc n] (rv):

$$\text{ldc } rv\ n$$

It is assumed that there is a convention for representing boolean values. Below, the values of this type will be represented, as usual, by *false* and *true*.

First, the translation of instructions evaluating expressions is considered. There are two cases: unary and binary operations (function calls are considered below).

For these two cases, it is necessary to consider the register-allocation operation implemented by the compiler. This is required because it is essential to keep track of the value computed by the register-machine instructions (the two-stack machine's instructions always place the result on the top of the stack). This forms part of the mapping between the top few stack elements and the register machine's registers.

For present purposes, the registers used to hold operands and results will be restricted to the I registers r_0, r_1 and r_2.

[e unop]:

$$\mathcal{T}(\text{e}) \to r_s$$
$$(\text{unop}) \ r_s \ r_d$$

here, the symbol **unop** denotes the unary operation to be performed.

In the two-stack machine, the top element of the stack is removed, operated upon and replaced. In the register machine, the value in register r_s is operated upon, the result being stored in register r_d. For the register machine, it is not necessary that $r_s = r_d$.

[e2 e1 binop]:

$$\mathcal{T}(e2) \rightarrow r_{s_2}$$
$$\mathcal{T}(e1) \rightarrow r_{s_1}$$
$$(\texttt{binop})\ r_{s_1}\ r_{s_2}\ r_d$$

In the two-stack machine, the top two elements of the stack are popped and an operation is performed upon them; the result is pushed onto the stack. In the register machine, the first operand is placed in register r_{s_1}, the second in r_{s_2}; the result is stored in register r_d. It is not necessary that either $r_{s_1} = r_d$ or $r_{s_2} = r_d$.

[jmp l]:

$$\texttt{goto}\ l$$

The translation is immediate given the definition of the two instructions.

[jeq l]:

$$\mathcal{T}(e) \rightarrow r_s$$
$$\texttt{if\_true}\ r_s\ l$$

The two-stack instruction expects the value determining whether the jump is performed to be on the data stack, σ_d. The register machine instruction expects the value to be in a register.

Assuming register $R_I(r_s)$ in the register machine holds the value *true*, the jump will be taken; otherwise, the instruction pointer is incremented. This corresponds directly to the two-stack machine's instruction: if the top value on the stack is *true*, the jump is performed, otherwise not.

[jne l]:

$$\mathcal{T}(e) \rightarrow r_s$$
$$\texttt{if\_false}\ r_s\ l$$

The justification for this translation is similar to that for jeq. The value being tested is, in this case, *false*: that is the only difference.

[getlocal n (rv)]:

$$\texttt{add rl n r0}$$
$$\texttt{ibgetnthrr r0 rv}$$

The offset to the local variable is n. The code works by adding the offset to the pointer to the local variables on the i stack. The stack is indexed and the result stored in register r_v (this register should not contain useful data when the sequence starts).

The two-stack transition is:

$$\langle g, d, c, p, \sigma_c, \sigma_d, i, \texttt{getlocal}\ n \rangle \rightarrow \langle g, d, c, p, \sigma_c, v \cdot \sigma_d, i + 1, \kappa(i+1) \rangle$$

where $\sigma_d(d + n)$.

The important register-machine transition is:

$$\langle M, R_C, R_I, i, S_C, S_I, \text{ibgetnthrr ro rd} \rangle \rightarrow \langle M, R_C, R'_I, i{+}1, S_C, S_I, \kappa(i{+}1) \rangle$$

where r_o and $r_d \in R_I$, $n = R_I(r_o) + 1$, $[S_C(n)) \mapsto r_d]R_I = R'_I$. The instruction indexes stack S_I and stores the datum in register r_d. (Remember that indexing, for the instruction, is zero-based.)

In the two-stack machine, $v = \sigma_d(d + n)$. The two-stack register d corresponds to the register-machine register r_l, so $d = r_l$. The value of $r_d = S_I(r_l + n) = \sigma_d(d + n)$.

[setlocal n (rv)]:

```
add rl n r0
ibsetnthrr r0 rv
```

The two-stack transition is:

$$\langle g, d, c, p, \sigma_c, v \cdot \sigma_d, i, \text{setlocal } n \rangle \rightarrow \langle g, d, c, p, \sigma_c, \sigma'_d, i + 1, \kappa(i + 1) \rangle$$

where $\sigma'_d = [v \mapsto (d + n)]\sigma_d$.

The more important register-machine transition is:

$$\langle M, R_C, R_I, i, S_C, S_I, \text{ibsetnthrr ro rs} \rangle \rightarrow \langle M, R_C, R_I, i{+}1, S_C, S'_I, \kappa(i{+}1) \rangle$$

where the operands are as for ibgetnthrr and $R_I(r_o) = n - 1$, $S_I = v_m \cdot \ldots \cdot$ $vn \cdot \ldots$ and $S'_I = v_m \cdot \ldots \cdot v_{n+1} \cdot R_I(r_s) \cdot v_{n-1} \cdot \ldots$. (Recall that indexing, for the instruction, is zero-based.)

Again, $r_l = d$, so the location at which the value is to be stored is $r_l + n = r_o$. The result is $\sigma'_d(d + n) = S'_I(r_l + n) = v$.

[getparam n (rv)]:

```
add rp n r0
ibgetnthrr r0 rv
```

The two-stack transition is:

$$\langle g, c, d, p, \sigma_c, \sigma_c, i, \text{getparam } n \rangle \rightarrow \langle g, d, c, p, \sigma_c, v \cdot \sigma_d, i + 1, \kappa(i + 1) \rangle$$

where $v = \sigma_d(p + n)$.

Again, the important register machine transition is:

$$\langle M, R_C, R_I, i, S_C, S_I, \text{ibsetnthrr ro rs} \rangle \rightarrow \langle M, R_C, R_I, i{+}1, S_C, S'_I, \kappa(i{+}1) \rangle$$

where the operands are as for ibgetnthrr and $R_I(r_o) = n - 1$, $S_I = v_m \cdot$ $\ldots \cdot vn \cdot \ldots$ and $S'_I = v_m \cdot \ldots \cdot v_{n+1} \cdot R_I(r_s) \cdot v_{n-1} \cdot \ldots$. (Again, indexing is zero-based.)

The offset of the start of the parameter area on S_I is stored in r_p. Therefore, the offset of the required parameter is given by $r_p + n$. Register r_p corresponds to the two-stack machine's p register, so $r_p + n = p + n$ and $\sigma_d(p + n) = S_I(r_p + n)$.

The next pair of translations deal with global variables. In the two-stack machine, there is a register, g, that contains the storage area for globals; in the register machine, it is the M register. As noted above, the two are identified.

[getglob n (rv)]:

$$\texttt{add rg ra}$$
$$\texttt{lda rv ra}$$

The two-stack transition is:

$$\langle g, d, c, p, \sigma_c, \sigma_d, i, \texttt{getglob } n \rangle \rightarrow \langle g, d, c, p, \sigma_c, g(n) \cdot \sigma_d, i + 1, \kappa(i+1) \rangle$$

The important register-machine transition is that for lda.

$$\langle M, R_C, R_I, i, S_C, S_I, \texttt{lda r a} \rangle$$
$$\rightarrow \langle M, R_C, [M(R_I(a)) \mapsto r]R_I, i + 1, S_C, S_I, \kappa(i+1) \rangle$$

In the two-stack machine, $v = g(n)$, while it is $M(r_a)$ in the register-machine code. Since $g = M$, $g(n) = M(r_a) = v$. Assuming the top of the stack is represented by register r_v, then $v \cdot \sigma_d$ corresponds to r_v.

[setglob N (rv)]

$$\texttt{add rg N ra}$$
$$\texttt{stor ra rv}$$

The two-stack transition is:

$$\langle g, d, c, p, \sigma_c, v \cdot \sigma_d, i, \texttt{setglob } n \rangle \rightarrow \langle [v \mapsto n]g, d, c, p, \sigma_c, \sigma_d, i + 1, \kappa(i+1) \rangle$$

The significant register-machine transition is that for stor.

$$\langle M, R_C, R_I, i, S_C, S_I, \texttt{stor r a} \rangle$$
$$\rightarrow \langle [R_I(r) \mapsto R_I(a)]M, R_C, R_I, i + 1, S_C, S_I, \kappa(i+1) \rangle$$

where r and a denote registers (here assumed to be in R_I).

The effect of this instruction is $g'(n) = v = [v \mapsto n]g$ in the two-stack machine. In the register machine, it is $M' = [R_I(r_r) \mapsto R_I(r_a)]M$. Since $g = M$ and $R_I(r_a) = n$, $[v \mapsto n]g = [R_I(r_r) \mapsto R_I(r_a)]M$.

The following instructions deal with routine call and return. Here, matters become somewhat more complex (as is to be expected). For these instructions, it is better to rely upon diagrams since the register-machine's calling convention involves a permutation of the elements stored in the base of the new stack frame.

[frame L P]:

$$\texttt{cpush rp}$$
$$\texttt{cpush rl}$$
$$\texttt{cpushc L}$$
$$\texttt{cpushc P}$$

The effect of the **frame** instruction is just to alter the σ_c stack in the two-stack machine. In the register machine, it alters the state of the stack S_C. In the two-stack machine, the effect of executing **frame** is:

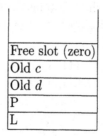

("Old" denotes values for the caller—this is the convention adopted in this book.) The register machine's **call** instruction pushes the return address onto the S_C stack when executed. There is no need to allocate a slot for it on the stack when executing the translated **frame** code. The register machine's control stack is therefore:

Now, $r_l = d$. There is no need, as noted above to store the equivalent of the c register. However, the pointer to the parameter area in the caller's context must be saved.

[call $P]:

```
cpop r0 % r0 = P
sub itop r0 rp
cpop r0 % r0 = L
add rp r0 rl
call $P
```

After executing its **call** instruction, the two-stack machine's control stack is now:

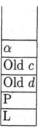

Here, α denotes the return address.

When the register machine's call instruction terminates, its control stack has the following form:

Here, α_r is the register machine's return address. Note that α and α_r denote the return address for the two-stack routine and its translation into register-machine code, respectively.

Apart from the different stack organisation, the register machine's call instruction differs by setting the r_l and r_p registers: $r_p = itop - L$ and $r_l = r_p + L$.

[ret]:

```
cpop r0 % r0 := return address
cpop rl
cpop rp
setr rp itop % return the data frame pointer
cpush r0 % replace return address on c stack
ret
```

This instruction sequence just re-arranges the control stack by popping off the information placed there by the translations of the two-stack machine's frame and call instructions. As long as the data is popped in the reverse order to that in which it was pushed, and as long as the correct registers are reset, all is well.

The data frame pointer (previous top of stack S_I) is reset to point to the old start-of-parameter pointer. The return address must be pushed back onto the control stack so that the register machine's ret instruction will work properly.

[retval]:

```
ipop rl % rl := return value
cpop r0 % r0 := return address
cpop rl
cpop rp
setr rp itop % return the data frame pointer
cpush r0 % replace return address on c stack
ipush rl % replace return value on i stack
ret
```

When this instruction is executed, the value to be returned is on the top of the S_I (data) stack. The code follows the ret instruction just presented. The sole difference is that the value to be returned is popped from the stack

S_I and must be stored in a register temporarily until the data frame of the routine that is returning has been removed from the S_I stack; then the value to be returned is pushed onto the S_I stack.

[switch]:

```
      -- Code for Exp
      switch
      jmp $L1
      ...
      jmp $Ln
$L1:  -- Code for case 1
      jmp $end
$Ln:  -- Code for case n
      jmp $end
$end: ...
```

For the register-based virtual machine, this must be translated into:

```
      -- Code for exp, leaving result in register rv
      go_on rv n ($L1, ..., $Ln)
$L1:  -- Code for case 1
      jmp $end
      ...
$Ln:  -- Code for case n
```

The correspondence between these two code fragments is so close that no comment is deemed necessary.

7.10 More Natural Compilation

Given the code produced by a direct translation of the ALEX stack-based virtual machine instructions, it is interesting to ask what code produced by a compiler that directly generated for the RTM would look like. In this section, this is addressed.

The production of a compiler for the RTM would have taken too much time. Instead, the code is produced in a way that seems natural.

First, it is necessary to define the conventions for the code. It was decided to pass arguments in the integer stack. Local variables would be assigned to registers r0 to r15. If a routine required more than sixteen local variables (a relatively uncommon case), the least used locals would be stored on the i stack and loaded into registers when needed, perhaps causing more heavily used locals to be spilled onto the stack. A compiler performing a reasonable level of optimisation could implement this strategy.

Registers r15 to r31 are to be used as working registers.

The decision to pass parameters on the stack has the implication that the number of parameters to a routine is potentially unlimited. Also, given that ALEX uses a call-by-value evaluation régime, updates to parameters are not possible. Furthermore, value parameters tend to be accessed rather less frequently than local variables.

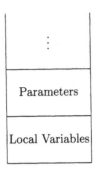

Fig. 7.6. *Integer stack organisation.*

Inside a called routine, the integer stack is organised as follows. First, the parameters are stored. Then come those local variables that must be stored on the stack. A pointer to the start of the parameters is maintained in a register, as is a pointer to the start of the local variables. The parameter pointer is, by convention, stored in control register c0; the pointer to the locals is stored in control register c1. This scheme is shown in Figure 7.6 (as is usual in this book, the stack grows downwards).

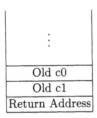

Fig. 7.7. *Control stack organisation.*

The control stack organisation exploits the properties of the `call` instruction: it pushes the return address onto the control stack. The values of the parameter pointer (c0) and the locals pointer (c1) are stored in the control stack below the return address. This is shown in Figure 7.7.

It might be better if the return address were under the other two values. This could be arranged if routines adjusted the stack when called. This protocol is not adopted here because, to some, it is a little counter-intuitive.

Local variables are allocated to integer registers, as noted above. They are allocated in registers r0 to r15. In the *add2* routine, there is only one local, *z*, so it is stored in register r0. A decent compiler could exploit this and use registers r1 to r31 as workspace. Here, a fairly simple complier is assumed, so the workspace is confined to registers r16 to r31.

```
% r0 = z, fp + 0 = y, fp + 1 = x
% Set the number of locals.
$add2: ldc c1 0
% z := 0
ldc r0 0
ibgetnthr c0
ipop r16        % r16 := y
setr c0 c2
incr c2
ibgetnthr c2
ipop r17        % r17 := x
add r17 r16 r0 % z := x + y
% now set the return-value register
setr r0 c31
% return sequence
cpop c16        % c16 := return address
cpop c1         % c1  := old locals ptr
cpop c0         % c0  := old params ptr
setr c0 itop
ret             % return to caller
```

Fig. 7.8. *RTM code for add2's body*

ALEX only allows one value to be returned from a function. This value could be returned on the integer stack. However, this compiler returns it in a register. This is, in general, a good way to return a value because returned values are very often immediately assigned to variables. Even when they are immediately used in an expression, moving the returned value from one register to another is, in general, faster than operating on the stack. Register c31 is allocated to the returned value. With the exception of registers c0 and c2, the other control registers are free for use.

The code for the body of *add2* is shown in Figure 7.8. Comments follow the convention adopted in this book.

The code to perform the call *add2(1,2)* is shown in Figure 7.9.

It is interesting to see what a more realistic piece of code would look like. The source code is:

```
a := 1;
b := 2;
zz := 0;
zz := add2(a,b);

% a = r0, b = r1, zz = r2
```

```
% Code for add2(1,2)
cpush c0
cpush c1
% push arguments
ipushc 1
ipushc 2
call $add2
```

Fig. 7.9. *RTM code for the call add2(1,2).*

```
% setup
ldc r0 1 % a := 1
ldc r1 2 % b := 2
ldc r2 0 % zz := 0
% Save local variables
setr lp c15
ipush r0 % save r0
ibsetnthr c15
ipush r1 % save b
incr c15
ibsetnthr c15
ipush r2 % save zz
incr c15
ibsetnthr c15
% save state
cpush c0
cpush c1
% call add2
call $add2
% on return, c31 = addr2's z
% restore locals
setr lp c15
ibgetnthr c15
ipop r2
incr c15
ibgetnthr c15
ipop r1
incr c15
ibgetnthr c15
ipop r0
% locals restored
setr c31 r2
% returned value overwrites z
```

This code is, again, sub-optimal. Note how the variable **zz** in the outer context is set, saved and restored, only to be the target of an assignment. This sequence could be optimised out.

The above code fragments employ a single calling convention for all functions. This is not what a decent compiler would do. The fragments are the way they are just to show how a simple compilation scheme would produce code for the register machine. As any assembly programmer knows, each routine's calling sequence should be handled on its own merits—optimising compilers can do this, as well.

The point of the code sequences is to provide an alternative view of what register code can look like. The amount of stack consumed by this code is less than that consumed by a simple translation from the stack machine's instructions.

7.11 Extensions

The example register machine can be extended in any way one wants. In particular, it can be extended to support objects and (pseudo-)concurrent processing in ways analogous to those presented in Chapter 5. As Parrot shows, it is also possible to introduce instructions to invoke complete virtual machines.

8

Implementation Techniques

The rationale for virtual machines is that they are processors supporting one or more programming languages in a hardware-independent fashion. What makes virtual machines different is that they are software processors. The implementation of such processors is an important topic in its own right. Although virtual machines can be used as the context within which to discuss important theoretical issues such as the mapping between language semantics and implementation, the adequacy of instruction sets and compiler correctness, to mention but three, it should not be forgotten that they are, after all, a mechanism for *implementing* a programming language (or an application or an operating system) on a target platform. This section is concerned with a discussion of some of the more common approaches to implementation. Each of the implementation techniques discussed below requires a translater or compiler that does more or less work (indeed, some, such as compilers for register machines, do a considerable amount of work). What will be of concern here is only the *runtime system* that is used to execute the virtual machine instructions generated by the translater or compiler.

The implementation techinques discussed here have, with one exception, no generally accepted names. The names given to them below are, therefore, purely for the purposes of this book. The approaches are:

- Direct implementation;
- Translation;
- Threaded code.

As will be seen, there are many variations on these themes. In particular, the *translation* approach can take many different forms.

This chapter is divided into two main sections. The first deals with stack-based machines while the second is concerned with virtual machines based on the register-transfer model. The stack-based approach is considered first because there has been more work on it. As a consequence, many of the techniques have already been tried for stack machines and remain to be attempted in the other model.

8.1 Stack-Based Machines

```
while not halt loop
   instr := code[ip];
   opcd := opcode(instr);
   case opcd of
      ....
      when ADD: ...
      ....
      when LAND: ...
      ....
      when HALT: halt := true;
      ....
      default: ...
         ....
         halt := true;
      ....
   endcase;
endloop;
```

Fig. 8.1. *A typical virtual machine main loop.*

8.1.1 Direct Implementation

The virtual instructions for ALEX were specified as small pieces of Algol-like code associated with an opcode. In a direct implementation, these code pieces are collected into a **switch** or **case** statement. The opcode is used as the label into the case statement. The case statement as a whole is executed inside a loop. This loop usually terminates when a flag is set by the code that is being executed (often this is implemented as a **term** or **stop** instruction).

Figure 8.1 is a schematic example of this approach. The loop shown in this figure has a structure that is very often found in virtual machine main loops. In the code in the figure, the instruction is first fetched from the code vector. Then, the opcode is extracted using the function (macro) **opcode**. The opcode is expected to be a small integral value that is used by the following **case** command, which has one branch per opcode. The figure shows three cases: that for addition (ADD), that for logical "and" (LAND) and the instruction that halts the virtual machine (HALT). The actions taken in the first two cases are not shown—generally, they would pop the operands from the stack, perform the operation, push the result back on the stack and increment the instruction pointer by the appropriate amount. The **default** case is outlined, as well; this is the case that would be selected if an unknown opcode is encountered—as shown in the figure, the loop enclosing the code is made to halt (in addition, other actions, for example, dumping the stack) might occur.

For direct implementation, the compiler or translator converts source code into a sequence of instructions whose opcodes are numerical values that cause the **case** statement to branch to the piece of code that implements that instruction.

The direct implementation approach is employed by BCPL, Pascal and non-JIT Java systems. It is also the approach at the kernel of the Smalltalk-80 system. It is a general approach and involves the implementation of the entire virtual machine as a separate program. In many ways, it is the standard approach.

The advantages of this approach are its simplicity and the fact that the entire virtual machine (usually a relatively simple program) are under the implementor's direct control. On cached architectures, care must be taken to avoid cache reloads if the control loop is very large. This approach does, however, lead to relatively low levels of runtime performance, as witnessed by the attempts to optimise Java programs.

8.1.2 Translation

By translation is meant the translation of the code generated by the virtual machine to some other format. This is really a family of approaches, as will be seen.

Translation to another language

The simplest translation mechanism is as follows. The source language is translated not into bytecodes or virtual machine instructions but into another programming language (the *target* language), for example C. The virtual machine's primitives are implemented as either macros or procedure calls and the target language's control structures are used to implement the control structures of the source language.

This approach requires first the translation of the source language to the target language, thus expanding macros or generating calls to the procedures implementing the virtual machine's instructions. It then requires the compilation of the target language program that is thus generated. Finally, it requires linking the generated program with runtime libraries as appropriate. The runtime libraries, in essence, implement a simulation of those parts of the virtual machine other than the instruction set. The resulting program can also be somewhat large and it can be very hard to ensure that a simple translation performs well on cached and pipelined architectures.

The translation of the source for the *add2* function (repleated in Figure 8.2) is shown in Figure 8.3. The source language is ALEX and the target is C. In the example, the instructions of the original ALEX virtual machine are implemented as C macros and expanded when the C program is compiled. The original instructions are shown as comments in the C code. The example also shows how C's control structures are used to implement those in ALEX.

```
let fun add2 (x,y) =
  let var z = 0
  in
    z := x + y;
    return(z)
  end
```

Fig. 8.2. *The (very) simple ALEX function (again).*

```
/* $add2:  */
/* pushc 0 */
sp    := sp + 1;
s[sp] := 0;
/* setlocal 0 % z := 0 */
s[fp + H + 0] := s[sp];
sp := sp - 1;
/* getparam 1 % get y */
sp    := sp + 1;
temp1 := s[fp + 3];
s[sp] := s[fp + H + temp1 + 1];
/* getparam 0 % get x  */
sp    := sp + 1;
temp1 := s[fp + 3];
s[sp] := s[fp + H + temp1 + 0];
/* add                  */
s[sp - 1] := s[sp] + s[sp-1];
sp := sp - 1;
/* setlocal 0 % z := x + y */
s[fp + H + 0] := s[sp];
sp := sp - 1;
/* getlocal 0 */
sp := sp + 1;
s[sp] := s[fp + H + 0];
/* reti = ret */
s[fp + 2] := s [sp]; % overwrite num params
sp := fp;
fp := s[sp + 1];
swap; /* call swap as a routine or macro */
ip := s[sp + 1];
```

Fig. 8.3. *ALEX stack VM code for add2 translated into C.*

Luckily, ALEX and C have control structures that are quite close, so there is no problem with the translation in this case.

```
/* size 1 2 */
if (H + 1 + 2 + sp) >= SL then error fi
sp := sp + H
s[sp] := 1
s[sp - 1] := 2
s[sp - 2] := fp
sp := sp + 1
/* pushc 2   */
sp    := sp + 1
s[sp] := 2
/* pushc 1   */
sp    := sp + 1
s[sp] := 1
/* frame 1 2 */
fp := sp - (1 + H + 2 + 1)
/* call $add2 */
s[fp] := 'size(call ep)' + ip
ip    := ep
/* return point: */
```

Fig. 8.4. *C code calling add2(1,2).*

The code that would be generated for a call to *add2* is shown in Figure 8.4 where the return address calculation contains a quoted subexpression. In an implementation, this would be replaced by a literal that the compiler looks up in an internal table.

Assembly language can be used as the source language for the instruction set. This was the approach adopted for the FPM functional programming system [7]. The instructions of the virtual machine were implemented as macros in VAX assembly language, expanded and assembled, then linked with a library to form an executable.

An advantage of this approach is that it can exploit any optimisations performed by the target language translator, in particular non-local optimisations. It also has the advantage that a language can be implemented reasonably quickly. One major disadvantage is that the approach requires a separate compilation and linkage process that does not relate in any way to the source language. Thus, it is possible for target language and linker error messages to be generated by an incorrect source-to-target translation or mistakes at the linkage step. Errors not relating directly to the source language can be most annoying, requiring the programmer to have knowledge of the target *as well as* the source language.

A second disadvantage of this approach is that it is not well suited to source languages whose semantics are distant from the target. In such cases, a greater amount of support from the libraries is required. However, it can be seen that there will be cases in which simple translation becomes extremely difficult or even impossible, for example when a highly concurrent language is mapped onto a sequential one (implementing context switching is a case in point); there might also be severe difficulties when using the approach to implement hybrid logic languages (which require suspension of functions when not all arguments have been evaluated).

A third disadvantage comes from the fact that the intermediate representation (the target-language code) is seldom an optimised representation. Thus, the target-language program can contain unwanted data movements and unwanted transfers of control. This can happen, for example, at the boundaries between the macros that implement virtual machine instructions.

Translation to another VM

This is an approach that has been suggested for the Parrot virtual machine for Perl. It is a generalisation of the concept of translating one intermediate representation to another within a compiler.

The virtual machine that actually executes is one whose instructions are simple and fast or are, in other ways, more powerful. The source program is first translated into its own virtual machine code. The output of this stage is then translated to the form required by the target VM. The translation process is the same as code generation in a conventional system. A translation from JVM bytecodes to Parrot instructions is an example of this process. As can be seen from a comparison of the JVM instruction set and the corresponding Perl instructions, operations such as register allocation must be performed; also data movement instructions are inserted to do things like register spilling. An example of such a translation is given in outline for the ALEX and RTM virtual machines (see Section 7.7).

The translation approach has the disadvantage that the compilation process is often more complicated. The counter-argument is that it can be separated into independent stages that run only when required. It also has the advantage that more global optimisations can be performed on the intermediate representation (JVM code in the case of JVM to Parrot translation). This approach also affords opportunities for dynamic compilation and other JIT techniques. The combination of a direct translation interpreter and a lower-level one is also possible and one that can be somewhat appealing in some cases (e.g., those in which performance and high-levels of portability are both required—native code compilation being a technique that opposes portability).

Using a JIT implementation

This is a hybrid solution employed by many of the more recent Java systems.

The usual way to implement a Just In Time (*JIT*) implementation is to compile a program unit when it is first referenced or called; the compilation process translates the program unit into native code. The input code (either source code or, better, virtual machine instructions) is compiled into a buffer that is allocated in the heap. When the unit is later referenced, the native-code representation in the buffer is executed.

Although JIT code is an improvement over many other approaches, it still suffers from a number of problems. One problem is that it involves the compilation of program components of a standard kind: for example, in Java the unit of JIT compilation can be a method or an entire class, while in a procedural language the natural unit is an entire routine. The approach also imposes the overhead of compiling all program units when they are referenced; it does not distinguish between units that are frequently referenced and those that are seldom referenced. Thus, the overhead imposed by the compilation mechanism is always incurred when code is referenced. The overhead imposed by compiling virtual machine instructions to native code is certainly less than that imposed by a full compilation from source, it is still a significant factor at runtime.

The JIT approach also suffers from the fact that it does not perform global optimisations. It operates only locally in a manner reminiscent of the translation process employed by the FPM system and suffers from the same faults.

A more sophisticated approach to JIT is based on obtaining usage statistics for each construct in a program, then translating only the most heavily used parts (which could be individual commands such as loops or selections), leaving the rest as virtual machine instructions. This approach is sometimes called *dynamic compilation*. The problem is that the usage statistics must be derived from somewhere. In a stand-alone approach, code is loaded first as virtual machine instructions and the native-code translator is applied only after these instructions have been executed. This has the implication that code has the same performance as the other methods discussed here for the first few times it is used. During these first few uses, statistics are gathered to determine which sections of code are to be translated to native code. There is the problem that the time during which the virtual machine instructions are first executed constitute the *only* time that that particular piece of code is executed.

An alternative approach is to gather usage data during testing or off-line use of the code. This second approach seems less satisfactory in general for reasons that should be clear.

8.1.3 Threaded Code

This is, again, a family of approaches. There are many variations and optimisations on this theme and it is possible to conbine a form of direct implementation with threaded code. Threaded code was introduced by Bell [9] (originally for an implementation of FORTRAN); the approach was adopted for the implementation of FORTH and has become widely known in that role.

Optimising a direct translation

In this approach, the case statement structure of the direct translation method is retained in the sense that each virtual machine instruction is implemented as a piece of implementation language code. This code is placed inside a control loop, just as in the direct translation case. The difference is that, instead of using a small numerical value to represent a case label (i.e., the use of a bytecode operation code), a *pointer* to the entry point of the implementing code is used. This requires the translator to have access to the addresses of the entry points or for the code generated by the compiler to be pre-processed when it is loaded into the virtual machine.

This approach has the advantage that it obviates the need for a jump table in the virtual machine's compiled code. Virtual machine instructions are interpreted by jumping to the corresponding piece of code. This is clearly quicker because it removes the indirection in compiled code. There can be problems, however, when optimising this approach for cached and pipelined architectures.

This appears to be an approach best suited to assembly language implementations. The GNU C compiler, however, permits a fairly direct implementation of this approach: with the appropriate switches set, labels are treated as first-class values.

This approach is a simple way of threading code.

Fully threaded code

In the original paper on threaded code [9], Bell describes a computer that uses the following steps to execute code:

1. S, the value of the pcth word of memory, is fetched.
2. a) The routine starting at location S of memory is executed.
   b) The value of pc is incremented by one.
3. Goto 1.

A machine operating in this way, he calls a "threaded-code computer".

To construct a machine like this in software, the following is required. First, the implementing machine's pc is ignored and replaced by a general register, R.

The algorithm above can be replaced by the following:

1. Transfer control to the routine beginning at the location whose address is the value of the Rth word of memory.
2. Increment R by one.

In PDP-11 assembly language, this is implemented as:

```
JMP \@(R)+
```

on the MIPS, it is:

```
lw   $2, 0($4) # assume $4 is the instr. ptr
addu $4, $4,4  # increment the instruction ptr by one word
j    $2        # execute next instruction
#nop           # branch delay slot
```

Step 1 of the VM algorithm corresponds to steps 1 and 2(a) of Bell's algorithm, while step 2 corresponds to Bell's remaining steps. If a computer has an instruction that can increment a register and can load the *pc* through two levels of indirection, it is possible to have an extremely compact implementation of the above algorithm.

The above code (and two-step algorithm) is the **next** routine that always appears at the end of each operation in a FORTH program.

There is, however, a choice: primitives can end with the **next** routine or can share a copy and jump to it. On modern processors, though, the shared **next** routine not only costs a jump but also dramatically increases the misprediction rate of the indirect jump. Shared **next** is not a good idea on most current hardware.

The idea is that all primitive (virtual machine instructions) are implemented as threaded code. The code that is output by the compiler consists of references to the entry points of the instructions. Each instruction ends with the **next** routine to transfer control to the next instruction in code memory.

It should be noted (as, indeed, Bell does in [9]) that arguments to threaded code routines can be passed on stacks or by any other possible discipline.

This is the approach historically taken by many FORTH systems. It can be adapted with relative ease to any language; indeed, the original implementation of code threading was used in a FORTRAN system.

8.2 Register Machines

The techniques available for implementing virtual machines based on the register-transfer model are roughly the same as those for stack-based machines. A stack-based implementation must handle the stack and a very few registers as well as what might be called "instruction decoding". Above, the focus was on the instruction decoding part of the task because there are usually so few registers. An implementation of a register-based virtual machine, on the other hand, requires implementations of the register sets and of the instruction decoding mechanism. Initially, this section will concentrate on the representation of (possibly multiple) register sets and then will move onto a discussion of instruction decoding.

8.2.1 Register sets

One problem that is immediate when considering register machines is that they can require multiple register sets, each of which contains more registers than are provided by the target hardware. A direct implementation method for a stack-based machine can try to arrange for all virtual machine registers to be allocated to machine registers. This can be done in C and some of its derivatives and in Ada, for example; in other languages, it cannot (even so, if the hardware processor has only a few registers—like the X86—the C or Ada compiler might not be able to ensure that all machine registers can be maintained in hardware registers at all times).

The natural way to implement a register set is as a vector of single registers. For example, an integer register set can be implemented as an integer vector. Accessing such a vector requires indirection, as does a stack. There is, in the linear vector case, no overhead incurred by increment, decrement and test of the top pointer, so there is already a performance gain. Single vectors also have the property that they can all be operated on together (e.g., when saving to a stack—an operation reminiscent of the IBM360 "store multiple" instruction). It is clearly advisable to arrange for all register sets to be stored in the fastest possible memory. Furthermore, the issue of locality can arise. The transfer of values between different register sets (whether of the same or of different types) should not require excessive re-loading of fast memory. In many languages, this merely means that all register sets should be declared without intervening variables (this is just a rough heuristic and the actual output of the compiler should be examined). In a similar fashion, transfers between registers should be as fast as possible; this implies that a machine with very large numbers of registers in a set should be redesigned.

8.2.2 Addressing

In a register-based machine, addressing is an issue. One reason for this is that a stack-based machine is a zero-address machine; almost every operand is found on the stack (in the ALEX virtual machine, data is usually on the stack, sometimes stored as a global). In a register-based machine, data can be located in many places, for example:

- On some stack;
- An operand to the current instruction;
- Stored in a register;
- Stored in flat memory;
- Pointed to by some other datum.

This suggests that data can be accessed in different ways; hence, there are different addressing modes, just as one finds in assembly code.

There is no translation problem in principle for these different modes: they can all be handled with some ease when translating the symbolic representation of the instruction set to the corresponding numeric ("binary") format. For example:

- Data on the stack is addressed using stack operations.
- An operand is binary literal data that is assembled into the binary code.
- An operand that is stored in a register can be accessed by naming the register in which it resides.
- Data in flat (i.e., non-stack) memory is accessed using addresses. Addresses can be represented by explicit labels or by offsets from known base addresses (e.g., the start of a table).
- Pointers are, after all, just addresses.

The problem is that either instructions are associated with exactly one addressing mode or more than one op (byte) code is required for each conceptual operation. The latter case is the norm for hardware instruction sets which are usually defined in terms of a set of bit fields (Intcode and Cintcode for BCPL is defined in an analogous fashion, see [45] for more information). One field names the basic operation to be performed (e.g., load, store, move, compare, add). There is a separate field for each operand, stating its addressing mode. While this is an optimal arrangement in hardware, it can be costly (in terms of time) in software. Furthermore, without care, instruction lengths can become rather long.

For example, assume that the address length of the underlying machine is 32 bits (so that a hardware pointer can be used without manipulation). Assume that the following addressing modes are possible:

- Immediate;
- Absolute;
- Indexed;
- Indirect;
- Indexed Indirect.

In the worst case, three bits are required to encode these modes. Assuming 64 instructions (not an unreasonable assumption), the opcode field requires six bits. Also, assume that 3-adic instructions are used (as they are in Parrot and the register-transfer machine described above), so the worst case is:

$$6 + (2 \times 32) + (2 \times 3) = 76 \text{ bits}$$

This is an awkward number of bits for an instruction. Of course, this is the worst case and a more optimal arrangement can be found; however it does indicate that care must be taken when integrating addressing modes with the instruction set.

Depending upon how the instruction set decoding is implemented, it might be better to adopt a scheme that is closer to that used for stack-based or RISC machines. This was essentially the scheme adopted for the example register machine described above. This is a general approach that associates one addressing mode with one opcode. Clearly, this puts pressure on the instruction space if a small number of bits (say eight) is allocated for the opcode. One clear way to handle this is to extend the allocation to 16 bits.

It must be remembered that, if the virtual machine works by translation to some other form, the number of bits required for an opcode is not necessarily the actual number of bits of runtime storage. If the register machine is implemented as a threaded-code device, the runtime representation of each opcode will require the same number of bits as the hardware representation of an address.

Similarly, if virtual machine addresses are represented at runtime by actual hardware addresses, the size of an instruction at runtime can be much larger than if they are represented as offsets into a byte vector.

8.2.3 Translation to Another VM

The possibility of translating register machine code to something more "fundamental" exists but has not, or so it would appear, been used. Again, there is the possibility of translating register-machine code into an equivalent form in some low-level language (C or even assembly language).

Translation of register machine instructions to the instruction set of the underlying hardware is also an option. There is no *a priori* reason to ignore JIT techniques as an aspect of this. An interesting alternative is to use JIT to translate stack-machine instructions into those for a register machine.

The possibility of translation to another kind of virtual machine is an interesting one, as is the idea of using threaded code to implement register-transfer machine instructions.

There are cases in which translation from register code to stack machine code appears viable: testing code is a case in point. The reason for this is that compilation to a stack machine is considerably less costly than translation to a register machine. During development, turnaround is of importance. For performance, though, such a translation would appear to be of dubious utility.

8.3 Using Transitions

In this section, the use of transition-based specifications is considered. In previous chapters, state transitions have been used to specify the operations of various virtual machines:

- The single-stack ALEX machine;
- The two-stack ALEX machine;
- The Harrison Machine virtual machine;
- The register-based virtual machine.

The transitions for the two-stack ALEX machine were used to define a translation to the register-based machine. That is clearly one good use for them. This chapter is concerned with the process of building virtual machines; transitions are a specification, so it should come as no surprise that they are of use in the construction process.

Before moving on, it is important to note that the sets of transitions given in various places above need to be augmented in a variety of ways. The Harrison Machine shows one of these: it contains transitions that determine how to stop the virtual machine. It is also necessary to include transitions that describe (or define) the *error* states of the virtual machine, so that they can be flagged or so that exceptions can be raised. In general, the addition of error transitions is a straightforward process; above, they were omitted partly for this reason but also because their inclusion would have cluttered the presentation unduly.

Now, it should be clear that transitions can be used either formally or informally. The latter consists of using the transitions as a high-level specification and simply converting them to working code. There is nothing wrong with this: a recent version of the Harrison Machine was constructed using the transitions presented in Chapter 6.

Virtual machines should be correct as far as the semantics of the language they implement (execute) is concerned. This is clear. The author's preferred criterion is that the virtual machine should be derived formally from the semantics of the language, ideally automatically (work has been done on this [16, 17]), a process which, unfortunately, has proved to be rather more difficult than it would appear.

Until such time as it becomes possible to automate the process, more traditional methods must be applied. Transitions can assist in the formal derivation of virtual machines by acting as a high-level specification that can be converted into a model-based notation such as VDM [26], Z [46] and B [2]. This turns out not to be all that difficult and is quite transparent, particularly in specification notations that employ pre- and post-conditions, such as VDM and B. The left-hand side of each transition acts as a precondition, while the right-hand side can be treated directly as a specification of the operation or as a postcondition.

The translation into Z has been attempted by the author for the Harrison Machine transitions as well as for the single-stack ALEX virtual machine with good results. Unfortunately, lack of space prevents the inclusion of the Z schemata in this book; the reader might care to attempt this for themselves.

8.4 Concluding Remarks

Although virtual machines, in the form of abstract machines, have been around for a long time, they have mostly employed the stack-based approach.

Only recently has the proposal of the Register-Transfer Model been taken seriously. As a consequence, many techniques have been identified and applied in the construction of stack-based virtual machines. The approach based on registers is, on the other hand, far less well explored. Translation of compiler intermediate code to register machines is well-established but the construction of software machines using many registers has not.

In this chapter, a number of implementation techniques have been proposed and discussed. It is clear that there is a considerable amount of work to be done in this area.

9

Open Issues

The purpose of this chapter is to give one view of how virtual machines might develop in the future. Anyone who attempts anything like this is likely to get things almost entirely wrong, so the reader is warned that no guarantees are given. Instead, the reader should read the following as a collection of ideas as to where things might go. Some of the ideas might turn out to be dead ends, some pure speculation, while others might be more promising. *Caveat lector!*

The developments outlined below can be divided into those of a more theoretical interest and those of more pragmatic importance. Many of the ideas presented below are inter-related, so the reader is warned that they are only roughly grouped.

It is also worth noting that there is a great deal to be said about some of these topics. There is a temptation to write enormous amounts about some of them[1] but, it is hoped, what follows is indicative of profitable future work.

9.1 Security

Security is currently a big issue. Clearly, when a virtual machine is used as a component in an open system, such as the JVM often is, there is a security issue. From this, it is obvious that more security measures will be added to virtual machines to ensure that "malicious" code cannot be loaded by or from sources that are not trusted.

The standard way of looking at security is to examine the code executed by a virtual machine. For example, the JVM's security mechanisms include one verifying that code does not access local files. Another standard technique is to add digital signatures to code; virtual machines verify the signature before loading the code. Another technique is to refuse connections from sites that have been established as insecure or malicious.

---

[1] There are some topics that interest the author a great deal and there are issues that seem to have some promise. These topics are not necessarily of interest to anyone else, of course!

There are arguments in favour as well as against the kinds of security afforded by Java and similar systems. One argument runs that it is not possible to ensure security using compiled code alone, only source code can be verified. The other argument is that compiled code is exactly what is to be run, so it contains all the necessary information. Unfortunately, in neither form can the following attack be detected (at least, as far as the author is aware). A routine or method allocates an enormous vector (say, 1024K words) and performs some test or other; if the test evaluates to true, the routine or method calls itself recursively, thus allocating another huge vector. Even worse is the case of mutually recursive routines or methods, one of which allocates a large amount of store, the other serves merely to obfuscate the issue. The test can be arbitrarily obfuscated; what matters is that it evaluates to true a good many times (the code should never terminate—another problem). Static checking of code of any kind will never detect this. The only sensible way to handle behaviours like this is to isolate it from the rest of the system. The problem is that code like that just described uses a central system resource.

Language design also plays a part in security. Java excludes pointers and a number of other "dangerous" features (hence the topic that follows this one).

It is clear that more secure virtual machines will appear in the near- and mid-term.

9.2 New Languages

It could be said that there are already too many programming languages. It can certainly be said that there are many languages that look the same. One problem that we face is that the languages we have are not terribly good; programming language design is a difficult process at the best of times.

New langues are often associated with virtual machines, particularly when the language is not of the von Neumann type. There is a vast literature on declarative and other languages that do not fit the standard mould and the reader is directed to it.

As noted as part of the last topic, language design can also relate to security. It is to be expected that new languages with security features will appear in the coming years; many of these languages will execute on virtual machines.

9.3 Typed Instruction Sets and Intermediate Codes

The JVM attempts to provide some type information in its instruction set. There are many reasons for wanting a typed instruction set. Here are just a few:

- In an untyped instruction set, instructions can be overloaded. For example, the "add" instruction might be overloaded to handle integers, floating point numbers and strings. Inside the code that implements the "add" operation, there have to be two type tests (one for each operand) that check that the operands are of compatible types. These type tests cost space or time or both. Runtime type tags, such as those used in most LISP implementations, can be used. It does seem, however, that separate instructions are best.

- In an untyped instruction set, it is not really possible to point to an instruction and be exactly sure about what it does. The "add" example can be integer addition, floating point addition, a combination of these two, or string concatenation. This is semantic ambiguity. It has the implication that the input to a virtual machine cannot be proved.

- In a typed instruction set, each instruction has a fixed type and performs a fixed operation. Not only is this simpler, it is faster at runtime (by omitting type tests, coercions, and so on), even though it does consume more space. However, when, e.g., instrumentation and introspection are concerned, typed instruction sets offer the advantage that the machine is performing exactly one task at a time and this can be directly related to the input code.

There is also a connection with the intermediate codes used in compilers generating code for virtual machines. In some of these, the intermediate code carries type information. The final translation to virtual machine instruction removes this type information when performing instruction selection. This is valuable information that could usefully be passed to the virtual machine.

Typed instructions put pressure on the instruction space in the sense that for each untyped instruction representing a polymorphic operation (e.g., addition), there will be more than one instantiation of that instruction in a typed system. For example, the addition operation would need to be instantiated for (at least) integer, floating point and string (boolean "or" can also be interpreted as an operation with the same properties as addition). This has the implication that the number of opcodes in use increases significantly and reduces the number of opcodes available for other operations; this is particularly painful in a space with 256 points; it is naturally eased in a larger space, say of 64K points (16-bit opcodes).

Of course, the runtime representation of instructions might be different from that output by the compiler. Elsewhere in this book (Chapter 8), the possibility of using, say, threaded code methods to implement instruction decoding has been discussed. In threaded code, opcodes are replaced by pointers to entry points in code. In a threaded-code implementation (unless it is an implementation on a machine with an address space that can be represented by a byte), there is more space for operation codes than there is in a single byte. What has been called the "direct" method for implementing virtual machines appears to prefer small opcodes, although there is no *a priori* reason for this.

9.4 High-Level Instructions

The Java VM, as was seen in Chapter 3, has an instruction set consisting of the instructions for simple operations together with instructions that perform complex operations. The simple instructions implement arithmetic operations and jumps. The complex operations implement operations such as:

- Object creation;
- Array reference;
- Variable access and update in classes and instances;
- Method invocation.

In the development of the example ALEX virtual machine (Chapter 4.2.5), instructions were added for vector manipulation. Procedure call and return are also handled by relatively complex instructions.

It is to be expected that higher-level instruction sets will appear with time. There are cases where this can be expected:

- When specific data structures are to be manipulated: for example, matrix or image operations, operations on processes (threads or tasks), as well as those provided by the JVM. Specific instructions might also be provided to implement such functions as:
  - Database query and update;
  - Remote procedure calls;
  - Setting up and using stream-based communications channels.
- When sequences of more primitive instructions repeatedly occur in code, it is worth combining them into single instructions.

9.5 Additivity and Replacement

Compiled code presents a problem: when a piece of it needs to be replaced, the whole image needs to be reprocessed. Direct editing of code (patching) is extremely error-prone and frequently introduces new errors. Relocatable code still requires offsets to be correctly adjusted. Dynamic linkage is also only a partial solution. Java gets round this problem by a dynamic linkage process on a per-class basis; event-driven software is easier to modify at the routine level but poses its own problems.

9.6 Compiler Correctness

Industrial people pull faces and mutter about academic irrelevance when issues like compiler correctness are mentioned; they are the first to phone their legal teams when compilers (and other software) fails to work! Compiler correctness *does* matter and has proved to be a hard problem. There are only a few successful examples, one of which is [47].

Virtual machines can be of assistance in the correctness proof in a variety of ways, some direct, some indirect.

Some might see the following as obvious, a virtual machine implements the instruction set of a machine that is often considerably more abstract than the hardware on which it runs. Therefore, the code generator for a virtual machine target is not as complex as that for a native code runtime. Typically, virtual machines are designed for a single language, so there is the possibility of a closer semantic match between language semantics and virtual machine instructions than between semantics and hardware instruction set. This implies that any proofs of correctness will be easier (and ease of proof tends to lead to comprehensiveness of proof—we're only human, after all!)

If the remarks about typed intermediate codes and instruction sets are accepted, the correctness proof is eased. However, and this is a little indirect, if the compiler is organised as a set of transformations between intermediate codes that carry different information. For example, higher-level transformations correspond more closely to the source language while lower-level ones contain information such as addresses, while intermediate ones might be organised in terms of continuations. This organisation suggests that the overall correctness proofs (as well as others) can be divided into stages, thus simplifying the process.

It is also possible to consider that each intermediate code is a code for a virtual machine, so a semantics can be given for each. This clearly relates to correctness.

(In a very modest way, this book contains a number of different instruction sets that have been related to each other. It has been shown, in the relatively informal argument of Section 7.9, and more extensively in Appendix A, that the translation is correct in the appropriate sense.)

9.7 Dynamic Code Insertion

This is a bit of a hobby horse of the author. The idea is that code should be compiled only when it is required. Unlike JIT where the entire program is presented and compiled when required, dynamic code insertion involves the direct insertion of newly generated instructions into the virtual machine's instruction stream; these instructions might also be stored somewhere else for subsequent execution.

Dynamic code insertion allows the system to do a number of things that appear a bit strange unless one has been a LISP programmer. In LISP, it is possible to construct pieces of code and store them, executing them only when they become needed. If they are not required, they are collected as garbage. A natural extension of this idea is that a program is written that writes bits of code as and when they are required; when doing this, one usually arranges matters so that the code can be modified on the fly. (This is not necessarily as dangerous as it appears and can, in principle, be formally specified.)

9.8 Instrumentation

Debugging code[2] is introduced into compiled code by inserting instructions to instrument it. This affects the behaviour of the original code. In some extreme cases, the introduction of debugging code can lead to behaviours that mask the faults under investigation. In a similar fashion, timing code alters the behaviour of the code being investigated and, as anyone who has timed code knows, the time taken to execute the added code has to be removed from the time reported by it. This is not particularly satisfactory.

Rather than *add* code to an existing program or module to assist in debugging, it appears less intrusive to turn a switch and let the environment within which the code executes produce the necessary information. Very often, the necessary code already exists in a virtual machine and is turned off. When testing a virtual machine, it is common to dump the registers and the top few stack locations so that they can be inspected to verify that the virtual machine is performing correctly. When the virtual machine is delivered, the code is commented or edited out or placed inside a conditionally compiled region of the source (#ifdef in C and C++ or using a macro that expands to a comment). This code could be used to dump debugging information.

Checkpointing and other debugging tools can similarly be integrated within virtual machine code and activated using a switch.

Code timing is always a problem because it takes some time for the code performing it to execute. If this code is already present in a virtual machine, it can, again, be revived from development. Timing, however, can only inform the programmer about the performance of the algorithm that has been coded—very often, it is already known when the algorithm has bad properties. However, timing can be included more reliably in a virtual machine.

There is increasing (and welcome) demand to include assertions and other correctness-oriented constructs in programs. An assertion typically tests a program-specific condition and, if the test fails, causes an exception (termination in the case of the standard C library routine). Assertions could be linked into a more friendly exception mechanism and they could be linked to virtual machine mechanisms (e.g., warning of low stack space or of low memory).

Virtual machines, in principle, allow one to get right inside the executing code of a program. This could be exploited to help debugging and testing, as well as instrumenting running programs. In particular, array bounds checking and similar operations can be performed "for free" by a virtual machine without interfering with the execution of code. This level of instrumentation

---

[2] This section is written by someone who tries *never* to use debugging tools. Disturbance of code is one reason why this policy was adopted; another is that the cause of most problems is not in the behaviour of compiled code but in the source—a closer examination of the source and a period spent thinking about it more often reveals the source of an error than watching registers change. Sometimes, though, debugging tools are useful, particularly when tracking what appears to be a compiler error.

can also include information about storage usage, the turnover of store and so on. It is arguable that it can be fed back into the compilation process so that optimisations can be performed. The tight coupling of a compiler with a virtual machine is necessary for this (some object to this because it is too reminiscent of LISP environments that do not permit the development system to be separated from delivered code).

Instrumentation can deliver information about which routines are being called, as well as information about the actual parameters. It can also intercept stack frame operations (perhaps allowing modification at runtime).

Flexible instrumentation can be handled by adding hooks into the virtual machine's code. Care has to be taken to ensure that the hooks cannot be abused (i.e., by inserting malicious code). These hooks could also be useful in the construction of virtual machines supporting reflective programs.

9.9 Including more Information about Source Code

Smalltalk and Objective-C, as well as interpreted object-oriented languages like LOOPS [11] and the Poplog system [42], retain information on program units that is derived from the source. Java, Smalltalk and Objective-C have runtime data structures that record information about class variables and inheritance structures; they also have method tables that translate method selectors to method code. The Poplog virtual machine is based on the idea that functions and data structures are represented at runtime by structures that contain a variety of information about these structures.

In a similar fashion, the Dylan language supports a controlled form of introspection. Programs can, at runtime, determine, for example, the types and arities of methods. Similar operations are provided for classes. This information is derived from runtime data structures describing the entities that have been loaded into the system.

Equally, the CORBA standard for the middleware used by some distributed systems contains data about the interfaces presented by objects.

The inclusion of information normally associated with source code has a number of advantages. As noted above, it can assist in introspective and reflective functioning and it can be used profitably in distributed systems. It can also be used to help support operations such as:

- Serialization of data;
- Verification of dynamic linkage.

Furthermore, meta programming and dynamic compilation make use of source code-derived information.

Source information can be used to great effect when combined with instrumentation. The data provided by the instrumentation can be presented in a form that directly relates to the source code, thus making the results more easily interpreted.

9.10 Integration with Databases

The integration of virtual machines with databases is already established. Java permits code to be loaded from files, from network connections, from code servers and from databases. Java, by its serialization mechanism, also allows class instances to be stored on databases, thus permitting a kind of code freezing. Code and application servers assist in the construction of distributed applications.

More generally, virtual machines can be augmented by orthogonal persistence, thereby allowing large amounts of data to be retained in a format that is accessible to the virtual machine's instructions. Traditional database applications typically require special-purpose code to be written to access the data in its stored format and to convert it to the format used by the code. Persistence avoids this.

Persistence also assists in the development of distributed applications. Data can be stored in a virtual-machine-dependent format and accessed by any instance of that virtual machine running on that network (or on any machine on Earth, in orbit around it or elsewhere in the solar system, if it runs on the Internet).

The combination of code servers and persistence clearly support integrated networked applications with components of applications (if they can still be so called) executing anywhere.

The freezing of the state of a program as it executes on a virtual machine is just an extension of the usual interpretation of persistence. Thus, a piece of code can execute for a while before all or part of its state is frozen and stored until later. Frozen code can later be unfrozen on the same or on another host (assuming the database is networked, a not unreasonable assumption); code freezing is also useful in mobile code systems (see Section 9.12).

If virtual machines can be executed by "virtual VMs" or by code morphing, or by other techniques not yet considered, it becomes possible for virtual machines to be stored in code servers. It also becomes possible for a virtual machine to be frozen and then moved elsewhere or to be stored until it is required at some later time. The distinctions between *a* virtual machine, an *instance of* a virtual machine and an instance of a *virtual machine state* thereby become necessary.

9.11 Increased Inter-Operability

Inter-operability appears to divide into a number of cases:

1. Inter-operability of components of distributed applications;
2. Inter-operability of different applications/systems.

Quite clearly, the first case is already served in part by integration with persistent stores as discussed in Section 9.10.

Inter-operability, more generally, is a complex problem that is very difficult to solve. Two important issues are protocols and data formats; it is clear that common protocols and data formats must be employed before systems can communicate. Unfortunately, there is insufficient space in this chapter to explore these in any more depth, so the last observation must suffice.

9.12 Code Mobility

As Java has shown, if every platform on a network has a virtual machine with the same instruction set, a given piece of code can be executed anywhere on that network. The next step from this is for code to move from place to place. The term "code mobility" is often taken to refer to code running on mobile phones, in bicycles, vacuum cleaners or lawn mowers that communicate with other pieces of code. However, there is another sense in which the code moves from processor to processor in a network.[3]

To do this, the code must be sure that there is a suitable virtual machine on every machine it might land on (or, equally, that its code can be dynamically translated to something that can run on the target machine). Once it has landed, the code has to acquire resources as it executes on its new processor. In addition, it has to determine where next to migrate; this requires knowledge of the network, including:

- The load at each candidate node;
- The resources at each candidate node, especially specialised devices;
- The performance of each candidate node;
- The security constraints at each candidate node.

Why should code migrate? Here are some answers:

- Resources: Some hosts have resources not available elsewhere. It is clearly quicker and easier to access a resource locally than remotely.
- Load balancing: This is really part of the resource problem. Code might move because the load on its local host might increase, making progress difficult. Under such conditions, the code might decide to move to another processor where things are less busy.
- Security: A particular application might have security constraints imposed upon it. For example, if code is moving around, it is far harder to locate it and intercept its data. If a large application is composed of mobile components, it becomes much harder to target. Naturally, the communications channels required by the code must change as it moves. (If both parties to a communication are mobile, there is an obvious problem—and a security hole!)

---

[3] This is the sense adopted by people working with "software agents".

- Environmental problems: If there is a hurricane threatening your machine, it might be a good idea for your survival to move to a machine where the weather is a bit better. Similarly, if your owner is going to move office/house, it makes better sense to move there rather than stay behind. (Perhaps this might be referred to as "survival"—scary!)

There is another point about mobile code that is, perhaps, not discussed very often. It is this: if code is mobile, it is not necessary for the processors upon which the code executes also to host certain applications. In the list above, the first item is "resources" and resources could include applications such as accounting packages and databases, as well as printers, special-purpose display devices and specialised data-capture devices. However, some pieces of code can be carried along with the mobile code, thus obviating the requirement that it be provided by the host system. Indeed, the components required by a mobile application could be distributed and mobile (with all the attendant problems).

An alternative to migration is that a central piece of code performs certain tasks but, to perform others, it creates modules that it executes on other processors on the same network. To do this, it transmits the code to the other processors and communicates only with them.

An even more radical proposal is that mobile code carries its own virtual machine with it!

However it is done, mobile code poses a huge number of security problems. Some problems are:

- The code could corrupt main store.
- The code could corrupt data on disk.
- The code could flood communications networks.
- The code could replicate itself and crash its host.
- The code could transmit confidential data to other sites.
- The code could reveal the location of resources that the host would prefer to keep under wraps.
- The code could replicate and send itself to hosts to which it should not migrate.

9.13 Small Platforms

There is a demand to execute code on small platforms. Small platforms are used in areas such as ubiquitous computing (including wearable systems), PDAs, mobile (cellular) telephones and embedded processors.

Small platforms are characterised, at least at present, by relatively small main stores, low performance processors and little, if any, backing store. The processor power issue is easing with time (but *power consumption* remains an issue, one that is not relevant to this book). Network connections in some form are increasingly common. The problem remains that small platforms are just that: small. This has implications for virtual machines that might execute on them. Some of these implications will now be considered.

In this book, it has been assumed that there is a heap storage mechanism with a garbage collector, so that allocation problems are not an issue for the virtual machine. When storage is at a premium, the space occupied by a sophisticated storage management mechanism is clearly one of the first components to review. Without garbage collection, static allocation becomes the norm, with dynamic allocation under program control.

Next, the virtual machine itself is a piece of software that resides in main store, taking up space that could be used for application software. However, a virtual machine is a flexible concept. Thus, a virtual machine could be constructed that has instructions for common application operations. This is entirely in line with the idea that virtual machine instructions are designed to support the main semantic constructs of some programming language. The idea that application-specific operations be included as virtual-machine instructions is similar to the (heretical?) idea that LISP, Snobol or APL programs are bits of control structure that manage calls to application-specific routines (be it list, string or matrix manipulation).

Compact code is clearly of benefit on small platforms. Compactness was an issue for the BCPL Intcode/Cintcode systems. The original Intcode machine is more graphic in this respect with operation codes being specified as a collection of bit masks. Some common instruction sequences are also collected into a single Intcode operation, thus abbreviating code with little overhead.

Instruction selection is also of benefit. It is not necessary always to have floating-point instructions. Similarly, the role of the stack can be reduced. Instead of using it for expression evaluation, it can be restricted to routine call; this can be done when there are sufficient general-purpose registers for arithmetic and logic operations. A machine like this can omit a number of low-level stack operations, replacing them with higher-level ones.

It has also been pointed out that relative jumps (branches) are more compact than absolute ones.

The main loop of a virtual machine tends to be quite small. It is the supporting code that can be large. There are places where the size of the entire system can be reduced.

The format used to store programs can be another source of complexity. Some virtual machines expect code to be input in a symbolic form that is assembled into the virtual machine's store. The JVM expects code to be in class-file format. This, as has been seen, is complex and consumes a large amount of space (it is garbage collected when the class is no longer of use). If programs are stored as "binary" code, they do not require this additional apparatus and can just be loaded into code store using a simple load loop.

The in-lining of storage management calls can also improve the footprint size. If it can be determined that a heap-allocated structure only has a lifetime commensurate with the block in which it is allocated, an explicit release call can be compiled into the end of the block.

There is no reason at all why an instrumented virtual machine could not be used to develop code for small platforms. Indeed, such virtual machines could simulate the entire small platform. There are many commercial products that simulate the processors used in embedded applications; the current proposal is just an extension of these but using a higher-level instruction set.

Finally, the translation of one virtual machine to another or the compilation of virtual machine code to another for (C or assembler macros) is another technique that might produce good results. In this scheme, the code is developed in a conventional cross-platform development system, but one that uses a virtual machine providing application-specific operations as instructions. The resulting code can then be macroed or compiled to the other form for final delivery. This does tend to obviate one of the best features of virtual machines: the ease with which code can be updated.

Embedded processors are becoming larger, in terms of address width, and faster. There are limits to both. Moore's Law cannot apply indefinitely: the physical limitations are beginning to hurt. Similarly, there is a limit to the amount of storage to be expected from an embedded processor. Faster processors and more store mean greater power consumption. A mobile (cellular) telephone the size and weight of *War and Peace* might have been acceptable once but no longer. All of this implies that virtual machines, when used in embedded systems, will still have to be tailored.

9.14 Real-Time VMs

There is already considerable interest in using virtual machines in real-time environments. Java was originally intended as a real-time system for what amounts to a ubiquitous computing environment but was released as the language for the Web. More recently, Sun has released real-time variants.

Small platforms are often used for real-time applications, so there is common ground to explore and many of the issues are the same. Here, the repertoire of primitives and the time taken to execute code are the focus.

The introduction of pseudo-concurrent execution led to the inclusion of appropriate data structures and primitives. The data structures represented the process abstraction, message and process queues. The primitives included those for process management and for inter-process communication. In real-time systems, inter-process communication is clearly of great importance, as is speed of execution. The cost of context switching is also an issue.

For virtual machines, the speed of operation (instruction) execution is a critical factor, as is storage management. There is a trade-off between high-level instructions that take a comparatively long time to complete and those that are at a lower level and are fast. Again, one advantage of a virtual machine is that frequently used operations can be implemented as instructions and thereby taken out of application code.

It is often claimed by practitioners that heap storage is too slow and too large for real-time systems. The author remembers a time when assembly language was claimed to be the "only" way to build real-time systems; most real-time work is now done in C, Ada or some other procedural language. The argument about heaps will probably go the same way. Heaps are just extremely convenient, even if they are never going to be as fast as hand-allocated store; compilers also alter storage arrangements when heavy optimisation is used.[4] Modern storage management techniques such as generational scavenging can be relatively fast.

9.15 Code Morphing

As its name suggests, code morphing is code transformation or translation, typically on a dynamic basis. This is a process that has already been alluded to in a number of places in this book. A simple example is that of a program compiled to Java JVM bytecodes and executed on the Parrot RTM. To do this, the JVM bytecodes have to be translated into Parrot bytecodes. Usually, this is done as a static process that is performed before loading into the Parrot virtual machine. However, it is possible to do it dynamically as the code is executed. The JVM bytecodes might be read and translated and then passed to the instruction stream of the Parrot virtual machine; at the same time, the translated bytecodes are stored inside the Parrot virtual machine in case they are to be executed at a later time (e.g., iteratively called again).

This leads to the idea that more than one virtual machine could be present within a system (this totally contradicts the Parrot approach, of course, but Parrot represents one view of virtual machines, albeit an extremely sensible one). When required, code is morphed so that it runs on a virtual machine other than the one that was its original target.

9.16 Greater Optimisation

A big issue is the speed of compiled code and the compactness of representations. Optimisation is a clear issue but techniques such as JIT do not lend themselves to global optimisations. It has been noted that statistics-gathering operations have been proposed as part of dynamic compilation.

It is to be expected that more optimisation can be provided by virtual machines in the future. High-level and typed instructions can perform local optimisations. With more global information available (from module- or even entire program-level analyses), possibly also from source information stored

---

[4] A good assembly programmer will always win the space/time tradeoff against even heavily optimised C—horses for courses.

at runtime, better optimisation can be expected. Similarly, the techniques employed in instrumenting programs can be fed back into low-level compilation processes.

The translation of one virtual machine to another, such as that discussed elsewhere in this book (e.g., Sections 7.7, 8.1.2 and 8.1.3) could easily lead to performance improvements.

9.17 Operating System Constructs

It is painfully clear that operating systems[5] are beginning to bloat with new "features". Not all applications require these features, so their inclusion for the few is at the expense of the many. It seems more reasonable to reduce the size and complexity of operating systems with those additional features being introduced on a per-application or application family basis. Some readers will object that this is a return to the libraries that were so common in the operating systems of the 1960s, 1970s and early 1980s. It need not be so. However, this view is not entirely novel because a similar motivation was behind the development of the Oberon System [53] and its successors. This leads to the ideas of the next section.

There is, however, another trend that can be supported by virtual machines. That is the so-called *virtual* operating system (VOS). This is an operating system that runs, essentially, as an application program within another operating system. The idea of one operating system within another was pioneered by IBM's VM370 operating system. That system provided each user with a private copy of the machine's hardware and low-level features so that a complete operating system could be executed by each user. This turned out to be an extremely successful approach and VM continues to be supported today.

The VOS concept can be seen as an individual operating environment for one or more users that abstracts away from the underlying operating system by providing new or more appropriate facilities. For example, one VOS might provide monitors and condition variables; another VOS might provide a richer storage environment and flexible process management; yet another VOS might be tailored more towards multi-media operations.

It would appear that the virtual machine concept, as interpreted as an abstract machine, can be employed very much as a VOS. When describing the virtual machine for the parallel extensions to ALEX, a number of constructs were introduced. These constructs implemented processes, messages and other objects. This amounted to the implementation of a very small operating system kernel.

---

[5] No names! The reader will undoubtedly figure out which they are!

9.18 Virtual Machines for more General Portability

Some years ago, the author learned that systems like FrameMaker and MS Word were implemented in application-specific languages that were interpreted. When porting the application from one architecture to another, all that was done was to re-implement the interpreter. This is an example of a virtual machine being used for portability. It seems quite possible that other applications could be implemented in this way.

9.19 Distributed VMs

The ACTOR languages were intended to run on a *distributed* virtual machine [32, 50]. Each of the primitives was implemented as an actor that resided within the distributed memory of the ACTOR machine. The idea was that the code of an actor would send a message containing its arguments to the primitive actor; the latter would return a message containing the result of performing the operation. In some versions, the interpreter was physically as well as logically distributed.

It is not suggested that arithmetic, string, vector, list or class operations be distributed in the various ACTOR machines. What is suggested is that special operations could be distributed. For example, matrix operations might be provided by special sites. These sites would support a virtual machine that performs these operations (as well, probably, as a common core); other sites could perform, say, robotic manipulator control; another site could offer theorem-proving primitives, while yet another does heuristic search. Other examples could be found—those just made are intended to be illustrative, not realistic. The basic idea is that networks are there to distribute functionality. It is not in tune with this idea for each networked virtual machine to offer the same functionality, if that means providing special-purpose operations at every site.

How might this be done? One clear way is that code is compiled in the normal way. The compiled code can contain instructions for the special-purpose operations. A virtual machine that is not capable of performing these operations invokes them at the remote site. The results are recorded locally or, possibly remotely, to be consumed later.

9.20 Objects and VMs

Objects are very popular. It is natural to ask whether a virtual machine can be implemented using objects. The answer is clearly "yes".

The Parrot virtual machine outlined in Chapter 7 already makes good use of what amounts to object-oriented techniques. It uses objects to represent new data types. It uses them as a common base for implementing new non-primitive data types. As has been seen, it does this by introducing a protocol that objects must obey.

There are other ways to exploit objects. The Harrison Machine, for example, has been implemented in C++ and in Java. These implementations posed fairly standard software-engineering problems but were, otherwise, quite straightforward. The Java implementation caused a few nasty problems as far as the circular type relationships were concerned but that was due to the fact that the Harrison Machine is a reflective system. These particular problems were distinct from those relating to the general problem of building a virtual machine.

An interesting observation was made: the main loop and the state (stacks, queues, environments, etc.) can also be implemented as objects (Java, being a pure object-oriented language, *forces* them to be implemented as objects). This implies that these components can be treated as independent objects. It also implies that they can be manipulated as collections—an entire virtual machine in a particular state (i.e., taken as a whole) or as a virtual machine loop (the part that implements the instructions and that iterates over the sequence of instructions it executes) *together with* an object that represents the current state. This, in turn, implies that it should be possible to switch states just by handing a different state-representing object to the main loop and taking it away again. It also has another implication: the entire virtual machine can be treated as an object. Quite where this leads is, at present, unclear: it is an area for future research, although it might well relate to the next (and final) topic.

9.21 Virtual VMs

The basic idea of a *virtual* virtual machine is of a general environment that executes virtual machines. It is a concept that has been explored in some detail by researchers at INRIA in France [19, 6]. Their Virtual Virtual Machine is an environment for the execution of "bytecoded" applications in any suitable language. The system contains support (libraries and toolkits) for particular languages, e.g., Java and Smalltalk, running on a virtual processor that has its own virtual operating system. The system has been used as the basis for the work on mobile code systems [29].

Work on code transformation appears relevant in this area, as does the representation (implementation) of individual virtual machines as data structures. One relevant idea is the derivation of the main loop and instruction interpretation components of a virtual machine from their specification. The author has experimented with this idea using transitions to specify instructions and has produced a general method (finding second-order differences between the two sides of a transition). The translation of code from the format required by one virtual machine to that required by another is also an apparently relevant issue.

It is one thing to morph code from one instruction set to another. A radical alternative is to morph the virtual machine itself. This is not quite as bizarre as it might appear: during the development of the Harrison Machine, it became clear that it might be possible to alter its virtual machine so that it ran different instruction sets at different times. The idea was developed in a little detail but never fully.

9.22 By Way of a Conclusion

This chapter contains a lot of suggestions, some that could be done today (or tomorrow) and some that require a lot of work. Some ideas might turn out to be unreasonable and others sensible. The ideas are offered merely to stimulate others to think seriously about virtual machines and be imaginative as they do so.

One thing to remember about virtual machines is that working with them can be enormous fun.

The concept of the virtual machine has come a long way since the SECD machine's appearance in 1964. It has grown larger; it provides more facilities. At the same time, it retains the core concept of executing a sequence of commands, just such as a physical machine. This core property can be a source of blindness, making one think that compiler-related issues are the *only* ones of merit. Around the core, there are issues and problems that relate to areas like storage management (specifically heap management but also more generally in terms of storage management encountered in operating systems), security, databases, distributed applications, and so on. There is clearly a lot of work remaining.

A

Compiling ALEX

A.1 Introduction

This appendix contains a specification of the rules for compiling ALEX source code to virtual machine code. Both the single and dual-stack virtual machines (see Chapter 4) are the target for this compiler; where necessary, alternative compilation rules are given.

A.2 Notational Conventions

In this section, the notation employed in the compilation rules is defined. The notation is relatively standard (it is similar to that employed in [38] and employs what amounts to a strongly-typed functional language (semantically sugared typed λ-calculus); it should be readily converted to a language such as OCaml.

In order to define the schemes, some notation is required:

- $\mathcal{E}[\![\cdots]\!]$ to represent the compilation of an expression.
- $\mathcal{C}[\![\cdots]\!]$ will be used to represent the compilation of a command.
- $\mathcal{D}[\![\cdots]\!]$ will be used to represent the compilation of a declaration. This has four associated schemes:
  - $\mathcal{D}_P[\![\cdots]\!]$ for procedures;
  - $\mathcal{D}_F[\![\cdots]\!]$ for functions;
  - $\mathcal{D}_V[\![\cdots]\!]$ for variables;
  - $\mathcal{D}_C[\![\cdots]\!]$ for constants.

The schemes are associated with a parameter, written ρ. This is the compile-time environment (often called the *symbol table*) and it will be referred to here as just "the environment". The environment contains information about the constants, variables and routines defined in a program. Because ALEX is lexically scoped, the environment is also: it is a sequence of environment objects. Environment objects are defined as:

$$P = \langle L, P, E \rangle$$

where L is a set of locally defined entities and P is a set of parameters and E is the entry point of the routine that this environment represents (the main program also has an entry point).

The *global* (or *outermost*) environment ρ_g is defined as:

$$\rho_g = \langle L_g, \emptyset, e_m \rangle$$

where L_g is the set of local declarations (which are, therefore, the global variables) and e_m is the entry point of the main routine. The parameters of the outermost program are empty for the time being (although we might want, as an extension, to allow some parameters, e.g., file names).

In addition, some functions are required:

$$numparams : P \to \mathbb{N}$$

$$numlocals : P \to \mathbb{N}$$

The compile-time environment is a sequence of environment objects, so has type P^*. The empty environment is written $\langle \rangle$; it is called the *arid* environment and will be denoted *arid*.

There are two functions and two predicates defined over the compile-time environment:

$$pushenv : P \times P^* \to P^*$$

$$lookup : \mathsf{Ident} \times P^* \to P$$

The *lookup* function looks up an identifier (denoted Ident) in the environment. It is a recursive function. If it finds no such identifier, it signals an error.

The symbol *error* uniformly denotes a compile-time error. For present purposes, no distinction is made between the various kinds of error that can be encountered while compiling an ALEX program.

A conditional construct is employed that might be unfamiliar to some. It takes the form:

$$exp_c \ \to \ exp_t, \ exp_f$$

where exp_c is an expression returning a value of type boolean (it is the *condition*), exp_t is an expression that is evaluated if the condition evaluates to *true* and exp_f is an expression that is evaluated if the condition evaluates to *false*. It must be noted that the true and false expressions are separated by a comma ("*,*").

In addition a binding construct, let is employed. It has the form:

$$\text{let } bdg_1 \text{ and } \ldots bdg_n \text{ in } exp$$

where the bdg_i $(1 \leq i \leq n)$ are bindings and exp is the body. The bindings take the form:

$$var = exp$$

where var is a variable and exp is an expression (possibly containing lets). The order in which the bindings occur in a let expression are not, in general, significant.

A.3 Compilation Rules

In this section, the compilation schemes for ALEX are presented. The point of them is to define how an ALEX compiler (should anyone really want to build one!) should compile the various constructs that define it.

For an integer constant:

$$\mathcal{E}[\![n]\!]\rho = \texttt{pushc} \ (tointernal \ n)$$

where the function $tointernal$ converts the syntactic representation of an integer to its internal representation.

For a literal string constant:

$$\mathcal{E}[\![l]\!]\rho = \texttt{pushc} \ (lookup\_lit \ l \ \rho)$$

where $lookup\_lit$ is a function that looks up the address of the literal in the current compile-time environment.

The $\mathcal{O}$ scheme performs a lookup of its argument in the current environment for the runtime equivalent. Its definition can be reduced to a table lookup, so its details are ignored here.

$$\mathcal{E}[\![\texttt{unop } e]\!]\rho = \mathcal{E}[\![e]\!]\rho; \ \mathcal{O}[\![\texttt{unop}]\!]\rho$$

$$\mathcal{E}[\![\texttt{e1 binop e2}]\!]\rho = \mathcal{E}[\![\texttt{e1}]\!]\rho; \ \mathcal{E}[\![\texttt{e2}]\!]\rho; \ \mathcal{O}[\![\texttt{binop}]\!]\rho$$

$$\begin{aligned}
\mathcal{E}[\![\texttt{funcall } f(\texttt{e1}, \ldots, \texttt{en})]\!]\rho = \\
function \ f \ \rho \ \to \\
\quad \texttt{let } n_p = numparams \ f \ \rho \\
\quad \texttt{and } n_l = numlocals \ f \ \rho \ \texttt{in} \\
\qquad \texttt{save } n_p \ n_l \\
\qquad \mathcal{E}[\![\texttt{e1}]\!]\rho \\
\qquad \ldots \\
\qquad \mathcal{E}[\![\texttt{en}]\!]\rho \\
\qquad \texttt{frame } n_p \ n_l \\
\qquad \texttt{call } (entrypoint \ f \ \rho), \\
\quad error
\end{aligned}$$

This scheme, like the one for procedure call, needs a little refinement when library routines are provided. This will be considered below when library routines are introduced. In both this case and the one for procedure call, if two-stack code is desired, the **save** instruction has to be removed and a **frame** put in its place.

$$\mathcal{E}[\![v]\!]\rho =$$
$$\quad global \; v \; \rho \; \rightarrow$$
$$\qquad\qquad \texttt{getglobal} \; (lookup\_addr \; v \; \rho),$$
$$\qquad error$$

$$\mathcal{E}[\![v]\!]\rho =$$
$$\quad local \; v \; \rho \; \rightarrow$$
$$\qquad\qquad \texttt{getlocal} \; (lookup\_addr \; v \; \rho),$$
$$\qquad error$$

$$\mathcal{E}[\![v]\!]\rho =$$
$$\quad vparam \; v \; \rho \; \rightarrow$$
$$\qquad\qquad \texttt{getparam} \; (lookup\_addr \; v \; \rho),$$
$$\qquad error$$

$$\mathcal{C}[\![v := e]\!]\rho = \mathcal{E}[\![e]\!]\rho; \; \texttt{setlocal} \; lookup\_addr \; v$$

$$\mathcal{C}[\![\text{if } e \text{ then } c]\!]\rho = \mathcal{E}[\![e]\!]\rho; \; \texttt{jne \$next}; \; \mathcal{C}[\![c]\!]\rho; \; \texttt{\$next} :$$

$$\mathcal{C}[\![\text{unless } e \text{ do } c]\!]\rho = \mathcal{E}[\![e]\!]\rho; \; \texttt{jeq \$next}; \; \mathcal{C}[\![c]\!]\rho; \; \texttt{\$next} :$$

$$\mathcal{C}[\![\text{if } e \text{ then } t \text{ else } e]\!]\rho = \mathcal{E}[\![e]\!]\rho; \; \texttt{je \$1}; \; \mathcal{C}[\![e]\!]\rho; \; \texttt{jmp \$next}; \; \texttt{\$1} : \mathcal{C}[\![t]\!]\rho; \; \texttt{\$next} :$$

$$\mathcal{C}[\![\text{loop } c]\!]\rho = \texttt{\$start} : \mathcal{C}[\![c]\!]\rho; \; \texttt{jmp \$start} :$$

$$\mathcal{C}[\![\text{while } e \text{ do } c]\!]\rho = \texttt{\$start} : \mathcal{E}[\![e]\!]\rho; \; \texttt{jne \$next}; \; \mathcal{C}[\![c]\!]\rho; \; \texttt{jmp \$start}; \; \texttt{\$next} :$$

$$\mathcal{C}[\![\text{until } e \text{ do } c]\!]\rho = \texttt{\$start} : \mathcal{C}[\![c]\!]\rho; \; \mathcal{E}[\![e]\!]\rho; \; \texttt{jne \$start}$$

$$\mathcal{C}[\![\text{for } i := e0 \text{ to } e1 \text{ step } e2 \text{ do } c]\!]\rho =$$

$\mathcal{E}[\![e0]\!]\rho$

```
dup
setlocal lookup_addr i
```
$\mathcal{E}[\![e1]\!]\rho$
```
geq
jeq $end
```
$loop : $\mathcal{C}[\![c]\!]\rho$
$\mathcal{E}[\![e2]\!]\rho$
```
getlocal lookup_addr i
add
dup
setlocal lookup_addr i
```
$\mathcal{E}[\![e1]\!]\rho$
```
geq
jeq $end
jmp $loop
$end :
```

This is pretty horrid!

Let's make use of the compiler to patch it up and make something a bit more elgant. First, let the compiler declare a local variable for each of i, e0, e1 and e2. The locals will be named ti, t0, t1 and t2; the *offset* function will still be used in the scheme. These variables are used to reduce evaluation as much as possible.

$$\mathcal{C}[\![\text{for } i := e0 \text{ to } e1 \text{ step } e2 \text{ do } c]\!]\rho =$$
let $\rho_1 = declvar\ t2(declvar\ t1(declvar\ t0(declvar\ ti\ \rho)))$ in

$\mathcal{E}[\![e2]\!]\rho_1$
```
setlocal lookup_addr t0
```
$\mathcal{E}[\![e1]\!]\rho_1$
```
setlocal lookup_addr t1
```
$\mathcal{E}[\![e0]\!]\rho_1$ dup
```
setlocal lookup_addr ti
jeq $end
```
$loop : $\mathcal{C}[\![c]\!]\rho_1$
```
getlocal lookup_addr ti
getlocal lookup_addr t0
add
dup
setlocal lookup_addr ti
getlocal lookup_addr t0
geq
jeq $end
jmp $loop
$end :
```

$$\mathcal{C}[\![\text{exitloop}]\!]\rho = \texttt{jmp \$next}$$

$$\mathcal{C}[\![\text{nextloop}]\!]\rho = \texttt{jmp \$start}$$

$$\mathcal{E}[\![\text{proccall } p(\text{e1}, \dots, \text{en})]\!]\rho =$$
$$\textit{procedure } p \, \rho \; \rightarrow$$
$$\text{let } n_p = \textit{numparams } p \, \rho$$
$$\text{and } n_l = \textit{numlocals } p \, \rho \text{ in}$$
$$\texttt{save } n_p \, n_l$$
$$\mathcal{E}[\![\text{e1}]\!]\rho$$
$$\dots$$
$$\mathcal{E}[\![\text{en}]\!]\rho$$
$$\texttt{frame } n_p \, n_l$$
$$\texttt{call } (\textit{entrypoint } p \, \rho),$$
$$\textit{error}$$

$$\mathcal{C}[\![\text{return}]\!]\rho = \texttt{ret}$$

If e is of type int:

$$\mathcal{C}[\![\text{return e}]\!]\rho = \mathcal{E}[\![\text{e}]\!]\rho; \; \texttt{retval}$$

If e is of type bool:

$$\mathcal{C}[\![\text{return e}]\!]\rho = \mathcal{E}[\![\text{e}]\!]\rho; \; \texttt{retval}$$

If e is of type bool:

$$\mathcal{C}[\![\text{return b}]\!]\rho = \mathcal{E}[\![\text{e}]\!]\rho; \; \texttt{retval}$$

Finally, if e is of type array of int:

$$\mathcal{E}[\![\text{return e}]\!]\rho = \mathcal{E}[\![\text{e}]\!]\rho; \; \texttt{retval}$$

In all other cases, it compiles to an *error*.

A scheme for compiling sequences of commands is also required:

$$\mathcal{C}[\![\text{seq}(\text{c1}, \dots, \text{cn})]\!]\rho = \mathcal{C}[\![\text{c1}]\!]\rho; \; \dots \; \mathcal{C}[\![\text{cn}]\!]\rho$$

$$\mathcal{D}[\![\text{defproc ident}(\text{p1}, \dots, \text{pn}) \text{ be d}]\!]\rho =$$
$$\text{let } \rho_1 = \textit{decparams } \langle \text{p1} \dots \text{pn} \rangle \; \textit{arid} \text{ in}$$
$$\text{let } \rho_2 = \texttt{pushenv } \rho_1 \, \rho \text{ in}$$
$$\text{let } \langle m, \langle c, \rho_3 \rangle \rangle = \mathcal{L}[\![\text{d}]\!]\rho_1 \text{ in}$$
$$\langle c, \textit{decproc ident } n \, m \, \rho \rangle$$

$$\mathcal{D}[\![\mathsf{deffun\ ident}(\mathsf{p1}, \ldots, \mathsf{pn})\ =\ \mathsf{d}]\!]\rho =$$
$$\mathsf{let}\ \rho_1 = decparams\ \langle \mathsf{p1} \ldots \mathsf{pn}\rangle\ arid\ \mathsf{in}$$
$$\mathsf{let}\ \rho_2 = \mathsf{pushenv}\ \rho_1\ \rho\ \mathsf{in}$$
$$\mathsf{let}\ \langle m, \langle c, \rho_3\rangle\rangle = \mathcal{L}[\![\mathsf{d}]\!]\rho_1\ \mathsf{in}$$
$$\langle c, decfun\ \mathsf{ident}\ n\ m\ \rho\rangle$$

$$\mathcal{D}[\![\mathsf{decvar\ v\ :=\ e}]\!]\rho =$$
$$\mathsf{let}\ \langle a_v, \rho_1\rangle = decgvar\ \mathsf{v}\ \rho\ \mathsf{in}$$
$$\langle \mathcal{E}[\![\mathsf{e}]\!]\rho;\ \mathsf{setglobal}\ a_v, \rho_1\rangle$$

$$\mathcal{D}[\![\mathsf{decconst\ c\ :=\ e}]\!]\rho =$$
$$\mathsf{let}\ \langle a_c, \rho_1\rangle = decgcon\ \mathsf{c}\ \rho\ \mathsf{in}$$
$$\langle \mathcal{E}[\![\mathsf{e}]\!]\rho;\ \mathsf{setglobal}\ a_c, \rho'\rangle$$

$$\mathcal{L}[\![\mathsf{let\ decs\ in\ c}]\!]\rho =$$
$$\mathsf{let}\ \langle n, \langle c, \rho'\rangle = \mathcal{L}_S[\![\mathsf{decs}]\!]\rho\ \mathsf{in}$$
$$\langle n, \langle c\ddagger\mathcal{C}[\![\mathsf{c}]\!]\rho', \rho'\rangle\rangle$$

$$\mathcal{L}[\![\mathsf{c}]\!]\rho = \langle 0, \langle \mathcal{C}[\![\mathsf{c}]\!]\rho, \rho\rangle\rangle$$

$$\mathcal{L}_S[\![\mathsf{dec1} \ldots \mathsf{decn}]\!]\rho =$$
$$decseql\ \langle \mathsf{dec1} \ldots \mathsf{decn}\rangle, \rho\langle\rangle$$

where:

$$decseql\ d\ \ddagger\ \langle\rangle\ \rho\ C =$$
$$\mathsf{let}\ \langle c, \rho_1\rangle = \mathcal{L}_1[\![d]\!]\rho\ \mathsf{in}$$
$$\langle c\ddagger C, \rho_1\rangle$$
$$decseql\ d\ \ddagger\ \langle d_1, \ldots, d_n\rangle\ \rho\ C =$$
$$\mathsf{let}\ \langle c, \rho_1\rangle = \mathcal{L}_1[\![d]\!]\rho\ \mathsf{in}$$
$$declseql\ \langle d_1, \ldots, d_n\rangle\ \rho_1\ c\ddagger C$$

$$\mathcal{L}_1[\![\mathsf{Ident\ :=\ e}]\!]\rho =$$
$$\mathsf{let}\ \langle a, \rho_1\rangle = declvar\ \mathsf{Ident}\ \mathsf{in}$$
$$\langle \mathcal{E}[\![\mathsf{e}]\!]\rho_1;\ \mathsf{setlocal}\ a, \rho_1\rangle$$

$$\mathcal{L}_1[\![\mathsf{Ident\ =\ e}]\!]\rho =$$
$$\mathsf{let}\ \langle a, \rho_1\rangle = declcon\ \mathsf{Ident}\ \mathsf{in}$$
$$\langle \mathcal{E}[\![\mathsf{e}]\!]\rho_1;\ \mathsf{setlocal}\ a, \rho_1\rangle$$

Finally, we have the $\mathcal{G}$ scheme for the main program. In ALEX, the main program is just the body of the top-level let. Notice that an environment is supplied. This will contain library constants, variables and routines, which are considered to be global. The body of the main program is just a command.

$$\mathcal{P}[\![\mathsf{letdec1} \ldots \mathsf{decn\ in\ c}]\!]\rho =$$
$$\mathsf{let}\ \langle c, \rho_1\rangle = \mathcal{D}_s[\![\mathsf{dec1} \ldots \mathsf{decn}]\!]\rho\ \mathsf{in}$$
$$\mathcal{C}[\![\mathsf{c}]\!]\rho_1$$
$$\mathsf{halt}$$

where:

$$\mathcal{D}_s[\![\mathsf{dec1} \ \ldots \ \mathsf{decn}]\!]\rho =$$
$$decseqlg\langle\mathsf{dec1} \ \ldots \ \mathsf{decn}\rangle \, \rho, \langle\rangle$$

and:

$$decseqlg \ d \ddagger \langle\rangle \ \rho \ C =$$
$$\mathsf{let} \ \langle c, \rho_1\rangle = \mathcal{D}[\![d]\!]\rho \ \mathsf{in}$$
$$\langle c \ddagger C, \rho_1\rangle$$
$$decseqlg \ d \ddagger \langle d_1, \ldots, d_n\rangle \ \rho \ C =$$
$$\mathsf{let} \ \langle c, \rho_1\rangle = \mathcal{D}[\![d]\!]\rho \ \mathsf{in}$$
$$declseql \ \langle d_1, \ldots, d_n\rangle \ \rho_1 \ c \ddagger C$$

B

Harrison Machine Compilation Rules

B.1 Introduction

This appendix contains a specification of the compilation rules for the Harrison Machine language described in Chapter 6. The notation employed is similar to that used for the ALEX compilation rules.

B.2 Compilation Rules

With the VM transitions established, we can define the compilation rules for the Harrison Machine's rule language.

An outline instruction set for the Harrison Machine is shown in the Appendix C, where he instruction's mnemonic name is shown together with a brief explanation of its function.

In this Appendix, we adopt the following notational conventions. Items printed in this font represent abstract syntax items. Items printed in this font are Harrison VM instructions, literals and labels.

The first compilation scheme is the $\mathcal{V}$ scheme for the compilation of literal values. As presented below, it deals only with integer and boolean values for illustrative purposes.

$\mathcal{V}[\![0]\!] = \text{push0}$
$\mathcal{V}[\![1]\!] = \text{push1}$
$\mathcal{V}[\![n]\!] = \text{push n}$
$\mathcal{V}[\![\text{true}]\!] = \text{push1}$
$\mathcal{V}[\![\text{false}]\!] = \text{push0}$

Next, there is the $\mathcal{O}$ scheme. This is the scheme that defines the compilation of the various primitive operators defined in the rule language. It is, in essence, just a table lookup. Again, not all cases are included; they can be inferred from the instruction set summary.

$\mathcal{O}[\![+]\!] = \texttt{iadd}$

$\mathcal{O}[\![-]\!] = \texttt{isub}$

$\mathcal{O}[\![*]\!] = \texttt{imult}$

$\mathcal{O}[\![/]\!] = \texttt{idiv}$

$\mathcal{O}[\![\text{minus}]\!] = \texttt{iminus}$

$\mathcal{O}[\![\text{rem}]\!] = \texttt{irem}$

$\mathcal{O}[\![\text{and}]\!] = \texttt{land}$

$\mathcal{O}[\![\text{or}]\!] = \texttt{lor}$

$\mathcal{O}[\![\text{not}]\!] = \texttt{lnot}$

The $\mathcal{V}$ and $\mathcal{O}$ schemes return single instructions.

Next, we define the $\mathcal{R}_P$ scheme, the scheme defining library routine call compilation. Most implementations of the VM have used an escape mechanism to call library routines (which have usually been written in the same language used to implement the VM). The escape mechanism consists of executing a primcall instruction whose (single) operand is an unsigned integer denoting the library routine. This scheme looks up the identifier of the library routine (r) in the environment (ρ) using the lookup function $lookup_R$. The reader should not confuse this function with the function $lookup$ which looks up variable names in the environment; one big difference between them is that $lookup$ returns a pair of natural numbers, while $lookup_R$ returns a single natural (see below).

$$\mathcal{R}_P[\![r]\!]\rho = \texttt{primcall} \; (lookup_R \; r \; \rho)$$

The $\mathcal{E}$ and $\mathcal{C}$ schemes are the major elements of this part of the description. These schemes return sequences of instructions and labels (by convention, labels are identifiers with prefix $). In the compilation schemes below, juxtaposition of instructions vertically represents concatenation; where horizontally presented, instructions will be separated by a single semicolon.

The compilation scheme for expressions, the $\mathcal{E}$ scheme, is as follows:

$\mathcal{E}[\![\text{ident}]\!]\rho \quad\quad = \texttt{getvar} \; (lookup \; \text{ident}, \rho)$

$\mathcal{E}[\![\text{unop e}]\!]\rho \quad\quad = \mathcal{E}[\![e]\!]\rho; \; \mathcal{O}[\![\text{unop}]\!]\rho$

$\mathcal{E}[\![\text{e1 binop e2}]\!]\rho = \mathcal{E}[\![e2]\!]\rho; \; \mathcal{E}[\![e1]\!]\rho; \; \mathcal{O}[\![\text{binop}]\!]\rho$

$\mathcal{E}[\![f(v1...vn)]\!]\rho \quad = \mathcal{E}[\![v1]\!]\rho; \; ... \; \mathcal{E}[\![vn]\!]\rho; \; \mathcal{R}_P[\![f]\!]\rho$

Note that the scheme uses the $lookup$ function. This is a function from identifiers to lexical addresses that looks up an identifier in the compile-time environment and returns its runtime address. The runtime address is composed of a pair, (f, o), where f is the *frame offset* and o is the *variable offset* within the frame.

Also, it should be noted that error cases are not included in these schemes. In particular, the cases for undeclared variables, incorrect function arities and undefined functions are all omitted; this is for reasons of clarity of presentation.

The first part of the $\mathcal{C}$ scheme, the command compilation scheme, now follows.

$\mathcal{C}[\![abort]\!]\rho$ $= \mathtt{jmp} \; \$\mathtt{Term}$
$\mathcal{C}[\![skip]\!]\rho$ $= \langle\rangle$
$\mathcal{C}[\![suspend]\!]\rho = \mathtt{suspend}; \; \mathtt{jmp} \; \$\mathtt{Start}$

The above schemes refer to two labels: $\mathtt{\$Term}$ and $\mathtt{\$Start}$. These are conventional names used in the specification. Label $\mathtt{\$Start}$ conventionally labels the start of a rule's pattern code, while $\mathtt{\$Term}$ labels its last instruction (usually a **term** instruction). The use of these labels will become clear below.

The rule for **skip** merely generates the empty instruction sequence.

Next, we define the scheme for assignment. Like the above schemes, it is quite easily comprehended.

$$\mathcal{C}[\![x := e]\!]\rho = \mathcal{E}[\![e]\!]\rho; \; \mathtt{setvar}(lookup \; \mathsf{x} \; \rho)$$

It is, however, worth noting that the environment parameter, ρ, refers to the environment produced by the compiler (the symbol table, in other words) and *not* to the environment maintained by the VM.

We now come to the schemes for the compilation of if and do. Necessarily, these are relatively large for the reason that they produce reasonable quantities of output code. Even so, they are, really, quite easily understood. It should be noted that there are various optimisations that can be applied to both if and do but, in order to be brief, we omit them here.

$\mathcal{C}[\![if \; e1 \rightarrow s1]\!] \ldots [\![en \rightarrow Sn \; fi]\!]\rho =$
$\qquad\qquad\qquad \mathcal{E}[\![e1]\!]\rho$
$\qquad\qquad\qquad \mathtt{jne} \; \$\mathtt{L}_2$
$\qquad\qquad\qquad \mathcal{C}[\![s1]\!]\rho$
$\qquad\qquad\qquad \mathtt{jmp} \; \$\mathtt{Lend}$
$\qquad\qquad\qquad \$\mathtt{L2} :$
$\qquad\qquad\qquad \ldots$
$\qquad\qquad\qquad \$\mathtt{Ln} : \mathcal{E}[\![en]\!]\rho$
$\qquad\qquad\qquad \mathtt{jne} \; \$\mathtt{Lend}$
$\qquad\qquad\qquad \mathcal{C}[\![sn]\!]\rho$
$\qquad\qquad\qquad \$\mathtt{Lend} :$

The if command compiles into the code that one would expect. In essence, it works by evaluating each condition expression, e1 ... en, in turn. If a test evaluates to false, the next condition is evaluated; if it evaluates to true, the corresponding command is evaluated and control immediately passes to the end of the construct. This is implemented by inserting a label before the compiled code for each condition expression. After each command, there is an unconditional jump to the end of the entire if.

In some versions of the rule language, we defined additional conditionals such as if-then-else. These can be compiled using the obvious source-to-source transformation.

$\mathcal{C}[\![\text{do } e1 \to s1]\!] \ldots [\![en \to sn \text{ od}]\!]\rho =$

$$\$Lstart : \mathcal{E}[\![e1]\!]\rho$$
$$\text{jne } \$L2$$
$$\mathcal{C}[\![s1]\!]\rho$$
$$\text{jmp Lstart}$$
$$\$L2 :$$
$$\ldots$$
$$\$Ln : \mathcal{E}[\![en]\!]\rho$$
$$\text{jne } \$Lend$$
$$\mathcal{C}[\![sn]\!]\rho$$
$$\text{jmp } \$Lstart$$
$$\$Lend :$$

The do command is similar to the if conditional. The most obvious difference is that do is iterative. The compiled code for do begins with a label ($Lstart). The conditional expressions are chained together as in if; if control reaches the last conditional and it fails, control passes out of the do by jumping to the end label, $Lend. To produce iterative behaviour, after the compiled code for each command, an unconditional jump to the start of the do is inserted.

Source-to-source transformations of the obvious kind can be used to define other kinds of iterative command in terms of do for example, when and until (in this present context, of course, the symbols "when" and "until" cannot be used).

We next consider procedure calls.

$\mathcal{C}[\![p(e1, \ldots, en)]\!]\rho = \mathcal{E}[\![e1]\!]\rho \ \ldots \ \mathcal{E}[\![en]\!]\rho; \ \mathcal{R}_P[\![p]\!]\rho$

Procedure call is compiled in the obvious way: the actual parameters are compiled (at present, the rule language supports only call-by-value parameters). Then, the procedure name is compiled using the $\mathcal{R}_P$ scheme for compiling primitive routines (which generates a `primcall` instruction). As with functions, we ignore the cases in which the identifier p is not a library procedure; we also ignore errors involving incorrect arity.

Next, we come to the cause command. This consists of compiling the expressions that provide values to be passed in the event structure. Then, the $\mathcal{T}$ scheme is used to generate the code for the event type. We do not define the $\mathcal{T}$ scheme in this Appendix (it involves the compilation of event structure definitions for use by the compiler, a process we prefer to omit because it is not relevant to the overall presentation).

$\mathcal{C}[\![\text{cause}(t, e1, \ldots, en)]\!]\rho = \mathcal{E}[\![e1]\!]\rho; \ \ldots \ \mathcal{E}[\![en]\!]\rho; \ \mathcal{T}[\![t]\!]\rho; \ \text{mkev}; \ \text{cause}$

The use of the `mkev` and `cause` instructions in sequence should be noted in the above scheme.

The last $\mathcal{C}$ scheme we require is the one for compiling sequential composition. It is quite simple:

$$\mathcal{C}[\![\mathsf{s1}; \mathsf{s2}]\!]\rho = \mathcal{C}[\![\mathsf{s1}]\!]\rho;\ \mathcal{C}[\![\mathsf{s2}]\!]\rho$$

Next, we introduce the $\mathcal{D}$ scheme for the compilation of let constructs. This scheme is interesting and supports a number of variations. To start, we introduce an additional scheme:

$$\mathcal{D}_D[\![\mathsf{declare}(\mathsf{v1} := \mathsf{e1}; \ldots \mathsf{vn} := \mathsf{en})]\!]\rho =$$

> newenv n
> $\mathcal{E}[\![\mathsf{e1}]\!]\rho$
> setvar 0 0
> . . .
> $\mathcal{E}[\![\mathsf{en}]\!]\rho$
> setvar 0 $(\mathsf{n} - 1)$

The scheme begins by introducing a new frame in the environment using the **newenv** instruction (the operand to **newenv** is just the number of variables declared by the let). The variables declared by the let are initialised using the $\mathcal{E}$ scheme for the expressions, then assigned to the appropriate variable using **setvar** (note that the frame offset is always zero—**setvar** and **getvar** index the environment from the top downwards). This establishes the environment in which the body is to be executed. (We will use the $\mathcal{D}_D$ scheme below when dealing with rules.)

We then have:

$$\mathcal{D}[\![\mathsf{let}\ \mathsf{v1} := \mathsf{e1}; \ldots \mathsf{vn} := \mathsf{en}\ \mathsf{in}\ \mathsf{s}]\!]\rho =$$

> $\mathcal{D}_D[\![\mathsf{declare}(\mathsf{v1} := \mathsf{e1}; \ldots \mathsf{vn} := \mathsf{en})]\!]\rho$
> $\mathcal{C}[\![\mathsf{s}]\!]\rho'$
> drop

First, the $\mathcal{D}_D$ scheme is used to establish a new environment of the correct size. Next, the $\mathcal{C}$ scheme is used to compile the body of the let in the environment composed of that in force immediately outside the let plus the variables declared by it; this is denoted by ρ' in the scheme. The previous environment is re-established by the **drop** instruction appearing at the end of the compilation scheme.

Now, there are some choices to be made. The environment in which the body is compiled (and executed) cannot be altered; it must be as described above and it must be discarded at the end of the body. In the above scheme, we have assumed that the expressions that initialise the variables in the declaration part are compiled (and executed) in the environment that was in force at the point at which the let was entered. This has the implication that, within the initialising expressions, there can be no references to any of the variables that are declared by the let. It is possible, on pain of more complex semantics, to permit mutually recursive declarations. We prefer, here, not to do this because of its complexity.

We continue with a presentation of the rules used to compile rules to virtual machine code. We will start with the schemes for compiling the patterns that can appear in rules. The process can be divided into an operation to test the type of the event being matched, and then two other operations: one to extract the value stored in an event at a given offset and a second to test the value stored in an event (this second operation will be referred to as "binding").

First, the schema for testing the type of an event is given by:

$$\mathcal{P}[\![t]\!]\rho = \texttt{getev}; \ \texttt{etype}; \ \mathcal{E}[\![t]\!]\rho; \ \texttt{ieq}; \ \texttt{jne \$fail}$$

The event structure is pushed onto the caller's stack (getev) and the type field extracted by etype. The expression, t, is intended to evaluate to an integer denoting an event type. The value derived from t is then compared, using ieq, with the value of the type field in the event. If the two values are identical, control falls out of the bottom of this scheme; otherwise, control passes to the label $fail.

The scheme for assigning the value stored at some index in the event is as follows:

$$\mathcal{P}_E[\![x < -e]\!]\rho = \texttt{getev}; \ \mathcal{E}[\![e]\!]\rho; \ \texttt{getpe}; \ \texttt{setvar} \ (lookup \ x, \rho)$$

Here, x is the variable into which the value will be assigned and e is an expression which evaluates to an integer index into the event's data vector (which is pushed onto the caller's stack by the getpe instruction). The assignment is performed by the usual operation.

Finally, the operation for testing the value stored at a given index in the event's data vector is the following.

$$\mathcal{P}_E[\![x? = e]\!]\rho = \texttt{E}[\![e]\!]\rho; \ \texttt{getev}; \ \mathcal{E}[\![x]\!]\rho; \ \texttt{getpe}; \ \texttt{ieq}; \ \texttt{jne \$fail}$$

The expression x is evaluated to produce an index into the event's data vector (the value is extracted using getpe as above). The expression e is evaluated. If the value stored in the event is identical (using ieq) to the one computed, control drops out of the bottom of this scheme; otherwise, control is passed to the failure continuation denoted by $fail.

We use the notation $\mathcal{P}[\![p]\!]\rho$ to denote the compilation of an entire pattern, p, composed of a type test followed by zero or more test and binding expressions. The instruction immediately after a compiled pattern's code is executed if an event satisfies the pattern test; failure continues at a point labelled $fail. This makes the compilation of pattern code extremely simple; it does make the compilation of rules a little harder to understand.

Next, we give the compilation schemes for rules *when used as commands*. As noted above, rules can constitute part of rule bodies; thus, they are commands. When rules are considered commands, they execute in a context pro-

vided by the declarations in force at the point of the rule's definition. This
makes the definition of the various schemes relatively simple. There is, though,
the constraint that a rule that is executed as a command should always wait
until the *next* virtual machine cycle before it executes. For this reason, each
compilation scheme for a rule as a command begins with the **suspend** instruction.

We allow all rule forms to appear as commands, so we will give the compilation schemes for each. The schemes for top-level rules will be given below.
The reason for this order is that when rules are used as commands nested
within commands, their compilation schemes are a little simpler than those
for rules at the top level.

The easiest rules to compile are the always and next rules.

$$\mathcal{R}_C[\![\text{always do s}]\!]\rho =$$
$$\qquad \text{suspend}$$
$$\qquad \text{\$Lstart : mkrdy}$$
$$\qquad \mathcal{C}[\![\text{s}]\!]\rho$$
$$\qquad \text{suspend}$$
$$\qquad \text{jmp \$Lstart}$$

The always rule executes its entire body on each virtual machine cycle.
Each time the body executes, the rule should wait until the next virtual machine cycle before executing again. This is the reason for the second **suspend**
instruction. The rule executes a **mkrdy** instruction when it has looped back to
$Lstart in order to make itself a rule that is ready to execute.

$$\mathcal{R}_C[\![\text{next do s}]\!]\rho = \text{suspend; mdkrdy; } \mathsf{C}[\![\text{s}]\!]\rho$$

The next rule is used to ensure that its body is executed on the immediately
succeeding cycle of the virtual machine; the body is executed only once. The
next rule compiles into instructions that first suspend the rule and then, on
the next virtual machine cycle, makes itself a ready rule (using **mkrdy**).

$$\mathcal{R}_C[\![\text{when p do s}]\!]\rho =$$
$$\qquad \text{suspend}$$
$$\qquad \text{\$Lstart : } \mathcal{P}[\![\text{p}]\!]\rho$$
$$\qquad \text{mkrdy}$$
$$\qquad \text{jmp \$ok}$$
$$\qquad \text{\$fail : notrdy}$$
$$\qquad \text{jmp \$Lstart}$$
$$\qquad \text{\$ok : } \mathcal{C}[\![\text{s}]\!]\rho$$

A when rule has a pattern, p, and a body, s. If the pattern matches the
current event, the body is executed on that VM cycle; otherwise, the rule is
suspended so that it can be tested again on the next VM cycle. This is the
first rule we have encountered that employs a pattern.

When the rule is executed, the pattern is first evaluated (using the $\mathcal{P}$ scheme defined above). If the match is successful, the mkrdy instruction places the rule in the set of ready rules; otherwise, the notrdy instruction is executed. If the notrdy instruction is executed, when the rule is tested on the next VM cycle, control will start at the instruction immediately after notrdy. This is a jump which causes control to pass to a point where the pattern is evaluated. If, on the other hand, the match was successful, when the ready rule is run to execute its body, the first thing done is to jump to the start of the body's code. When the body has terminated, control passes out of the rule.

$\mathcal{R}_C[\![\text{unless p do s}]\!]\rho =$

```
        suspend
$Lstart : P[p]ρ
$ok : notrdy
jmp $Lstart
$fail : mkrdy
C[s]ρ
```

The unless rule is, in a sense, the complement of when: it is executed only when its pattern is not satisfied by the current event. This duality is reflected in the use of the $fail label. If control directly passes out of the pattern-matching code, the pattern has not been satisfied by the current event. For this reason, the rule is made not ready (by the notrdy instruction) immediately *after* the pattern code. The $fail label, on the other hand, denotes success for unless rules, so the instruction labelled $fail is mkrdy (which makes the caller a ready rule) after which the body, p, is executed.

$\mathcal{R}_C[\![\text{since p do s}]\!]\rho =$

```
        suspend
$Lstart : P[p]ρ
mkrdy
jmp $ok
$fail : notrdy
jmp $Lstart
$ok : C[s]ρ
suspend
jmp; $ok
```

Like until, since requires the repeated execution of the body, s, of the rule. The biggest difference between them is that since evaluates its pattern before its body is executed, while until evaluates its body first. The scheme for since is, in many ways, similar to that for when. When the body, s, has been executed, the rule suspends (using suspend) and then jumps back to the start of the body.

$\mathcal{R}_C[\![\text{until p do s}]\!]\rho =$

        suspend

        \$Lstart : $\mathcal{C}[\![\text{s}]\!]\rho$

        suspend

        $\mathcal{P}[\![\text{p}]\!]\rho$

        jmp \$ok

        \$fail : mkrdy

        jmp \$Lstart

        \$ok :

The until rule executes its body at least once before it evaluates its pattern. The pattern is always executed on the *next* VM cycle, so the body ends with a suspend instruction. If the pattern is satisfied by the current event, control should pass out of the rule (by jumping to \$ok). If the pattern is not satisfied, the body should be executed again, so the rule is made ready (mkrdy) and control is passed to the start of the body when the ready rules are executed.

We permit alt rules to appear as commands. The compilation of the rules that are components of an alt is very close to the above schemes, the only difference being the way in which failure is handled. To compile an alt, the rules are chained together so that the pattern of a rule is only evaluated if the pattern of the previous rule has failed. We use the failure continuation to do this chaining. This means that each compilation scheme ends with the label to which control is passed when the pattern's evaluation fails. As usual, the unless rule, uses the complementary approach to handling failure.

The scheme for compiling an alt command's rules is called the $\mathcal{R}_{CA}$ scheme. We first give the schemes for the rule forms that we currently permit inside an alt command.

The schemes are as follows. It should be observed that, after the successful execution of a rule's body, control is passed to the end of the entire alt command.

$\mathcal{R}_{CA}[\![\text{when p do s}]\!]\rho = \mathcal{P}[\![\text{p}]\!];\ \text{mkrdy};\ \mathcal{C}[\![!][\text{s}]\!]\rho;\ \text{jmp \$endalt};\ \$\text{fail} :$

$\mathcal{R}_{CA}[\![\text{unless p do s}]\!]\rho =$

        $\mathcal{P}[\![\text{p}]\!]\rho$

        jmp \$next

        \$fail : mkrdy

        $\mathcal{C}[\![\text{s}]\!]\rho$

        jmp \$endalt

        \$next :

$\mathcal{R}_{CA}[\![\text{since p do s}]\!]\rho = \mathcal{P}[\![\text{p}]\!]\rho;\ \text{mkrdy};\ \$b : \mathcal{C}[\![\text{s}]\!]\rho;\ \text{jmp \$b};\ \$\text{fail} :$

It should, of course, be noted that each failure label, here written \$fail, is generated by the compiler and guaranteed to be unique. (A similar remark applies to all labels in the compilation schemes given here.)

$$\mathcal{R}_{CA}[\![\text{next do s}]\!]\rho = \texttt{mkrdy}; \mathcal{C}[\![!][\![s]\!]\rho; \texttt{jmp \$endalt}$$

The next rule is permitted inside alt commands as a kind of optional default action to be executed when no other rule applies. It is considered legal for an alt command to contain no next rule. However, alt commands can contain *at most* one next rule.

The alt command itself is very simple:

$$\mathcal{C}[\![\text{alt r1}, \ldots, \text{ rk}]\!]\rho = \texttt{\$LLstart} : \mathcal{R}_{CA}[\![\text{r1}]\!]\rho \ldots \mathcal{R}_{CA}[\![\text{r1}]\!]\rho; \texttt{\$endalt} :$$

The scheme merely concatenates the code of each of the component rules. They are connected, as outlined above, using their failure labels. The scheme ends with the $endalt label to which every rule jumps after successful execution.

In the rule language, the top-level elements are always rules. We now move onto the compilation schemes for these rules. Top-level rules fall into two groups:

1. Those that have a set of outermost declarations;
2. Those that do not.

We start with the second group, for they are slightly simpler and show all the main points of top-level rule compilation. Again, we note that not all rule forms are permitted at the top-level: in particular, next rules are not permitted (for obvious reasons).

The always rule is the simplest of those that can appear at top level. The compilation scheme for always rules is as follows:

$$\mathcal{R}_T[\![\text{always do s}]\!]\rho =$$

```
$Lstart : arid
clear
$next : mkrdy
C[s]ρ
suspend
jmp $next
$Lterm : term
```

The first thing to observe is that the scheme, like all other top-level schemes, respects the semantics of the rule type. The scheme introduces an initial label and instructions to clear the runtime environment and the stack. Then the actual always code appears. At the end of this code is the $Lterm label and the term instruction; the abort command causes control to jump to the $Lterm label.

$\mathcal{R}_T[\![\text{when p do s}]\!]\rho =$

$\quad\quad\quad\quad$ \$Lstart : arid

$\quad\quad\quad\quad$ clear

$\quad\quad\quad\quad$ $\mathcal{P}[\![\text{p}]\!]\rho$

$\quad\quad\quad\quad$ mkrdy

$\quad\quad\quad\quad$ jmp \$ok

$\quad\quad\quad\quad$ \$fail : notrdy

$\quad\quad\quad\quad$ jmp \$Lstart

$\quad\quad\quad\quad$ \$ok : $\mathcal{C}[\![\text{s}]\!]\rho$

$\quad\quad\quad\quad$ suspend

$\quad\quad\quad\quad$ jmp \$Lstart

$\quad\quad\quad\quad$ \$Lterm : term

The scheme for top-level **when** rules begins with code to initialise the environment and stack. Then there is the code to implement the rule's behaviour. This is followed by the **term** code. It is worth noting, at this point, that **abort** (and, hence, **term**) are used to *terminate* rules, not merely to halt their execution. As can be seen from this example, when the body of a **when** (or **unless**) has completed, control passes back to the *start* of the rule, thus permitting it to be executed on a subsequent virtual machine cycle.

$\mathcal{R}_T[\![\text{unless p do s}]\!]\rho =$

$\quad\quad\quad\quad$ \$Lstart : arid

$\quad\quad\quad\quad$ clear

$\quad\quad\quad\quad$ $\mathcal{P}[\![\text{p}]\!]\rho$

$\quad\quad\quad\quad$ notrdy

$\quad\quad\quad\quad$ jmp \$Lstart

$\quad\quad\quad\quad$ \$fail : mkrdy

$\quad\quad\quad\quad$ $\mathcal{C}[\![\text{s}]\!]\rho$

$\quad\quad\quad\quad$ suspend

$\quad\quad\quad\quad$ jmp \$Lstart

$\quad\quad\quad\quad$ \$Lterm : term

The **unless** rule scheme also begins with initialisation, then the behaviour of the rule is compiled; finally, the termination code appears. In this case, as in all other cases of **unless**, matcher failure causes execution of the rule's body, while success causes a jump back to the start of the pattern code.

$\mathcal{R}_T[\![\text{since p do s}]\!]\rho =$

```
$Lstart : arid
clear
𝒫[p]ρ
mkrdy
jmp $ok
$fail : notrdy
jmp $Lstart
$ok : 𝒞[s]ρ
suspend
jmp $ok
$Lterm : term
```

Iterative rules like since and until are only a little more complicated. Like the other rule forms, they begin with initialisation code and they end with the term instruction. For the since rule, if the pattern code fails on a virtual machine cycle, there is a jump back to the rule's initialisation code to clear the environment and the stack. The body of the since is repeatedly executed. There is no jump back to the start of the rule's code for the reason that since rules should iterate forever (or until they are terminated by some event).

The until rule scheme now follows. Its form should be easily understood.

$\mathcal{R}_T[\![\text{until p do s}]\!]\rho =$

```
$Lstart : arid
clear
$l : 𝒞[s]ρ
suspend
𝒫[p]ρ
jmp $ok
$fail : mkrdy
jmp $l
$ok : suspend
jmp $Lstart
$Lterm : term
```

The other top-level form of rule is one in which a let encloses some rule (always, when, unless, since, until and alt). The schemes for these rules follows a general pattern, which we exemplify by the the following scheme for when rules that are enclosed in a let. We only give the essentials in the following.

$\mathcal{R}_{TAB}[\![\text{let d in when p do s}]\!]\rho =$

$\qquad\qquad$ \$Lstart : clear

$\qquad\qquad$ arid

$\qquad\qquad$ $\mathcal{D}[\![\text{d}]\!]\rho(= \rho')$

$\qquad\qquad$ $\mathcal{P}[\![\text{p}]\!]\rho'$

$\qquad\qquad$ mkrdy

$\qquad\qquad$ $\mathcal{C}[\![\text{s}]\!]\rho'$

$\qquad\qquad$ suspend

$\qquad\qquad$ jmp \$Lstart

$\qquad\qquad$ \$fail : drop

$\qquad\qquad\qquad \cdots$

The declarations are compiled using the $\mathcal{D}$ scheme immediately after the stack and environment have been initialised. The declarations create a new environment (denoted by ρ') which is used by the subsequent compilation schemes. If the pattern-matching operation fails, the environment that was added by the $\mathcal{D}$ scheme must be removed, hence the use of the **drop** instruction.

The other rule forms have a similar structure when wrapped in declarations. In every case, immediately after the environment and stack initialisation, the $\mathcal{D}$ scheme is used to compile the declarations. When the matching operation fails, the environment is dropped. We leave their elaboration to the interested reader.

At the top level, alt rules can occur. As with alt commands, it is necessary to thread the component rules together. We give the compilation schemes for when, unless and since components. We do not permit always or until as top-level alt components because of their iterative characteristics. We do permit since even though it is iterative; this is because it has a starting event that can be identified. Rules like always and until do not have identifiable start events when they appear at top level.

When a rule appears as an alt component, the main issues are the threading of the failure code and the action taken when a rule body successfully completes. We give the compilation schemes for the three rule forms that we currently permit inside top-level alt rules.

Before continuing, it is worth noting that all stack and environment initialisation will have been performed by the alt rule, so they are not required here.

$\mathcal{R}_{TA}[\![\text{when p do s}]\!]\rho =$

$\qquad\qquad$ $\mathcal{P}[\![\text{p}]\!]\rho$

$\qquad\qquad$ mkrdy

$\qquad\qquad$ $\mathcal{C}[\![\text{s}]\!]\rho$

$\qquad\qquad$ suspend

$\qquad\qquad$ jmp \$Lstart

$\qquad\qquad$ \$fail :

The first thing to note is that the failure continuation is used to thread the code. In this case, as in the case of alt commands, when a pattern's evaluation fails, control passes to the next rule in the alt. If the pattern succeeds and the body is executed, control passes to the jmp immediately after the body (denoted, as always by the $\mathcal{C}$ scheme). This jump makes a transfer of control to the start of the *enclosing* alt rule.

$$\mathcal{R}_{TA}[\![\text{unless p do s}]\!]\rho =$$
$$\qquad \mathcal{P}[\![\text{p}]\!]\rho$$
$$\qquad \text{jmp \$fail}$$
$$\qquad \text{\$ok : mkrdy}$$
$$\qquad \mathcal{C}[\![\text{s}]\!]\rho$$
$$\qquad \text{suspend}$$
$$\qquad \text{jmp \$Lstart}$$
$$\qquad \text{\$fail :}$$

The keen reader will have observed that this kind of unless rule follows the convention that pattern failure causes body execution, while pattern success causes rule failure. In this case, if the pattern's evaluation fails for an event, control passes to the \$fail label. This label is used, as in the other cases of alt components, to thread control. If the body *is* executed, control immediately passes back to the alt's initialisation code.

The last case is that of a since rule inside an alt. This case differs slightly in that control does not return to the start of the enclosing alt rule after the execution of the body.

$$\mathcal{R}_{TA}[\![\text{since p do s}]\!]\rho =$$
$$\qquad \mathcal{P}[\![\text{p}]\!]\rho$$
$$\qquad \text{mkrdy}$$
$$\qquad \text{\$b : } \mathcal{C}[\![\text{s}]\!]\rho$$
$$\qquad \text{suspend}$$
$$\qquad \text{jmp \$b}$$
$$\qquad \text{\$fail :}$$

Finally, we need the scheme for top-level alt rules. Like the schemes for alt that we have already seen, it is quite simple. Here it is:

$$\mathcal{R}_{T}[\![\text{alt r1, } \ldots, \text{rk}]\!]\rho =$$
$$\qquad \text{\$Lstart : arid}$$
$$\qquad \text{clear}$$
$$\qquad \mathcal{R}_{TA}[\![\text{r1}]\!]\rho$$
$$\qquad \ldots$$
$$\qquad \mathcal{R}_{TA}[\![\text{rk}]\!]\rho$$
$$\qquad \text{suspend}$$
$$\qquad \text{jmp \$Lstart}$$
$$\qquad \text{\$Lterm : term}$$

Here, we have the usual initialisation code. This is labelled $Lstart, as we now have come to expect. There follows the code produced by the compilation of the component rules. It should be noted that the compilation of a component rule plants the failure label for the implementation of threading. After the last rule in the alt scheme, there is a jump back to the start of the entire alt. The reason for this is that it clears all data off the stack and environment ready for the next attempt at matching its rules.

We currently do not permit next rules as components of top-level alt rules. We could do this with ease but it breaks the rule that we used to ban top-level until and always rules: their execution can be triggered by *any* event. The point of the alt is that it "chooses" between rules that could trigger on the current event. The excluded cases do not exhibit such behaviour and do not trigger on particular event types. This appears to violate our semantics for alt.

Our rule compilers do not prevent us from compiling these three rule forms inside top-level (or any other) alt rules. If we find good reasons to include them, we will do so (perhaps a little reluctantly).

C

Harrison Machine Instruction Set

In this Appendix, an instruction set for the Harrison Machine described in Chapter 6 is outlined.

primcall n Call primitive number n.

term Terminate the rule.

suspend Suspend the calling rule.

mkrdy Place caller in the Ready Set.

notrdy Place caller in the Waiting Set.

clone Clone this rule.

reset Reset the instruction pointer to zero.

getev Push the current event onto the stack.

etype Extract the type of the current event and push it.
The event must be on the top of the stack.

jmp L Jump to label L.

jeq L Jump to label L if top of stack is not zero.

jne L Jump to label L if top of stack is zero

push0 Push zero onto stack.

push1 Push one onto stack.

push n Push integer value n onto stack.

pop Pop stack.

dup Duplicate element on top of stack.

swap Swap the top two stack elements.

clear Clear the stack.

arid Create an empty environment.

newenv n Create a new environment frame of n elements and push onto environment stack.

drop Pop the top environment frame from environment. Discard the this frame.

setvar i j Set the jth variable in environment frame i.

getvar i j Get the value of the jth variable in environment frame i.

iadd Add top two stack elements. Push result.

isub Subtract.

iminus Unary minus.

imult Multiply top two stack elements. Push result.

irem Remainder.

idiv Integer division.

ieq Integer equality.

land Logical conjunction.

lor Logical disjunction.

lnot Logical negation.

halt Halt the processor. Set the termination flag.

Note:

- All arithmetic and comparison instructions operate on *integers*.
- The standard representation for *false* is zero; *true* is represented by one.

References

1. Abelson, H., and Sussman, G. J., *The Structure and Interpretation of Computer Programs*, MIT Press, Cambridge MA, 1985.
2. Abrial, J.-R., *The B Book*, CUP, 1996.
3. Aït-Kaci, H., *Warren's Abstract Machine*, MIT Press, Cambridge MA, 1991.
4. Appel, A. W., *Compiling with Continuations*, CUP, 1992.
5. Appel, A. W., *Modern Compiler Implementation in Java*, CUP, 1998.
6. Baillarguet, C., MVV: langage et système, plus qu'un mariage de raison, *Journées des Jeunes Chercheurs en Système*, Rennes, France, June, 1999.
7. Bailey, R. *FP/M Abstract Syntax Description*, Internal Report, Dept. of Computing, Imperial College, London, 1985.
8. Barratt, R., Ramsey, A., and Sloman, A., *Pop-11: A Practical Language for Artificial Intelligence*, Ellis Horwood, Chichester, England, 1985.
9. Bell, James R., Threaded Code, *Communications of the ACM*, Vol. 16, No. 6, pp. 370–72, 1973.
10. Blaschek, G., *Object-Oriented Programming with Prototypes*, Springer-Verlag, Heidelberg, 1994.
11. Bobrow, D. G., and Stefik, M., *The LOOPS Manual*, Xerox PARC, Palo Alto, CA, 1983.
12. Brinch Hansen, P., Structured Multiprogramming, *CACM*, Vol. 15, No. 7, pp. 574–578, 1972.
13. Craig, I. D., Reflecting on Time, *Proc. Intl. Congress on Cybernetics and Systems*, International Cybernetics Society, 1999.
14. Craig, I. D., HM paper from Freiburg, 2003. Event-based Introspection and Communcation, *ESSCS Annual Conference*, Freiburg, Germany, August, 2003.
15. Craig, I. D., *The Interpretation of Object-Oriented Programming Languages*, 2nd edn., Springer-Verlag, London, 2002.
16. Diehl, Stephen, *Semantics-Directed Generation of Compilers and Abstract Machines*, Ph. D. Dissertation, University of Saarbrücken, Germany, 1996.
17. Diehl, Stephen, A generative methodology for the design of abstract machines, *Science of Computer Programming*, Vol. 38, pp. 125–142, 2000.
18. Field, A. J., and Harrison, P. G., *Functional Programming* Addison-Wesley, Wokingham, England, 1988.
19. Folliot, B., Virtual Virtual Machine Project, Invited Talk, *Simposio Brasileiro de Arquitetura de Computadores e Processamento de Alto Desempenho* (SBAC'2000), 2000.

20. Friedman, D. P., Wand, M., and Haynes, C.T., *Essentials of Programming Languages*, 2nd edn, MIT Press, Cambridge, MA, 2001.

21. Goldberg, A., and Robson, D., *Smalltalk-80: The Language and Its Implementation*, Addison-Wesley, Reading, MA, 1983.

22. Gosling, J., Joy, B., Steel, G., and Bracha, G., *The Java Language*™ *Specification*, 2nd edn, Addison-Wesley, 2000.

23. Gries, D., *Compiler Construction for Digital Computers*, John Wiley and Sons, New York, 1971.

24. Henderson, P., *Functional Programming*, Prentice-Hall, Hemel Hempstead, UK, 1980.

25. Johnsson, T., Lambda Lifting: Transforming Programs to Recursive Equations, *Proc. Conference on Functional Programming Languages and Computer Architectures*, Nancy, France, pp. 190–203, 1985.

26. Jones, C. B., *Systematic Software Development Using VDM*, Prentice-Hall, Hemel Hempstead, UK, 1986.

27. Kahn, G., *Natural Semantics*, Rapport de recherche no. 601, INRIA, Sophia-Antipolis, France, 1987.

28. Kelsey, R., Clinger, W., and Rees, J., (eds.), *Revised⁵ Report on the Algorithmic Language Scheme*, available from www.swiss.ai.mit.edu/projects/scheme.

29. Khoury, C. and Folliot, B., Environnement de programmation actif pour la mobilité, *Journées des Jeunes Chercheurs en Systèmes*, Besançon, June, 2000.

30. Landin, P. J., The mechanical evaluation of expressions, *Computer Journal*, Volume 8, pp. 301–20, 1964.

31. Liang, S., and Bracha, G., Dynamic Class Loading in the Java Virtual Machine, *Proc. OOPSLA*, 1998.

32. Lieberman, H., Concurrent Object Oriented Programming in Act 2, in *Object-Oriented Concurrent Programming*, Yonezawa, A. and Tokoro, M., (eds), pp. 55–89, MIT Press, Cambridge, MA, 1987.

33. Lindholm, T. and Yellin, F., *The Java*™ *Virtual Machine Specification*, 2nd edn, Addison-Wesley, Reading, MA, 1999.

34. Milne, R., and Strachey, C., *A Theory of Programming Language Semantics*, Halstead Press, London, 1976.

35. Milner, R., *Communicating and Mobile Systems: the π-calculus*, CUP, 1999.

36. Noble, J., Taivalsaari, A., and Moore, I., *Prototype-Based Programming*, Springer-Verlag, Singapore, 1998.

37. www.parrotcode.org/docs/

38. Peyton Jones, S., *Functional programming implementation*, Prentice-Hall, Hemel Hempstead, England, 1987.

39. Peyton Jones, S., and Salkild, J., The Spineless, Tagless G-Machine, *Proc. ACM Conf. on Functional Programming Languages and Architectures*, pp. 184–201, 1989.

40. Pierce, B., and Turner, D., Pict: A Programming Language Based on the Pi-Calculus, in *Proof, Languages and Interaction: Essays in Honour of Robin Milner*, Plotkin, G., Stirling, C. and Tofte, M. (eds), MIT Press, Cambridge, MA, 1998.

41. Plotkin, G., *A Structural Approach to Operational Semantics*, Report DAIMI FN-19, Computer Science Dept., University of Aarhus, Denmark, 1981

42. www.poplog.org.

43. Reppy, J. H., *Concurrent Programming in ML*, CUP, 1999.

44. Richards, M., *The BCPL Manual*, available from: www.cl.cam.ac.uk/users/mr/BCPL.html.

45. Richards, M., and Whitby-Strevens, C., *BCPL: The Language and Its Compiler*, CUP, 1979.

46. Spivey, J. M., *The Z Notation* 2nd edn, Prentice-Hall, Hemel Hempstead, UK, 1992.

47. Stärk, R., Schmid, J., and Börger, E, *Java and the Java Virtual Machine*, Springer-Verlag Berlin Heidelberg, 2001.

48. Steele, Guy L., *Common Lisp The Language*, 2nd edn, Digital Press, 1990.

49. Stoy, J. E., *Denotational Semantics*, MIT Press, 1977.

50. Theriault, Daniel G., *Issues in the Design and Implementation of Act2*, MIT AI Laboratory, Tech. Rep. No. 728, June, 1983.

51. Wall, L., Christiansen, T., and Schwartz, R. L., *Programming Perl*, 2nd edn, O'Reilly, Sebastopol, CA, 1991.

52. Warren, D. H. *An Abstract Prolog Instruction Set*, Technical Note 309, SRI, Menlo Park, CA, 1983.

53. Wirth, N. and Gutkneckt, J., *Project Oberon—The Design of an Operating System and Compiler*, Addison-Wesley, Reading, MA, 1992.

Index